A Convert's Guide to
MORMON LIFE

A Convert's Guide to

MORMON LIFE

CLARK L. AND KATHRYN H. KIDD

Bookcraft
Salt Lake City, Utah

Library of Congress Catalog Card Number: 98-73235

ISBN 1-57008-520-X

Second Printing, 1999

Printed in the United States of America

*To Dick and Hazie Brown —
for your friendship, your example,
and your willingness to accept as Saints
those who aren't always saintly*

CONTENTS

ACKNOWLEDGMENTS

We would be remiss if we didn't thank a cast of thousands for their assistance in writing this book. Here are those grateful words:

Many heartfelt thanks to Scott Card, whose encouragement provided the inspiration to start writing this book, and whose well-placed phone calls kept the manuscript from languishing on a desk the way so many other books are wont to do;

To Mary Kay Stout, whose "intense" love of every tidbit of Mormonism gave us ideas in several areas;

To Michael E. Mitchell, BA (history), MA (modern European history), consulting instructor in world history with a specialty in 19th Century German history, and consultant in modern pharmaceutical reimbursement policy, for his acumen regarding the spiritual significance of Cheerios;

To Janece Ford, who provided numerous helpful insights about Relief Society and other things, and who cheerfully threw tares in with the wheat by adding outdated information about the Primary (a pox on you for moving to El Paso);

To Missy Hooper, who delivered the bad news that all the clever stuff Kathy had written about the Primary, based on Janece Ford's misinformation, was outdated and had to be jettisoned;

To Emma Gene Gentry, our Episcopalian proofreader, who was especially helpful in providing a non-Mormon's perspective and in asking questions for the question and answer sections;

To Dick and Hazie Brown, for letting us steal numerous books and manuals for research;

To Ben Brown, for the real scoop on how the funding of missionaries works;

To Cameron and Bev Anderson, for their insights into the inner workings of the Young Men, Young Women, and Cub Scout programs;

To "the Incognito Patriarch," who bailed us out on the section about patriarchal blessings;

To Bruce Kneeland, for his insights about the law of averages;

To Carla Child, for her help in reviewing the sections on music and Church education, and for her continued friendship, even though her evil husband, Dennis, has banished her to the wilds of Colorado;

To Dennis Child, pinochle demon, who didn't answer a single e-mail plea regarding this book, but who was an inspiration as we wrote the sections on bishops and Young Men presidents;

To Dale and Lynne Van Atta, on general principles, and to their son Dylan, whose experiences helped us write the missionary section;

To our friends at the Washington Temple, who were enthusiastic cheerleaders as the work progressed, and especially to Elaine Roueche, temple matron, for her information about silk flowers;

To Bishop Lance Moss, who gave us the highlights and lowlights of being a bishop, and who will find that his brand new house outside the ward boundaries is cursed;

And to the kind and friendly people at Bookcraft, primarily Cory Maxwell, Garry Garff, and Janna DeVore for having the insight to see why a book such as this one is needed.

INTRODUCTION

The Road Ahead

During 1997, some 317,798 courageous individuals made a gigantic leap of faith as they entered the waters of baptism and became members of The Church of Jesus Christ of Latter-day Saints. This number does not include the 75,214 new members whose families were already members of the Church and who were baptized because they reached the age of accountability—the age when people are mature enough to choose between right and wrong, which the scriptures tell us is eight years.

Most of these 317,798 pioneers were adults or young adults who were already members of the workforce, active in their schooling, or involved in raising families. Many of them were previously active in other churches; others had never been part of an organized religion but were searching for something to better their lives. Some of them may have almost given up in their search for a higher purpose in life, only to find in the LDS Church the answers they had been seeking.

Some of these converts received the restored gospel like a bolt from the sky, quenching a thirst that they didn't know existed and showing them a greater light than they had previously ever known. For others, the journey to baptism was a long process as a seed was planted in their souls and slowly grew until they could no longer deny its beauty and power.

The baptism of each new Church member represents the beginning of a marvelous new journey and adventure. But life in the Church can seem pretty overwhelming as the convert sees longtime members scurrying around doing hundreds of strange or intimidating tasks and speaking of things that the new convert doesn't understand. Many converts wonder how they will ever be able to be anything more than just the "newest member" of their local congregations.

Yet if they follow the path the Lord intends for them, they will grow, learn, and take on new responsibilities, for in the LDS Church all members are expected to be ministers and serve each other in the name of Christ. Within a surprisingly short period, new converts will become leaders and teachers—sturdy anchors in the kingdom of God. They will become better husbands, wives, fathers, mothers, children, and citizens of their communities. And they will look back in wonder at how quickly they made the journey that seemed so impossibly difficult at the start.

In the 19th century, when the Church was newly restored, new converts suffered much persecution, and some gave their lives for their faith. Others left behind family and friends to follow where the newfound gospel led them, and regardless of what their careers or plans had been before their baptism, they joined together at great sacrifice to build farms, settlements, and cities in the wilderness of the American frontier.

Although today's converts do not usually endure the physical hardships of early members, the tasks they are called on to perform can be equally heroic. Sadly, sometimes their former friends and even members of their own families turn away from them, and they are faced with the task of finding new friends or living with strained family relationships. Some converts must also break powerful habits such as drinking alcohol or using tobacco. These lifestyle changes occasionally cause conflicts with other family members, friends, and coworkers, although just as often they lead to increased respect.

Equally difficult, new converts must often make sacrifices in terms of time. Every hour spent in church service means less time for other activities and interests. As new converts begin to take joy in their ministry in the gospel, they will soon find a happy balance between personal time, family time, work time, Church time, and social time.

Those who grew up in the Church learned all these things from childhood on; it's as natural for them as breathing. But for you who are about to be baptized or who were baptized not that long ago, a road map—or at least a few highway signs—can give you much more confidence in navigating this confusing new territory.

Before baptism, you met with missionaries and possibly other members of the Church in your area. Probably you also attended one or more Church meetings. These discussions and meetings should have given you an understanding of the basic doctrines and principles of the Church. You will spend the rest of your life learning the gospel from the scriptures, from Church meetings, and from your own experiences as you are led and taught by the Spirit of God. Growth in the Church is a lifelong process, and not even the best missionaries could possibly prepare you for all of the new ideas and concepts to which you will be exposed.

Why We Wrote This Book

As Latter-day Saints with a combined experience of more than 65 years in the Church, we have often been involved in offering fellowship to new members. Yet that experience has intensified in the past few years as we have become acquainted with "Betty" and "John."

Our friendship with Betty is unusual in that we have never met face to face. A few years ago we met her on a computer network, and our conversations with her have been almost exclusively through e-mail. During our communications with her, and through the efforts of the missionaries and the members of the Church in her area, she and her husband joined the Church (that is enough of a story for a separate book!). As she grew in the gospel, we took great joy in reading her letters and watching the day-to-day progress she was making. We also tried to answer her questions about the wonderful but strange new community she was joining.

We met John in December of 1995 when he was baptized as a new member in our neighborhood. We were assigned to visit him regularly and help him to learn about the Church. Our visits with him over an 18-month period have let us watch his growth, curiosity, and enthusiasm for the gospel.

What overwhelmed us in dealing with these two new members was the great amount of new information they had to absorb and the number of questions these new teachings generated: *What is a calling? Am I still allowed to play poker as a church member? What are home teachers? What is a stake conference? What is a patriarchal blessing? Can my nonmember wife attend a ward social?*

Both Betty and John are intelligent people with a wide variety of talents, and they were already successful in many aspects of their lives. They were both well versed in the Bible and other religious teachings, but their studies had not familiarized them with the day-to-day life of average Mormons. Hearing their questions made us realize the steepness of the road that the new convert must travel.

Then President Gordon B. Hinckley came to a regional conference in our area, and we heard him encourage the Saints to help new converts find their way in the Church. After the conference, we thought about our experiences with Betty and John—and compared our own life experiences, as Clark is a lifelong Church member from Ogden, Utah, and Kathy joined the Church as a college student at Brigham Young University, after growing up as a Protestant in Mandeville, Louisiana. We realized that lifelong members—"lifers"—often don't realize how strange and confusing even the most ordinary aspects of Mormon life can be to a new member, while new members are often too shy to ask questions that might reveal how little they know.

That's when we thought of writing a book that could serve as a road map for investigators and converts—and also help longtime members as they offer fellowship to brand-new Latter-day Saints. Using our own experience in the Church and expanding on teaching materials we developed for Betty and John, we began to develop an outline for this book.

Years ago, we wrote several books to help people learn to use home computers; in working on this book we quickly realized that computer programming can be a lot simpler to explain than Mormon life!

What We Hope to Teach You

The Lord says that those who follow Him are different from the rest of the world, "a chosen generation, a royal priesthood, an holy nation, a peculiar people; that ye should shew forth the praises of him who hath called you out of darkness into his marvelous light" (1 Peter 2:9).

Anyone who has ever visited a Latter-day Saint meeting will probably admit it is a bit peculiar—hopefully not peculiar as in *odd*, but peculiar as in being different from other Christian sects. Some of the elements are similar, such as prayers and congregational singing, and yet many elements are unique to Mormon worship.

It is our hope that this book will serve to help explain many of these things that may seem strange to you and yet will eventually feel as natural and right as an old, comfortable pair of shoes. We will try to explain these new concepts not only as they apply to Sunday meetings but also as they fit into the entire spectrum of day-to-day Mormon life.

Although it is inevitable that some of the following chapters will mention doctrines of The Church of Jesus Christ of Latter-day Saints, we will try to avoid exploring those doctrines in any great depth. There are plenty of other resources, such as the scriptures and other official Church training materials, that will do a better job of that than we could ever hope to do. The place to learn doctrine is during your Sunday meetings and in the course of your individual study and prayer. We will try to direct the focus of this book more to the organization, programs, and culture of the Church—especially the things that others might perceive as peculiar. Although you will spend a lifetime learning the doctrines of the kingdom of God, learning about the culture, programs, and organization of the Church can help you gain confidence more quickly as you begin your service to the Savior within His Church.

How to Use This Book

In the LDS Church we have a language all our own. Throughout this book, we'll be using terms that may not be familiar to you. If you run across a strange word or phrase, look it up in the glossary at the back of this book. There is also an index, which you can use to cross-reference topics that are discussed in different parts of the text. If the index and the glossary don't tell you all you need, ask a Church member about any unfamiliar terms you read in this book or hear in your Church experience. Church members are always ready to help.

At the end of each chapter, you'll find a section of questions and answers that are often asked by converts. If the text of a chapter raises any questions in your mind, we hope at least some of those questions will be answered for you here.

We have tried to keep the tone of the text light to make the reading more enjoyable. We have also endeavored to explore the culture of the Church in a lighthearted way, trying to present an accurate picture of the typical convert experience. Although Jesus Christ is perfect and His Church is true, the daily life of the Church is conducted by imperfect people who are trying to achieve perfection. We would do a great disservice to you as a new convert if we tried to sugarcoat the journey you have embarked upon. As we said to one convert friend, it is better for you to see an accurate representation of the convert experience, warts and all, than to be disillusioned the first time someone doesn't live up to your expectations.

Having said that, we fully expect that 99 percent of your experiences will bless you, enlighten you, and bring happiness into your life and the lives of those you love. You will be able to look back on your baptism with great joy because it signified the start of a marvelous journey that will continue to delight and amaze you, not only throughout your life but throughout the eternities.

The Church is as varied as its millions of members, but what binds us together is the knowledge that the gospel is true. In serving each other, we are together following the Savior. In the Church we are "fishers of men"—and we are also the "fish"!

1

YOUR NEW WARD FAMILY

A Physical Entity

Even if you gave up friends and family to join the LDS Church, no Mormon is ever homeless. Every member of The Church of Jesus Christ of Latter-day Saints has a niche, and that niche can be found in his home congregation. Every member, from the President of the Church to the most recent convert, is assigned to a congregation according to his place of residence. Regular-sized congregations are called wards; smaller congregations are called branches.

Wards and branches are equivalent to parishes in the Catholic Church. Each ward is presided over by a bishop, and each branch is presided over by a branch president—much the same as parishes are presided over by a parish priest. The difference between a ward and a branch lies in the scope of the Church programs that are available to members. Because branches have fewer people to do the work, some of the organizations that would be found in a ward are scaled down, combined, or missing in a branch. But don't worry if you find yourself residing in a branch—there will be a good spirit there, you will be able to progress as a member, and there will be plenty of work for you to do.

Every effort is made to give each ward or branch a sense of identity by giving it a name that is unique to the area. In our area, for example, seven wards and a branch are named after the towns where the congregations reside, the ninth unit is named after the Algonkian Indian tribe who used to inhabit that particular area, and the tenth is named for the Shenandoah River. If you've joined the Church in an area that is

teeming with Church members, however, the people who organized your ward may have had no alternative but to give your
ward a number instead of a name. So you may find that you
reside in the Warrenton Virginia 2nd Ward, or the BYU 87th
Ward. There are well over 100 wards at Brigham Young University, for example—and there aren't that many geographical
features in all of BYU's hometown of Provo, Utah.

You'll learn in chapter 5 how multiple wards are joined
together to form stakes. For now, just remember that a stake is
a group of wards and that the leadership of a stake consists of
a stake president and his two counselors—together they comprise a stake presidency.

No matter whether your ward has a name or a number, the
local meetinghouse will be easy to spot for Church members
who are just passing through the area. Somewhere on the front
of each building is the name of the unit or units that worship
there, together with the full name of the Church: The Church
of Jesus Christ of Latter-day Saints. Although we may speak of
ourselves as Mormons or Latter-day Saints, or talk about being
LDS, the official name of the Church is the name that is posted
outside every building for people to see.

The other hallmark of our meetinghouses can be found by
looking heavenward. Our buildings usually have a spire that
reaches to the sky, but there's never a cross at the top of the
spire. If you used to be a Catholic, you're familiar with the
image of the crucifix, with Jesus hanging on the cross to
remind believers of His sacrifice. If you used to be a Protestant,
the crosses that played a part in your worship were bare of the
Savior, reminding you to focus on the resurrection rather than
the crucifixion itself. Although members of the LDS Church are
mindful of both the crucifixion and the resurrection, we believe
that the best way we can show the world who we are is not by
a crucifix or a cross, but by our actions. Matthew 7:20 says,
"Wherefore by their fruits ye shall know them." Each man or
woman who claims to follow the Savior is judged by his or her
works, whether they be good or evil. The symbol of our belief is
not to be found atop the steeple or in our meetinghouses or
around our necks, but in the works we perform.

The boundaries that define a ward are based on geographical features and man-made structures. A sample boundary

description might read like this: "The southern boundary of the Maple 1st Ward will run along Maple Street from Route 29 to the Snake River. The eastern boundary will run from the Snake River to the Henrico County line. The northern boundary will run from the Henrico County line to State Highway 7. The western boundary will run from State Highway 7 to Maple Street." The number of miles contained within a ward will vary according to the density of Church membership. In urban areas with large Latter-day Saint populations, a ward might cover just a few city blocks. In rural areas, it might cover hundreds of miles.

When you enter an LDS meetinghouse, you may be surprised at the plainness of the surroundings. Our meetinghouses are functional, designed for maximum use. In urban areas, there are often four or more wards that share a single building, so more attention is paid to acoustics than to aesthetics. The carpet on the wall may be the ugliest thing you've ever seen, but it does a great job of keeping one noisy group from disturbing others.

If you're dismayed by the plainness of your particular ward meetinghouse, you may get a different perspective if you realize the building may have been constructed by the volunteer labor of the people who are worshiping in the pew next to yours. Until recently, congregations were responsible for raising the money to build their own meetinghouses. Each family was assessed a percentage of the building cost. Individual families were often asked to make huge financial sacrifices—sacrifices that resulted in family members having to get paper routes or give up their vacations or defer their own home improvements or even sell their cars in order to raise money to build a church. And that wasn't all. After the money was raised, ward members were expected to do much of the actual construction.

Our own ward meetinghouse may be an architectural nightmare, but there's a certain amount of sentiment that comes from knowing our friends raised the walls and did the roofing with their own hands. We still remember the story about how a former bishop was on the roof nailing down the shingles in the middle of a blinding snowstorm. We're only grateful that we moved to Northern Virginia long after the meetinghouse was finished, so we can admire their sacrifice without having had to endure any personal experience of it.

In areas where there are few Church members, buildings are constructed in phases. The smallest phase begins with a large room that can be divided into a number of smaller classrooms through the use of accordion doors. The room is left open for sacrament meeting (the weekly worship service), but then the doors are drawn as the members go to their various classes. As Church membership grows, subsequent phases add a cultural hall (gymnasium) and a full-sized chapel (sanctuary).

In areas where there are large numbers of Church members (such as most major urban areas), the buildings will be full-sized when they are first constructed. The central feature of each meetinghouse is a large sanctuary that is usually rectangular in shape. We don't use the word *sanctuary,* however; we use the word *chapel* instead. Most chapels are sparsely decorated, with no flags or statues to adorn them. There are no candles, and no incense, either. Altars are found in our temples but not in our chapels. The only thing in an LDS chapel that resembles an altar is the table where the sacrament is blessed.

Most LDS chapels have an overflow area in the back to accommodate expanding congregations. Other areas of the building will contain the cultural hall and the classrooms used by the various organizations. There may be a baptismal font, there is always a nursery, and there is usually a room set aside for nursing mothers. There is a large meeting room for children, too. There will be a kitchen somewhere near the cultural hall, and there will be an office for each bishop whose ward shares the building. There will also be a room for clerical work; this is where financial contributions are processed and membership records updated. It's almost overwhelming to see how many separate rooms can be fit into one small meetinghouse, but Mormon meetinghouses are built to be used.

One thing you may notice when you enter an LDS meetinghouse for the first time is that you do not go directly from the outside into the chapel, but instead find yourself in a foyer. Foyers have an important function in that they are designed to be a place where Church members can meet and greet one another before they enter the chapel. In theory, by the time that members of the congregation have entered the chapel, they have finished their visiting and are ready to sit quietly and worshipfully in these sacred surroundings. In practice, however, the atmosphere in LDS chapels can become so boisterous that one can only imagine how much worse the situation would be without the buffer of the foyer.

Each LDS meetinghouse is different, and all of them seem confusing at first—especially if your ward is juggling with one or more other congregations to share a finite amount of space. But fear not—everyone gets lost at first. If you lose your way, all you need to do is ask for directions.

Social Connections

No matter how many brothers and sisters were raised in your family home, you inherited a huge extended family when you joined the LDS Church. The members of your new ward may not all be on your Christmas list, but they're considered to be your brothers and your sisters just the same. Indeed, Church members call one another "Brother Jones" or "Sister Smith," rather than Mr. or Mrs., when they aren't yet on a first-name basis. They may also use these terms to show respect to an older Saint. Even good friends occasionally refer to each other as "Brother X" or "Sister Y" when they're addressing each other in a Church setting.

When your bishop is out of earshot, you should refer to him as "Bishop Brown" (or whatever his surname might be) or as "the bishop." When you speak to him, you may call him "Bishop" without his last name. Other Church leaders might be referred to as "President Barker" or "Elder Johnson," and addressed as "President" or "Elder." But when you don't know a person's proper title, "Brother Jones" or "Sister Martin" is always correct.

We'd like to tell you that you'll be greeted by your new brothers and sisters with open arms, but this isn't always the case. If you were brought into the Church in the ideal situation, you attended the ward several times before your baptism date, and members of your new ward rejoiced with you at your baptism. But sometimes, eager missionaries or excited converts convince one another that the convert is so ready for baptism that he doesn't need to be immersed in the ward before he's immersed in the water. When that happens, a convert may first set foot in a Mormon meeting after he's already joined the Church, and he may get lost in the shuffle.

If you're one of those converts whose first visit to a Mormon ward was marked by indifference, we want to assure you that this indifference was entirely unintentional. LDS congregations are fluid. People move in and out of them as they move in and out of houses, so it's not uncommon for a ward to get three or four—or more!—new families into a ward every week during the summer. During the three months of summer vacation, a ward can easily lose sixty old members and acquire seventy-five new ones. And during the periods when people are likely to be moving, other people are likely to be visiting. You may have seen the sign on the front of your ward meetinghouse: "Visitors Welcome." Saints take that literally. If they're out of town on a weekend, Sunday will often find them visiting an LDS congregation in whatever place they find themselves. There can easily be a half-dozen adult visitors in a ward on a Sunday, in addition to all the people who are moving in and out. Even the most conscientious members of a ward are likely to be overwhelmed by the number of strangers who appear in a church meeting. Some of those new members are bound to fall through the cracks. As you grow in the Church, you will also find that most Latter-day Saints are very busy with family life and with all the various programs of the Church. What you might perceive as indifference is probably just a lot of activity.

Sometimes new ward members are ignored just because people assume somebody else is looking after them. A year ago, a terrific couple moved into our ward from overseas. They had been temple workers in the Orient (we'll discuss the temple in greater detail later), and both of them were vivacious, friendly, and smart. Recently they moved overseas again—after confiding that in the entire year they'd lived in our ward they'd never made a friend. Everyone who heard this was dumbfounded. We had all believed the couple were at the center of a social group in the ward and wouldn't be available if we called them. They were neglected for the same reason that beautiful girls often go dateless—everyone assumed they were occupied already.

If you feel lost in a new congregation, you can sit around feeling sorry for yourself or you can do something about it. When we first got married, we wasted several months as we waited for people in our new ward to include us in their activities. Nobody got around to doing it. When we saw that cobwebs were tying us to our chairs, we realized we had to make the first move.

One night, we got out a directory of ward members and started at the A's, calling every couple on the list alphabetically until somebody finally agreed to go out to dinner with us. It's embarrassing to admit that we got all the way to the K's before a couple finally accepted our invitation, but our perseverance was rewarded when they became our closest friends in that new ward.

When we were living in the same ward, another couple moved in from out of state and immediately held several large parties to which different groups of ward members were invited, just so they could get to know the ward members in a social setting. Within a month, they were at the center of every social activity that was going on within our ward boundaries. All it took was a little initiative on their part.

There are other ways to get to know the members of your new Church community. For a year or so, we used to bake bread or cookies every Sunday afternoon, and then take loaves of bread or plates of cookies to ward members we wanted to get to know. We made many friends through those Sunday visits, and we had a good time by ourselves before the visits as we baked the cookies or the bread and decided who we'd visit that day.

We also have a friend who has found that the fastest way to get immersed in a new ward is to join the choir. Many of the most devoted participants in the ward seem to be choir members. If you join the choir (and you don't have to be a Pavarotti to sing in a ward choir), you'll get to know these stalwarts who will soon welcome you in their other Church activities.

If sign-up sheets go around, asking for volunteers for one assignment or another, you may want to enlist yourself to do service projects as a way to meet other ward members. And the Relief Society (women's organization) homemaking meetings are essential for women to get to know other women in the ward. Once the women know each other, their families often become friends. Accepting ward callings (more about that in chapter 3) will also give you the opportunity to learn to love the people you serve. The more actively you participate, the more quickly you'll form friendships.

Social connections in a ward are vital for several reasons. First, your non-Mormon friends and family may not support you in your decision to join the Church. This may leave a void in your life that ward members can fill. But even if your extended family and friends support you wholeheartedly, there may come a time when your employment situation forces you to move away from the people you hold dear. When that happens, Church members who move into a new ward find they have an instant surrogate family to give them love and support.

When we moved to Virginia several years ago, most of the people at Clark's office were also recent transplants who had moved to the area from other states. It was amazing to see how much more quickly Clark adapted to his new surroundings than his coworkers did. When Clark's coworkers needed a new dentist or a good auto mechanic, they had to take their chances with the Yellow Pages. Clark just called a few people in his ward directory, and he soon had more recommendations than he could use.

Second, you'll find that Church activity takes a whole lot of your time. Although you may have been a rabid golfer or bridge player before your conversion, you'll probably find that as the months pass, you'll be spending less time with your old golf cronies or bridge partners. Nobody will demand that you give up your old activities, but you'll probably decide for yourself that other things are more important. You'll make friends inside your new ward solely by virtue of the fact that you spend so much time in their company. But beyond that, you'll find that your ward members understand the challenges and the blessings you're experiencing, and you'll turn to them instead of to people who don't share that common ground.

Third, ward members offer support to you when you need it. This support comes in a thousand different ways. Men in the elders quorum (men who are still young enough to have strong backs) are famous in every ward for the physical labor they perform helping families move into or out of their house or apartment—though we've heard of wards where it's the Young Men (boys from age 12 through 17 who hold the Aaronic Priesthood) who do the moving. Mothers may form children's play groups with one another to give each other some needed rest. Young Women (girls from age 12 through high school graduation) may volunteer to baby-sit free of charge for couples who attend the temple, or a teenager can sit with a mother whose husband isn't in church with her to help her ride herd on the kids. A member of the ward will often watch a house while the family members attend the funeral of a loved one, and Relief Society members will provide funeral dinners to those bereaved families.

Moral support comes in the form of a phone call just to say hello or a written note telling you what a good job you did when you taught a Relief Society lesson last week. It comes as an invitation to Christmas dinner if you're living in circumstances where you might otherwise spend the holiday alone. It comes as a secret present left on your doorstep, or a wave in the hallway as you move from meeting to meeting, or a casserole when you're sick, or a shoulder and a Kleenex when you've had a bad day.

Just as ward members should help you when you need warmth and friendship, you should also be ready to help those who need comfort from you. Think of your ward as being a bathtub full of water. Sometimes you'll let some water down the drain by accepting the kindnesses of your fellow ward members. Just as often, you'll be the one to put some water in as you reach out a hand of friendship to help others.

If you don't know who needs your help, keep your eyes and ears open. There's always someone who has difficulty and who needs a friend. If you're not good at discerning who needs something you can give, pray to be led to those in your ward who need your help. You'll be surprised how often those prayers are answered.

Finally, social connections in a ward give you the opportunity to learn from the people around you. New converts can learn much about the Church from spending time with Church members. If you're feeling lost as a new member of the Church, be sure to take advantage of this opportunity.

Spiritual Strength

If there's any place in the scriptures to find a blueprint of how a Latter-day Saint ward works, 1 Corinthians 12 is that scripture. In this chapter, the Apostle Paul compared the body of the Church to a human body. In a human body, all the parts work together by doing their separate assignments. The eye doesn't worry about whether it's doing a more important job than the heart. The feet don't wonder if the hands have higher status. Each part of the body concerns itself only with fulfilling its own function, and together those body parts work together for the benefit of the whole.

So it is in the Church. All of us have talents. Some people are gifted in music. Others are intensely interested in family history (genealogy). Others have a missionary zeal about food production and home storage. Some can teach; others are more adept at clerical work. Some are natural leaders; others spend their lives supporting those leaders by being good followers. Some touch us with the talks they give from the pulpit; others touch us with their acts of charity. Some feel a calling to do temple work; others are no less passionate about taking the youth on camping expeditions.

Every one of these gifts is vital, but their collective beauty is in their diversity. It would be a pity if a ward didn't have a choir director, but it would be a tragedy if everyone in the ward were only trained to lead the choir. A person who has no eyes will be forever unable to see, even if he has hundreds of hands. Similarly, the ward is most whole as long as it is balanced.

As a new convert, you may be wondering where you fit into the body of the Church. After she joined the Church in 1971, Kathy spent many years being firmly convinced that she was a canker sore on the tongue of whatever ward she happened to be in—an entity with no function other than to irritate the people who were actually doing the work. Eventually she realized that even canker sores serve a purpose (if only to remind you that you have a tongue!), and she became more at ease with her role.

If you find yourself being an earlobe in your ward body, be the best earlobe you can be.

When we visualize ward members as parts of a single body,

we realize that we are dependent on one another. Teachers can't teach if nobody comes to class. Bishops can't lead if nobody accepts a calling or comes to meetings. You only have two responsibilities as far as keeping the body of your ward together—you must perform your tasks to the best of your ability, and you must do all you can do to support others as they do the tasks they've been assigned. If all of us fulfill both of those responsibilities, our wards will run smoothly, no matter what particular assignments we happen to be doing at any particular time.

The other way you can derive spiritual strength from your ward is by sharing testimonies with others. Testimonies are declarations of belief that are given spontaneously by ward members during lessons and sermons or during the monthly fast and testimony meeting. But there's a wider definition of testimony, and that is when people show what they believe through their actions. Your actions can inspire others, just as their actions can inspire you. When you use other ward members as your examples, remember they aren't perfect—just as you aren't perfect. Follow their lead when they do right. When they make mistakes, try to overlook those mistakes and forgive the people who make them, just as you would have them forgive you.

Remember that one of the reasons we have a church is to give us an opportunity to meet together and grow spiritually by sharing each other's strength and experiences. That being the case, people who want to become more like the Savior should take full advantage of the benefits a ward can offer. If we were strong enough, we could teach and practice the gospel in our homes—and thus be less dependent on a formal church. But because we are not strong enough to stand alone, we will continue to have the Church as the primary vehicle through which the gospel is practiced and taught.

It is good to remember the relationship between the gospel and the Church so you can achieve the proper balance in your life. You will probably meet some members who become so involved in the Church that they forget about the gospel. Which is more important—going to church to hear a lesson on how to be a better Christian, or stopping by the side of the road to help a child in need? If you ever find yourself concentrating on the Church to the exclusion of the gospel, reevaluate your activities by asking yourself what the Savior would do.

Another spiritual pitfall is that some members believe they have progressed intellectually or spiritually beyond the level of the other ward members. They become intolerant of the Church as they come to believe the ward has nothing to offer them, so they reduce their participation in the organized worship and limit their contact with Church members. Eventually they find themselves at odds with Church teachings and doctrine, to their detriment and the sorrow of their families.

Both of these attitudes are dangerous in terms of your spiritual progression. You must strive to live the gospel in your home, your ward, your neighborhood, and your community.

What a Ward Isn't

A Ward Is Not a Community of People Who
Were Designed by a Cookie Cutter

Although the members of your ward share a common religion, you'll find that they're a surprisingly diverse group. One of the first things you'll learn when you join the Church is that if you look below the surface, no two Latter-day Saints are alike.

Think about it: Beyond a few basic beliefs that we all hold sacred, Church members are taught to study things out in their minds and to rely on personal revelation. Because we are given our freedom to choose, what constitutes Mormonism may vary widely from one person to the next. Beyond the core doctrines of the Church, we often create our own individual codes of conduct based on what brings us, as individuals, closer to God.

In any congregation, for example, there will be people who think it's a sin to drink cola soft drinks and go to movies with mature themes. Others will happily go to movies with mature themes, but they wouldn't dream of buying a Coke at the snack bar. There will be some who think cola is fine, but movies with mature themes are an abomination. And we'll have a couple who think if cola is bad, we shouldn't eat chocolate either, and to be on the safe side, we shouldn't go to any movie that's not specifically produced for children. And while we're at it, let's throw away the television too.

This is fine, as long as we all realize that our personal rules apply to us personally, and our household rules apply only within our household. We are given commandments and basic rules of conduct by the Lord, but the details of how we interpret and carry out those principles are between us, our families, and the Lord. Church members are not all expected to live their lives in accordance with the rules Brother and Sister Sanctimonious have worked out for their own household. We must all be patient with each other's differences, starting from the assumption that everyone is doing his best to live the gospel as he understands it.

Still, there are some areas where custom or tradition requires Church members to live up to certain basic minimums. If somebody tries to correct you, don't immediately assume that the person doing the correcting is judging you harshly or behaving improperly. You're new in the Church, and there may well be widely practiced customs that haven't become clear to you yet. For instance, you may not have noticed that in most wards in the United States, Mormon women wear skirts or dresses to church, or that there are certain words that Mormon men just don't use, even when there are no ladies present. When someone points out the custom to you, the intention is to spare you embarrassment, not to judge or condemn you. And sometimes there are customs in one part of the Church that aren't followed in other areas. If you join the Church in Hawaii, you'll be used to sacrament meeting speakers greeting the congregation with a cheery, "Aloha!" Try this on the mainland, and you'll see a lot of raised eyebrows in the congregation.

At the same time, don't assume that every "commandment" you're told about is doctrine, or you're headed for big trouble. Every ward seems to have at least one member who spends a lot of time thinking up extra commandments that nobody else has heard of. When you hear something that doesn't ring true, it's perfectly acceptable to mildly ask for the scriptural source of the doctrine so you can study it for yourself.

As Church members, we're so accustomed to having

anti-Mormons try to discredit us that we sometimes get paranoid about the motives of people who are on our side. Many of us have lost the ability to laugh at ourselves, and that's a pity.

When a ward member seems to be chastising you unfairly, remember that he—like you—is a human being. All of us are trying to live our religion the best we can. Sometimes we're gloriously successful, but sometimes we fail, and occasionally we really mess things up. When somebody offends you, remember that without the Atonement, none of us is worthy of exaltation. None of us has any reason to take himself so seriously that he can't laugh at his own mistakes or forgive the mistakes of others.

A Ward Is Not a Collection of Perfect People

We're in the process of becoming perfect, but we're all a long way from meeting that goal. There will be people in the ward who aren't as spiritually advanced as you are, and there will be people who are spiritually so far ahead of you that you'll be afraid you can never catch up. There will be people you like, but there will also be people you don't like—and there will no doubt be people who don't like you. When you run into someone who doesn't like you despite all your wit and your charm, just remember that even the perfect Savior had people who didn't like Him. That being the case, it's not surprising that we imperfect souls are occasionally unappreciated.

Sad to say, on a few rare instances you'll run into ward members whose behavior can only be described as out-and-out dishonest. These people probably don't think of themselves as evil; they rationalize their behavior by having a different set of ethics for business dealings. When it comes to financial matters, it is best to treat ward members as you would any other person trying to sell you something. Check out the details and do not feel any obligation to do business with them unless you're comfortable with the arrangements. You should be especially cautious when a person tries to leverage your ward association to force your involvement. "You can trust me, Brother Jones, we're in the same ward!" Or, even tackier, "I'm selling this to support my son on his mission." When you want to contribute to the missionary fund, you give the money to the bishop—you don't have to buy things from a missionary's family unless it's something you really want to buy.

If you get burned by a Church member in a business dealing, don't blame the Church. There isn't a whole lot your bishop can do, unless the person who bilks you is convicted in a court of law. If you're cheated, you can take some consolation from the fact that people who prey on the good faith of others will have to answer to a higher judge.

The longer you're a member of the Church, the more you'll learn about the principle of commitment. You've heard the old saying, "My family, right or wrong." The same thing should be said about wards. If your ward isn't perfect, the best course of action is to quietly try to change it through your example of faithfulness, patience, and kindness rather than to start a conflict or bail out. We should strive for the attitude of a new Church member who once stood up in our ward and said, "I love all of you—even the ones I don't like." Remember that it's the Lord's job to judge. Our challenge is to love one another unconditionally.

A Ward Is Not a Place to Solicit Clients for Your Business

Mormons work in every legitimate career. It's fine if you sell vitamins or real estate or cleaning supplies, or if you're a doctor, lawyer, or plumber. It's perfectly acceptable to mention to ward members what you do for a living. But that's as far as you can go. Once you start actively soliciting ward members to buy what you have to sell or to become your client, you've crossed the line. Using Church membership directories in any business-related endeavor is strictly prohibited.

That's not to say you can't hire Brother Pipes to do your plumbing for you if your toilet backs up. If someone in the ward offers a service you need, don't hesitate to call—as long as you're willing to pay the going fee for his services. Just remember that when you enter into a business arrangement with members, the normal rules of business apply. You should not expect a discount from Church members, and many Saints refuse to accept such discounts if they're offered. If the price a Saint charges nonmembers is fair and honest, then that is exactly the price that Church members should also pay.

Exceptions are made, of course, when a service is being shared with a family that is passing through hard times: at such times Saints must be willing to give and receive special treatment. Sometimes the bishop, Relief Society president, or quorum president will ask a member for a one-time donation of services. But in the normal course of affairs, no one should gain special benefits or suffer unusual costs because of Church membership. And no one should ever assume that a Church member will donate his professional services for free. Don't ask a Mormon doctor to diagnose you in the Church foyer, and don't expect the Mormon sign painter to donate both labor and materials to make signs for every ward event.

A Ward Is Not a Place Where You'll Be Doing Your Part If You Only Show Up on Christmas and Easter

No matter what religion you came from before you joined the Church, you're probably accustomed to sitting in the audience while watching the worship service as it is conducted by a minister or a rabbi or a priest. In our Church, it's the people in the congregation who do the work. If you stay home from your meetings, there is work that won't get done; there will be needs that won't be met. As a Church member, you're as responsible for the well-being of others in the congregation as those others are for you.

There's an old joke that has a particular application to Mormons. You've probably heard it a million times—it's the one about the chicken and the pig, sitting in a cafe and talking about the virtues of a balanced breakfast. The chicken says, "I don't know what the big fuss is all about. We should all give what we're asked." The pig replies, "That's easy for you to say. For you, it's an egg a day. For me, it's a total commitment."

Here's something you may want to tape to your refrigerator: In the breakfast buffet of life, Mormons bring the ham. You won't be asked to run the congregation the first day you step into an LDS meetinghouse, but you'll definitely be asked for more than an egg a day. Read about the law of consecration in the scriptures, or look in the index of this book to find the sections that talk about sustaining (supporting) ward leaders in their callings.

A Convert's Questions

Do all wards have geographical boundaries?

Most of the wards in your area are determined solely by geographical boundaries. On rare occasions, however, there are special interest wards whose boundaries are not strictly geographical. There may be wards to accommodate unmarried Church members who want to worship solely with other singles. There are sometimes deaf branches in areas with large numbers of people who are hearing impaired. Foreign language branches may be established for people meeting in one country but speaking the language of another. There are also servicemen's branches, which are established for the benefit of servicemen living overseas, as well as other branches that are formed as the need arises. If you have special circumstances that would make it hard for you to worship in a regular ward, there may be a ward that will fit your needs. But in many areas of the Church there aren't enough members to allow for the creation of specialized wards, and we simply do our best within the ward or branch where we reside.

Do the boundaries always stay the same?

Ward boundaries are determined by the size of a ward. Although theories about the optimum ward size change over time, the current belief is that the ideal ward has 300 to 350 active members. If a ward contains more than about 350 members, there are more ward members than there are positions to fill, and members may feel unneeded. A great effort is made to keep wards small enough that every ward member serves a vital role in the community, and this means that wards divide faster than yeast spores in warm dough. It's not unheard of for a family to live in four or five different wards—without ever moving from the family home.

What conditions cause the boundaries to change, and how is the change made?

The first thing you'll notice is that the chapel seems

awfully small during sacrament meeting and that the overflow area is being used more often than not. Next you may hear new ward members complain that they've been in the ward for three months, "and I don't have a calling yet!"

The third step is the activation of the ward rumor mill, which is always an interesting source of information. You'll hear rumors that the ward is about to split—often months or even years before it actually happens. People speculate whether two adjacent wards jointly give up regions to form a third ward, or whether your ward will simply split in two. And everyone will have a different theory of where the lines will be drawn and who will end up in what ward. This is a time of high drama, and many tears will be shed by people who don't want to see the fabric of their ward family torn apart.

If your ward is growing quickly but an adjacent ward isn't, one stopgap measure would be to realign the boundaries, reassigning a neighborhood from one ward into another to equalize the ward populations. A boundary realignment isn't nearly as fun to gossip about as a real ward split, but for those affected it can feel just as wrenching as if you had picked up and moved to another town!

Whether your ward splits or there's just a boundary realignment, the decision making will be conducted on a level higher than the bishop. One thing you can be sure of—the people who are gossiping about what could happen are almost always people who don't have the facts. The people who know what's going to happen—and when—generally keep their mouths shut and enjoy the rumors.

Once the decision has been made, an announcement will usually be made in sacrament meeting that the following week's sacrament meeting will be under the direction of the stake presidency (see chapter 5). This announcement can mean one of three things—either the bishopric is going to be changed, or the ward boundaries are going to be realigned, or both. If the ward boundaries are about to change, either through split or realignment, this sacrament meeting will often be a combined meeting attended by all the wards who will be affected. (Be sure to go early so you'll get a seat.)

After the sacrament service, the stake presidency will announce the new ward boundaries. Usually there will be maps or handouts showing exactly what the new ward boundaries are, together with ward lists showing which families will reside in each ward. If a new ward is created, a name will be announced for the new unit, and a bishopric will be chosen to lead it.

Your role as a member of the ward will be to raise your right hand to sustain (show your support of) the decisions that have been made. Even if the new boundaries seem to be putting you together with a bunch of strangers and cutting you off from your best friends in the old ward, realize that the boundary changes were done with everyone's best interests at heart and that the decisions were made after fasting and prayer on the part of the stake presidency and the bishops. When they drew the new boundaries, they were counting on you to be a stalwart member of the ward you've just been put into.

A ward division is one of those times when members have to take a leap of faith that everything will work out for the best. And when everyone works hard to serve the Lord and their fellow Saints in the new ward, everything turns out just fine.

All my friends ended up in the other ward. Can I go there?

The Church has a strict policy that your membership records will be maintained by the ward you live in. "Ward hopping" for trivial reasons—for instance, a preferred meeting time, a grudge against a ward leader, or avoiding unwanted responsibility—is strongly discouraged.

On rare occasions, circumstances in a ward make attending that ward almost impossible for a Church member. On those occasions, bishops and stake presidents are sometimes able to follow the old Mormon adage that "people are more important than programs," and exceptions are made to the rigid boundary rule.

Some of these unusual circumstances might include an elderly parent who doesn't drive and whose children live in an adjacent ward. The parent might ask that he be assigned to the children's ward in order to have a ride to church. Or a bitter divorce could make it so uncomfortable for two spouses to attend the same ward that if they were forced to do so, one of them would stop going to church. Exceptions will often be made in such a circumstance.

But if your only complaint is that your friends ended up on the wrong side of a boundary split, your best option is to make new friends in the new ward. You can be comforted by the knowledge that everyone in your new ward is missing at least one dear family who was torn asunder from them when the ward split. Everyone feels a loss to some degree. But at least you aren't walking into a ward where everyone is a stranger. You made friends in the old ward. You'll make friends in this one too. Although a ward division can be a sad occasion, it is also a positive sign that the kingdom of God is expanding in your area.

What happens if I move?

It isn't uncommon for Church members to choose their houses based at least in part on the ward they'll be attending. If you're the victim of a ward split that seems impossible to bear, moving may be an option. But most Church members move because their family outgrows their present house or a breadwinner changes jobs. Never fear; wherever you go, there will almost always be an LDS congregation to fill your needs.

When you move from one ward to another, it's a good practice to tell your ward membership clerk (the person who keeps track of membership records) where you're going to move. If you have the address and the phone number, give them to him. If not, a city and state will do. If you forget to do this, don't panic. The Church won't lose track of you. Notifying your ward membership clerk ahead of time is just a courtesy that will make his job a little bit easier. It's something you'd want done for you if you were the membership clerk and had to keep track of three hundred ward members who never seemed to live in the same place for more than fifteen minutes.

As you're looking for housing in your new hometown, you may want to look up the Church in a local phone book and ask the bishop to line you up with someone in his ward who can tell you about the area. Ward members can tell you which areas of town are crime free, which neighborhoods have several Church members in them, and which schools have a good reputation. And the trusty elders quorum can help you move into your new home if you don't have movers to do it for you. But just as often, Church members move to their new homes and then use the phone book to call the local ward. Whatever bishop you contact can tell you which ward you're in, and may even give you directions to the meetinghouse. Then you'll begin once again the exciting process of finding a community of brothers and sisters who are just like the ones you so tearfully left behind.

I've noticed Church members wincing when I say certain words. Is there a secret vocabulary nobody has told me about?

You'll find that Church members are conservative in their use of language. Most members of the Church don't use obscene language, but most people don't use four-letter words in churches of any denomination. There is one way Saints differ from members of other churches as far as language is concerned, however, and that may be what's tripping you up. Saints do not use the names of God or Christ in casual conversation. It's one thing to use those names when you're actually talking about God or the Savior, but it's another thing altogether to use those sacred names as an epithet when you stub your toe. In fact, if most Church members were given a choice of hearing blue language or hearing the name of God taken in vain, they'd prefer to hear the obscenities.

Even when the names of deity are used properly, they're used sparingly. Prayers begin with a petition to God the Father and close in the name of Jesus Christ, but it isn't recommended to use those names within the body of the prayer. Church members usually refer to "the Savior" rather than calling Him by name. If you're unsure of proper usage, listen to others in your ward or ask a trusted ward member. The only way you can learn is to ask, and people will always be glad to help you.

Why do Mormons fold their arms when they pray? It looks more hostile than worshipful to me.

The practice of folding the arms to pray is a cultural practice, not a doctrinal one, so there isn't any scriptural reference we can give you to tell you why it's done. But in the absence of any official policy, we'll give you a theory of how the arm folding might well have started.

Once upon a time, a desperate Primary teacher got tired of having her students whack each other every time their heads were supposed to be bowed in prayer. She wisely discerned that children whose arms were firmly tucked under their armpits would not be available to wreak mayhem on other children, so she had them fold their arms during prayers. The tactic was so wildly successful that it was adopted by the entire Primary— and then by parents outside the Primary, who realized that what worked with Primary classes would also prevent siblings from clobbering one another during family worship. These grateful parents told their friends outside the ward, who told *their* friends, and a tradition was born. Children who have grown up with the tradition believe that folding their arms is as integral to the ritual of prayer as bowing the head and closing the eyes.

We can only guess that the practice of arm folding sprang up during the late 1940s or early 1950s, because many adults who grew up in that period fold their arms when they pray. Older people usually don't do so. Also, nobody knew about body language back in the old days, so our legendary Primary teacher wouldn't have known that arms folded across the chest indicate hostility. All that would have concerned her was *preventing* hostility, and the folded arms were exactly what the doctor ordered.

Whether or not the theory is true, you may want to teach your children to fold their arms if they might otherwise run amok when their parents' eyes are closed in prayer. If you have no children it isn't necessary for you to fold your own arms – unless, that is, you're tempted to whack the person sitting next to you in Gospel Doctrine class.

Since I joined the Church, my whole life seems to have fallen apart. What's going on?

Most new converts report that life seems to take a dramatic turn for the better after baptism. When new Church members begin to follow the Word of Wisdom, they find themselves with greater health and a sense of better self-control. When they begin to pay tithing, they find themselves with increased financial blessings. When they begin to focus on family unity by holding family home evening, their children respond by choosing to live righteous lives. Church members expect this. After all, we've been promised blessings based upon our faithfulness and we expect the Lord to deliver.

But what many Church members don't understand is that smooth sailing isn't always based on virtue. It's all based on the law of averages. Church members *as a group* live longer than people who don't follow the Word of Wisdom, but individuals can get just as sick as people who smoke a pack a day. Tithepayers *as a group* can expect to have increased financial benefits by paying tithing, but individual Church members still face financial trials. And although children who have regular family home evenings will respond *as a group* by making proper choices, some children still occasionally take paths that lead to sorrow and sin. The key is to learn patience and humility and to realize that such problems are usually not sent from God as a punishment for our transgressions.

There's more than one reason why your baptism didn't bring the peace and joy you hoped it would bring. Your misfortunes could be the result of coincidence or design. They might be coincidental because everyone goes through tribulations in life, and you may be going through one of those periods. Or they could be a natural result of actions you've taken—actions that you didn't realize would have the effect they did. If you neglect to see a red light you're liable to get in an accident, whether or not you read your scriptures today.

If careful analysis of your situation tells you that you haven't done anything to deserve your current bad luck, look to see whether you're being singled out by design. God could be testing you to help strengthen you in a particular area. Trials in life teach us humility, and through humility we learn dependence on him. But sometimes the trials are sent to us by the Adversary, who uses discouragement as a tool to draw us away from God. These trials could come in the form of lost employment, poor health, or friends and relatives who ridicule us or even shun us after our baptism. It is not uncommon for new Church members to report an increase of such misfortunes prior to spiritual events such as baptism or a first visit to the temple.

If you're discouraged by the situation you're facing, take the matter to God in prayer. Sometimes he takes the trials away; other times he comforts us so that we'll be able to bear the burdens we have. All we can promise you is that if you endure, you will eventually be greatly rewarded—even if you don't receive a relief from your trials until the next life. Keep the faith.

2

CHURCH SERVICES AND OTHER MEETINGHOUSE ACTIVITIES

If you attended worship services in another church before you joined The Church of Jesus Christ of Latter-day Saints, you may have assumed LDS services would be somewhat similar. On the contrary, our meetings are unlike those of any other denomination. And there are also more of them. Mormons don't just run into church for an hour on Sunday, and our meetinghouses aren't dark for the rest of the week. Our faith is a growing, moving entity.

Our principal meetings take place during a three-hour block on Sundays. But there are also midweek meetings and classes of various sorts, as well as social occasions that appeal to young and old alike. Whenever you drive past an LDS meetinghouse, there are likely to be cars in the parking lot. When you hear Church members being referred to as "active," you can take it literally.

The Three-Hour Meeting Block

Sacrament Meeting

The most important meeting for members of The Church of Jesus Christ of Latter-day Saints is the weekly sacrament meeting. At this meeting, Church members partake of the sacrament (or communion) in remembrance of the Atonement.

After the sacrament, members of the congregation give inspirational messages.

In many wards, sacrament meeting is the first meeting of the congregation that is held on Sunday. In other meetinghouses, however, logistics demand that wards hold sacrament meeting at the end of their three-hour block. Whenever sacrament meeting occurs in your ward, the program is the same. The meeting will open with a hymn, which is followed by an opening prayer (usually referred to as the invocation) from a member of the congregation. There is much singing done in the LDS Church, and although you may be familiar with many of our hymns, others will be new and strange to you.

Sacrament meeting is customarily conducted by the bishop or one of his two counselors. After the opening prayer, ward business is finished before the remainder of the service begins. During this portion of the meeting, you may be asked to sustain (vote to support) ward members who have received new positions in the ward organization. This is done by raising your right hand when asked to do so. Hands are also raised to give a vote of thanks to people who have finished their service in a particular position. Anyone in the congregation can raise a hand to sustain or thank the people who serve, with the exception of former Church members who have been excommunicated and who have lost that privilege. If you attend sacrament meeting before you are baptized, you are welcome to raise your hand at the appropriate times. (For a more thorough explanation of the process of sustaining Church leaders, see chapter 3.)

After ward business is conducted, a hymn is sung to set the tone for the passing of the sacrament. The sacrament is passed by young men who first bless the bread and then take trays of bread to the seated members of the congregation. A similar process is then followed for the water (not wine!), as it is blessed and passed to the congregation. The prayers that are given are found in both the Book of Mormon and the Doctrine and Covenants, and they must be said perfectly. If a prayer is repeated, this means that some word or phrase was missed or said incorrectly, or an extra word or phrase was added.

The Mormon way of passing the sacrament may seem strange to people who are accustomed to taking communion in other churches. In many Protestant churches, communion is taken by anyone who professes a belief in the Savior, and in both Protestant and Catholic churches, worshipers who choose to take communion leave the congregation and walk to the altar in order to partake of the bread and grape juice or wine. In the LDS Church, only members of the Church in good standing are allowed to partake of the sacrament, but it is expected that anyone who is worthy to take the sacrament will do so. Thus it is more efficient to take the bread and the water to members of the congregation, rather than the other way around.

The sacrament is passed from one end of a pew to the other. A Church member usually takes the bread or the cup of water with his right hand and then uses his right hand to take the tray and pass it along the row to the next person. (Using the right hand for the sacrament is a custom rather than a law. If you find yourself holding a sleeping baby in your right arm when the sacrament is passed, the building isn't going to fall down around you if you use the left one.) If you attend church before your baptism and are unable to take the sacrament, just take the tray when it is offered to you and hold it so that the person sitting on the other side of you can take a piece of bread or a cup of water.

It may seem odd to you that although non-Mormons who love the Savior are not encouraged to take the sacrament in a sacrament meeting (although no one will stop them if they do), little children who have no concept of Christ's sacrifice are permitted to do so. Parents customarily give their children the sacrament as soon as they're able to chew the bread or to swallow the cup of water that is held to their lips by a parent. This is done to teach the children the importance of the sacrament. Young children may think of the bread and water as refreshments, and they'll raise a ruckus if the sacrament passes them by. However, as they grow older, they'll realize that the bread and water represent the body and blood of Christ.

As you progress in the Church, you might find that responsibilities or special occasions might take you to more than one sacrament meeting in a Sunday. When that happens, you may take the sacrament every time it is offered. It is always appropriate to contemplate the Atonement, even several times during the course of a single day.

Because of the sacredness of the sacrament service, those who attend are asked to quietly pray and meditate while the sacrament is being passed. Unfortunately, this doesn't always happen. The biggest complaint about sacrament meeting from new Church members is the lack of reverence in sacrament meeting, which is quite jarring to people who are accustomed to the solemnity of services in other denominations.

In many churches, children are segregated from adults, playing games in the nursery or participating in children's services so the adults can worship in peace. Latter-day Saints believe that children must be taught at a young age that Sunday is a day of worship. Children from birth on up are expected to be in church with their parents, and quite often these little ones take part in the program. Although you will find a traditional nursery operating in most wards, the nursery is not open for business during sacrament meeting.

Many families in the Church have several small children, and it can be difficult to keep an infant, a two-year-old, and a four-year-old content for a whole hour, especially for single parents or wives whose husbands must sit on the stand with the bishop. Sadly, there are also plenty of families with two able-bodied parents in the congregation who are either oblivious to the noise their children make or who don't know how to train their children to behave in church, and who let their children remain in the pews long after they should have been removed from the chapel. The result is that sacrament meetings in some wards are often more deafening than reverent. There's not much that you can do about the noise level, other than showing by the example of your own children that in most circumstances children can be quiet and happy when it is appropriate for them to be so. Some people can concentrate on the program despite the noise level, but if the din becomes unbearable for you, talk to the bishop or your home teachers to see if your ward can come up with a plan to help parents and children find a more reverent way to worship. (If you don't know what home teachers are, we'll tell you later.) If your attitude is one of helpful cooperation rather than criticism and complaint, you may find that people are more than willing to hear your suggestions.

After the sacrament service has ended, the remainder of the meeting consists of talks (sermons) that are given by members of the congregation or other invited speakers. Usually the talks are assigned weeks or even months ahead of time so Church members will have the opportunity to prepare a faith-promoting talk on a gospel subject. On rare occasions, however, a scheduled speaker may miss the meeting due to sudden illness or some other emergency. When that happens, bishops have been known to call people from the congregation and ask them to say a few words. It's always prudent to have a thought or two in mind, just in case.

One thing you'll never see in a Latter-day Saint meeting is the passing of a collection plate. Offerings and donations are not taken so casually that members of the congregation can dig into their pockets and pull out their spare change to give as an offering. You've probably already heard about tithing. If you want to read more about tithing and other contributions, there's a full description in chapter 8.

Fast and Testimony Meeting

Once a month, usually on the first Sunday of the month, the regular sacrament meeting is replaced by a fast and testimony meeting. This meeting gets its name because Church members are asked to abstain from food for two meals before the meeting. (See chapter 8 for a more complete explanation of fasting.)

If babies have been born into the congregation during the previous few weeks, each is given a name and a blessing at the beginning of fast and testimony meeting (see chapter 8). The naming and blessing ordinance is usually performed by the father, although any Melchizedek Priesthood holder can do it. Also, new convert members who have been recently baptized are usually confirmed as members of the Church in fast and testimony meeting. Otherwise, fast and testimony meetings proceed in the same order as sacrament meetings until the conclusion of the sacrament service. At that time, the person conducting the meeting stands and gives a brief inspirational thought to the congregation. This is known as bearing testimony. A testimony consists of a statement of beliefs, such as, "I testify to the truthfulness of the Book of Mormon," or "I have a strong faith in redemption through the Atonement." The person bearing his testimony may also tell of a spiritual experience he had recently or talk about a lesson he has learned.

The person conducting the meeting concludes his testimony by using the same words that close all talks that are given in an LDS sacrament meeting: "In the name of Jesus Christ, amen." Members of the congregation should then also say "amen" to signify that they agree with what has been said. At that point, he'll invite members of the congregation to come forward and share their testimonies as they are prompted by the Spirit to do so.

There are two basic rules for bearing testimony in a testimony meeting. Keep it short, and keep it humble. Don't try to impress people with travelogues or overwhelm them with your intelligence or your superior spiritual gifts, and don't make a habit of standing up every month to the exclusion of others who would like to bear their testimonies. If you are impressed to stand and make a few remarks, feel free to do so. As long as your testimony is brief and simple, the congregation will look forward to hearing what you have to say.

Primary and Sunday School

If sacrament meeting is held first in the three-hour block, at the meeting's conclusion ward members and visitors go to classes that are geared toward their respective age groups. Babes in arms accompany their parents, but from the time a child is 18 months old, there is a class that is geared to his needs. From age 18 months to three years, children attend the nursery. Here they are given activities based on their ability to participate. Regular Primary classes begin when children reach the age of three. By then, most of them are ready to sit still enough to listen to lessons that are prepared for their age group.

Although adults and children over age 12 attend two different meetings during the second two hours of the three-hour block, Primary lasts for both hours. The lessons and activities are usually excellent, and young children are willing listeners.

With the exception of the home, Primary is viewed as the most important teaching tool for Mormon children.

As a parent of a Primary child, you'll find that your child is often asked to recite a scripture or give a talk or a prayer during the portion of Primary when all the children meet together. Parents often leave their own classes to attend Primary just long enough to give moral support to the child who is in the spotlight.

Children graduate from Primary when they reach their 12th birthday. From that time forward, they attend Sunday School during this second hour of the meeting block. Lessons are once again geared to the age of the student, although most age groups should ideally be covering roughly the same lesson material every week. If the teachers stay on schedule, families can go home after church and discuss the day's lesson topic, with each member of the family able to contribute to the discussion.

Beginning with the 15-year-old course of study, Sunday School lessons are taught in four year-long cycles. As a new member of the Church, you may attend a Gospel Principles class for a brief time. (See chapter 8 for a fuller explanation.) Otherwise, you'll study the scriptures in a repeating, four-year cycle. A year is given to the Old Testament, with lessons supplemented by text from the Pearl of Great Price. This is followed by a year devoted to the New Testament. A year dedicated to the Book of Mormon comes next, with the last year in the cycle being spent on the Doctrine and Covenants. Then the cycle begins again.

Converts may be surprised at how much material is covered in one week of Sunday School. When she was a Protestant, attending a Protestant Sunday School, Kathy spent three years studying 1 Corinthians. It was a major culture shock for her to go to a Sunday School where whole books of the Bible were covered in the course of a single Sunday. But eventually she learned that she was expected to do additional scripture study alone, where she could go as quickly or as slowly as her interests dictated. In the LDS Church, lessons focus not as much on individual scriptures as on the moral lessons that can be learned from them. Sunday School lessons should supplement personal scripture study, not replace it.

Priesthood, Young Women, Relief Society

The remaining part of the meeting block finds ward members scattering in every direction. The men (and this includes boys age 12 and up) attend priesthood meeting. From age 12 through high school graduation, girls attend a meeting of the Young Women organization. And from high school graduation onward, women attend Relief Society. Unlike Sunday School, where lessons concentrate on an understanding of the scriptures, meetings that are held in this third hour focus on the challenges of life and how to overcome them. Adult courses of study focus on the teachings of latter-day prophets and the scriptures.

Priesthood holders belong to groups called quorums. At age 12, boys are called as deacons in the Aaronic Priesthood. When they reach their fourteenth birthday, worthy young men are allowed to hold the office of teachers. After their sixteenth birthdays, they may be advanced to the office of priest. The office of elder marks the transition from the Aaronic Priesthood to the Melchizedek Priesthood. A young man may be approved to be an elder at any time after his eighteenth birthday. Eventually, as they mature in the gospel, men will advance once again to become high priests. (For an explanation of priesthood offices and functions, see chapter 8.)

Priesthood meetings begin with opening exercises, which consist of an opening song, a prayer, any pertinent announcements, and other priesthood business. After all priesthood business is finished, boys and men divide into quorums to conduct quorum business. Priesthood advancements may be done during quorum meetings, too; often families will come from their other classes to see a son or husband ordained to his new calling. After the ordinations have been completed, family members are dismissed and the quorum members participate in their weekly lessons. These lessons focus on spiritually strengthening men of all ages as individuals, family members, and quorum members. (Ordinations may take place at other times as well, such as in the bishop's office following the meeting block.)

While the men meet in their priesthood quorums, the

young women hold similar meetings. They too meet in classes that are divided by age group. Beehives are girls aged 12 and 13, Mia Maids are 14 and 15, and Laurels are 16 and 17. The Young Women program serves the twofold purpose of strengthening each young woman individually and strengthening her family. Weekly lessons are devoted to these two purposes, as young women learn how to apply gospel principles in their daily lives.

All women who have reached the age of 18 are considered to be members of the Relief Society. The Relief Society is the oldest auxiliary in the Church, having been organized by the Prophet Joseph Smith in response to a revelation from God. From the beginning, the Relief Society has been the arm of the Church that has provided compassionate service to those in need; the *relief* in Relief Society refers to this foundation of charity. Sunday meetings cover a variety of topics that inspire women to spiritual growth, or give instruction on individual and family issues. Since the beginning of 1998, The Relief Society and the Melchizedek Priesthood quorums study from the same lesson manual in order to promote unified gospel study in the home.

Midweek Activities

As a member of The Church of Jesus Christ of Latter-day Saints, you'll find that you're likely to be over at the meetinghouse nearly any day of the week for one reason or another. The only exception to this is Monday, when no meetings are scheduled. Monday night is considered a family night throughout the Church, and members are strongly encouraged to spend the evening with their families in family home evenings. (A fuller explanation of family home evenings will be given in chapter 7.)

During the remainder of the week, there's a wide variety of auxiliary and other meetings that may be held in a ward meetinghouse. The following list is by no means all-inclusive, but it may give you an indication of why Church members are referred to as "active":

Seminary and Institute

High school students (grades nine through twelve) receive scriptural instruction in seminary classes that are held on school days throughout the school year. In areas where Church members are so numerous that they're under every cabbage leaf, students may be released from school to go to seminary in a building that is set aside for the purpose, with a regular faculty who teach seminary as a career. But in most areas, seminary is taught by ward members and is held in ward meetinghouses or in members' homes at an hour of the morning that is too early for most of us to contemplate. If you happen to drive by your meetinghouse at 6 A.M. on a weekday and see lights in the windows and cars in the parking lot, you'll know that seminary is in session.

A similar program known as institute is designed for college students, but is also open to anyone interested in taking the classes. Depending on the circumstances, institute may meet in a special building close to campus, or it may meet in a ward meetinghouse.

Scouts

The LDS Church has been traditionally involved in the Boy Scout program, at least in the United States. Boys begin Scouting at a young age—typically when they enter the Cub program as eight-year-olds or when they begin the second grade. They progress through the rank of Wolf and Bear until they reach age 10, when they are given a rank that may not be familiar to you—Webelos. (Webelos are not wild animals related to badgers. The name is an acronym that stands for "WE'll BE LOyal Scouts.") After graduation from Webelos, a boy officially leaves the Cub program and becomes a Scout.

From the time the boy receives the Aaronic Priesthood at age 12, his Scouting experience is linked with his priesthood quorum. Boys are encouraged to continue in Scouting through their mid-teenage years, and LDS troops have high percentages of Eagle Scouts. Scout meetings and activities are typically held in ward meetinghouses on weekday nights.

Young Men and Young Women

The Young Men program in the ward consists of the Aaronic Priesthood quorums (deacons, teachers, and priests), plus midweek activities that may include Scouting and other activities. Sunday is their day for spiritual instruction, but the midweek activities are more educational, recreational, or service oriented. Activities should be divided according to age group, but on occasion all the youth in the ward get together for activities. The basketball hoops in the cultural hall provide a strong attraction for young men to visit the meetinghouse on nights when no meetings are scheduled.

The Young Women program is similar, although it does not include Scouting. (The Church does not officially affiliate with the Girl Scout program.) Sunday classes concentrate on spiritual matters, while the midweek activity is more for fun, practical learning, and service. Classes should normally meet separately, but occasionally all age groups meet together, and sometimes they meet with the Young Men for a combined activity.

Relief Society Homemaking Meetings

Once a month, usually on a weekday evening, Relief Society women gather for an evening of social activity. The name "homemaking meeting" doesn't even begin to cover the range of activities that are accomplished at that monthly event. Often, a meal of some kind will be served to those who attend. Classes are also held in a range of subjects, from spiritual to whimsical. In homemaking meeting, women may learn to cook foreign food or plan their vacations. They may create works of art in a craft class or learn the principles of home storage. Although it is often difficult for women to attend homemaking meeting after a busy day, those who make the sacrifice are almost always glad they did.

Bishop's Meetings

If there is one place you can often find your bishop, it's in your ward meetinghouse. He has so many meetings in the building that he's usually in residence several times a week. If your Church responsibilities require that you attend a meeting in the bishop's office, please make every effort to attend. (He's already left the comfort of his home and is waiting for you.) And if you need to talk with your bishop outside a scheduled meeting, he's available by appointment through his executive secretary.

Libraries and Research

Most ward meetinghouses will contain a meetinghouse library, where teachers can go to get resource materials. These libraries aren't only open to teachers, however. Parents and other ward members can check out materials to use in home study. Written materials are available, as well as artwork and audiovisual aids. There's often a photocopier, too, but for some reason photocopiers in LDS meetinghouses are unfailingly temperamental. If by chance you find a photocopier that is in working order when you start printing, it will probably break before your printing job is done. Use that photocopier only when there's no other option, and never assume that it's in working order. Ward meetinghouse libraries are often open one evening per week for the convenience of Church members. Please don't ask ward librarians to make a special trip to the library for you. Instead, make every effort to visit the library when it's open for business.

Many ward meetinghouses are also equipped with a family history center, where ward members can go to do genealogical research. These libraries aren't just open to Church members; family history librarians often lament that there are more non-LDS patrons than LDS ones. If you don't know how to do genealogical research, don't despair. Somebody in the family history center will be glad to teach you, free of charge.

Social Occasions

One thing about Church members is that they look for any excuse to have a party. All you have to do is bring out the refreshments, and Saints come from miles around. Numerous social occasions are held in LDS meetinghouses, among them organized ward activities, weddings and wedding receptions, baptisms, and funerals. The following section gives a brief overview of what you can expect at these social events.

Ward Activities

One of the foundations of any ward organization is the ward activities committee. Members of this committee are faced with the challenging task of putting together social events that appeal to diverse Latter-day Saint congregations. Two major areas of focus are cultural arts and athletics. The activities committee may sponsor plays or roadshows or talent shows, but it is just as likely to sponsor basketball or baseball tournaments. There are also parties and picnics centered around holidays or other seasonal celebrations. Your activity committee's calendar of events is limited only by the imagination and the energy of the committee members. Ward activities are excellent opportunities to get to know the other members of your congregation, and they are also an ideal means to introduce nonmember friends to the Church.

Weddings and Wedding Receptions

The goal for LDS men and women is to have their marriages performed in temples rather than in ward meetinghouses (see chapters 7 and 9). However, there are numerous circumstances that may prohibit a couple from going to the temple to be married. When that happens, civil marriages may be performed in some part of a meetinghouse other than the chapel, or in a home. Marriages may be performed on any day except Sunday; receptions aren't scheduled on Sundays or on Monday nights.

Mormon wedding receptions offer wonderful creative opportunities for the mother of the bride, who has to devise a way to camouflage the basketball hoops in the ward cultural hall. No matter what she does, the cultural hall will still look like a basketball court when the reception is held. The polite fiction is that everybody pretends not to notice.

LDS receptions are similar to wedding receptions held in

other churches except that no liquor is served and nobody would even think of lighting a cigarette. In the United States, refreshments at an LDS wedding reception have a reputation for being sugary and caloric. Don't expect to dine on heavy hors d'oeuvres when your Mormon friends get married. However, you may find several varieties of nonalcoholic punch in an assortment of intriguing colors.

Baptisms

The ordinance of baptism is fully explained in chapter 8, but since baptisms are also considered to be social occasions, a brief overview here is also appropriate.

Baptisms can be held on any day of the week, with the exception of Monday night. Family, friends, and ward members may be invited. The baptism itself is brief, and there is usually a short spiritual program as well. Although a new Latter-day Saint used to be confirmed a member of the Church immediately after baptism, a recent change recommends that this should now be done on a later Sunday. (See chapter 8.) Depending on how it is done in your ward, young children who are baptized may either be confirmed immediately after baptism or on a later Sunday. Refreshments may follow the service.

Funerals

Before you joined the Church, your experience with death may have been limited. In the United States, death is made to be as impersonal as possible. When a person dies, his body is picked up by the mortuary staff and taken to the mortuary, where it is dressed and prepared for a funeral that is likely to be held on the mortuary premises and conducted by an anonymous clergyman or lay person who is affiliated with the mortuary and who may be unknown to the people who attend the funeral. Funerals are conducted so quickly that they often take place the day after a death, and the relatives of the deceased have no responsibilities except to choose the casket and pay for the services.

In the LDS Church, death is a function of life. It is a graduation of sorts, and although the family members and ward members grieve for the loss of the loved one, they also celebrate that loved one's life by taking an active part in the funeral.

Although the actual preparation of the body is done in accordance with local laws, Church members often dress the body for burial. When possible, adult members who have been endowed in a temple are buried in their temple clothes (see chapter 9). Clothing is placed on the deceased person by a family member if that is the family's preference; if not, deceased women are often dressed by the Relief Society president, and men are dressed by a man who is designated by the bishop. Some mortuaries (particularly in areas with large LDS populations) will have LDS staff members who are qualified to do this.

Family members take an active part in the funeral service itself. The funeral is usually held in the meetinghouse chapel, and it features speakers and musical numbers similar to a sacrament meeting. Because a funeral is a formal Church meeting, it is held under the direction of the bishop, and the bishop will control the content of the program. The bishop will usually defer to the wishes of the family however, provided the proposed program is in keeping with the spirit of a Church meeting. Typically, the speakers at the funeral are chosen by family members and often include the family members themselves and other ward members.

Although funerals are usually somber occasions, the family has some latitude in determining the tone of the funeral. We attended one funeral where the deceased man himself, an elderly gentleman who had plenty of notice that his death was imminent, performed at his own funeral. He taped himself singing his favorite songs and telling stories, and the tape was played to the delight of the mourners who attended. Although it's extremely unusual for a person to perform at his own funeral, it's quite common to hear laughter at a funeral service as fond memories of the deceased are recounted by those who speak.

Because family members take such an active part in the funeral, funeral services for Church members are usually held several days after a death. This gives the speakers time to prepare their talks, and it allows family members and friends to travel to the service from far-flung areas. Between the time of death and the day of the funeral, so much food is taken by ward members to the family of the deceased that no matter how many relatives arrive from distant cities, they never want for something to eat. In addition, family members and close friends are often provided a meal after the dedication of the grave and the graveside service. This meal, which can be held at the meetinghouse or at the family home, is usually prepared and served by Relief Society members.

Sharing a Building

It's a rare LDS ward that has a meetinghouse all to itself. Most of them are shared by at least two wards, and many of them by four or even more. This poses many a logistical nightmare for the people who want to schedule activities and who may have trouble finding enough free days in the month to squeeze everything onto the calendar.

When you attend church, you may find members of other wards using a different part of the building from the one where your meetings are being held. Occasionally there may be several groups sharing a meetinghouse at the same time. Great care is taken to make sure every congregation sharing the building has equal access to the meetinghouse. This includes rotating meeting schedules every year so no ward has the best schedule all the time. For example, your ward may meet from 9:00 A.M. to noon one year, from 11:00 A.M. to 2:00 P.M. the next year, and from 1:00 P.M. to 4:00 P.M. the year after that. Most wards rotate their schedules on January 1.

Another tactic to maximize space is to shift the order of the meetings. Your ward may hold sacrament meeting during the last hour of the three-hour block instead of the first hour so another ward can use the chapel while your ward is in the building. And each ward that meets in a building will probably have a different "activity night" when homemaking meetings and Young Men–Young Women meetings are held every week. If your ward auxiliaries meet on Tuesday night, your sister ward's activity night may be Wednesday or Thursday.

In order to maintain absolute fairness in the sharing of the meetinghouse, the wards that meet in the same building will take turns acting as agent ward over the meetinghouse. The bishop of the agent ward is called the agent bishop; he is responsible for coordinating any repairs or other changes to the meetinghouse during the year he acts as agent, and he is the final authority on any decisions that are made concerning the meetinghouse during his tenure. Each bishop will also call someone from the ward to serve as the building coordinator so that all the wards may coordinate their activities together. If you're in charge of an activity, it should be scheduled in advance with the building coordinator. Otherwise, the cooking class you've planned may be squeezed out of the kitchen by a wedding reception for somebody in another ward.

A Convert's Questions

What should I wear to church?

Although the trend in many churches is to attract worshipers by inviting them to "come as you are," members of the LDS Church still use the term *Sunday best*. In the United States, men generally wear jackets and ties to church on Sunday. Almost without exception, women and girls wear dresses to Sunday meetings. Modesty, not fashion, is the rule. Church members strive to present themselves in a way that won't distract from the worship of others and that will show respect for the Lord.

Boys are asked to wear ties and white shirts when they pass (distribute) the sacrament. This isn't a doctrine, and in most wards it isn't even a rule: it's a sign of respect for the ordinance they're performing. If white shirts are a custom in your ward, and if your son passes the sacrament, you may want to purchase a white shirt for him when your budget allows.

If you see someone who doesn't abide by these general outlines, don't shun him. Some people don't know better, some people can't afford to dress up, and some people may have physical handicaps that prohibit them from dressing in the prescribed way. It is also common for people to be visiting from out of town, only to realize they forgot to pack any nice clothes for church. People are more important than the clothes they are wearing. It's far more essential for a person to come to church at all than it is for him to come in the proper attire. Just as Church members strive to dress in a way that won't detract from the worship of others, it is equally true that we should be so involved in the act of worship that we don't even notice what other people are wearing.

A story is told about President Spencer W. Kimball, who led the Church during a period when miniskirts were all the rage. One day he was walking down the street with one of his associates when they were passed on the sidewalk by two girls who were wearing the shortest of skirts. The associate said, "Isn't that terrible! Those girls' skirts were so short you could see their underwear!" President Kimball responded, "I didn't notice. I was too busy looking at their beautiful smiling faces."

During other meetings throughout the week, circumstances should determine the attire that is worn. Baptisms, weddings, and funerals call for Sunday clothes, but other meetings may demand more casual dress. Early morning seminary, for example, may find teenagers in sweat suits, with their mothers in curlers waiting for them outside in the car. Many women wear slacks or jeans to Relief Society homemaking meetings or other events when the activities are strenuous or messy. If you dress modestly and use your common sense to dictate what should be worn to a Church-sponsored event, you probably won't go too far astray. But if you're still nervous, you can always check with others in your ward to see what they're going to wear on a particular occasion.

Why are there Cheerios all over the floor of the chapel?

Cheerios are so common in sacrament meeting that most Church members don't give them a second thought, but their presence may be confusing to newcomers. In many denominations, young children don't attend the Sunday worship service. But, as we've already noted in this chapter, LDS children attend sacrament meeting from birth onward. The presence of children can be a distraction to the spirit of worship under the best of circumstances, but the situation is complicated when wards share a building and children are forced to sit in meetings during times when they'd normally be eating or sleeping. Under those conditions, children tend to get cranky and noisy—not the optimum condition for them during an hour of enforced silence.

Cheerios are used by many mothers to keep the little ones occupied so they won't make even more noise during sacrament meeting than they already do. Most mothers choose Cheerios because they don't contain dyes that would stain the carpet in the chapel or sugar that might cause hyperactivity. And no, it isn't considered good form to eat your children's Cheerios. For adults, breath mints are considered the refreshment of choice.

Speaking of Cheerios on the carpet, who cleans the meetinghouse?

To an extent, you do. The heavy cleaning is usually done by a cleaning service that comes to the building at least once a week, at least in the United States. But if you're part of a group that meets in the building at any time of the week other than Sunday, the people who attend that activity are expected to clean up after it.

Remember that congregations share a building. If you leave the printed program from sacrament meeting on the pew, somebody else will have to move the program or sit on it. Even on Sunday, it's always wiser to leave a room cleaner than you found it. But during the week, keeping the meetinghouse clean is crucial. You may be tempted to leave a building in disarray if you have an activity on Tuesday night, especially if you're expecting the custodians on Wednesday morning. But you never know when the custodians will have to change their schedule, leaving the building untended before another ward's activity. It's always prudent to do the basic cleaning yourselves, just in case.

I'm not the slightest bit interested in learning how to be a homemaker. Do I have to go to homemaking meetings?

Lots of women stay away from homemaking meeting because they aren't interested in home arts, but they're missing the point of homemaking meeting. The hidden benefit of homemaking meeting is that it provides an opportunity for women to make friends with one another. When women are making a wreath or chopping vegetables, they are indeed honing their skills. But the crafts and cooking only exist to give women something to do with their hands as they spend a few hours of relaxation with other LDS women.

In homemaking meetings, women find kindred souls to befriend themselves and their families. They can find other ward members to share their joys and their sorrows. They can seek out women with husbands who have similar interests to those of their own husbands, or children who might be compatible with their own children.

If you're a new ward member and you're lucky enough to be a woman, seek out homemaking meeting at every opportunity. If you're a man, gently persuade your wife to go there. Your transition into a new ward will be greatly eased by your family's contact with homemaking meeting, and your interaction in an old ward will be continually strengthened by the time that is spent forging friends in that monthly gathering of women.

Why are Church members so obnoxious at sporting events?

One of the mysteries of our religion is why some people see fit to leave their Christianity at home when they pick up a basketball. Ideally, the people who play basketball or volleyball or whatever sport is played in a church setting should realize that the game is just a game and that the exercise and fun are more important than the win. Most people do understand that, but the ones who don't grasp the concept of sportsmanship are so visible—and so vocal—that they can't be overlooked. Rumor has it that more people have left the Church because of the poor sportsmanship of others than ever joined it because of the comradery displayed in the basketball games.

In many areas, poor sportsmanship by players has caused Church leaders to abandon sports programs altogether. If the Church still sponsors sporting events in your area, don't participate if your testimony can be shattered by learning that some Church members turn into fang-toothed monsters when they play competitive sports. And if you're one of the fang-toothed beasts who can't get any enjoyment out of a game unless you win, and who make that abundantly clear to everyone around you, please do everyone a favor and stay home.

My friends and I are Spanish, and ward socials aren't designed for us. Everything is geared to American tastes, with people standing around and talking and eating refreshments. For us, it's not a party without dancing. And we also feel uncomfortable with people who stand so far away from each other and don't touch each other the way we're accustomed to doing. How can we be more comfortable in our ward?

We can't promise you any miracles, but we can offer you a little advice. First, you need to look at what can realistically be changed, and what can't. It's a cultural habit for people of Anglo descent to stand farther away from each other than do people of Spanish descent. That's a fact of life. In this respect, all you can do is to realize that when Anglos back away from you, they're doing it because you're inside their comfort zone and not because they don't like you. By the same token, they should keep in mind that when you occasionally step inside their comfort zone, you aren't doing it to be obnoxious or pushy. It's the same way with touching. A lot of people like to be touched, but others are unaccustomed to it. If you touch someone who flinches, try not to touch that person again. But that person should realize you are exhibiting appropriate behavior for your culture and should make allowances for those cultural differences. This isn't a case of one thing being right and another being wrong. People are shaped by their culture, one way or another.

Now that we've mentioned what can't be changed, here's some advice about things that can. The roots of our church are definitely American, but there isn't a law that says all ward activities have to cater to Anglo tastes. Church members should be delighted when people of other cultures offer to share cultures with ward members, and there are many ways you can do it. Volunteer to teach a cooking class in homemaking meeting. Volunteer to be in charge of a ward Christmas party or other celebration. A Cinco de Mayo party may be ideal for you to host for the members of your ward. (People who were raised in other cultures can plan parties based on their own national holidays.) A Thanksgiving meal of your own traditional foods might be readily received by your ward activities committee. If you want dancing, volunteer to teach ward members how to dance.

It's unrealistic to think that every ward activity can be geared around your culture, especially if you're a small minority in your ward. But there should be several opportunities every year for you to be able to show your Anglo friends how to have a good time. Talk to your bishop to see what you can come up with or volunteer to serve on the ward activities committee. And be sure to take advantage of returned missionaries who served in your native land. They can often bring multicultural awareness to domestic wards and serve as a resource to people of various backgrounds.

If it's any consolation, there will soon be more Church members with Spanish roots than with Anglo ones. Bide your time.

Why didn't you tell us about the tabernacles the Church builds?

For many nonmembers, one of the few things they associate with the Church is the image of the Mormon Tabernacle Choir singing in the famed tabernacle on Temple Square in Salt Lake City. As a result of this, one might get the erroneous impression that the Church builds a lot of tabernacles. The Church does own several tabernacles, but they all date back to a time when a tabernacle was the only option for holding large church meetings.

Today, the tabernacle has been replaced with the satellite dish, as many Church buildings are built to accommodate regular broadcasts of meetings from Church headquarters. So, in a sense, millions of people are still gathering together, but they are using an electronic tabernacle rather than a physical one.

We would expect there will always need to be a tabernacle in Salt Lake City. In fact, plans to build a larger meeting hall just a stone's throw from the old tabernacle were announced in 1997. The Salt Lake Tabernacle is important because of its history, and also because conferences and other meetings are regularly held there and then beamed around the world via satellite. But for people who live away from Church headquarters, the "satellite dish tabernacle" is all the tabernacle they'll ever need.

Why do our meetinghouses have those tacky silk flowers all over the place?

Church members have an eye for beauty, and if it were possible their meetinghouses would be filled with artwork and murals and stained glass windows similar to those that are so conducive to worship in other churches. But ours is a practical religion, and meetinghouses are costly enough without adding expensive decorations. The rational alternative is flowers, but fresh flowers also cost a lot of money. It's hard to justify the cost of fresh bouquets or live plants, financed by tithing dollars, when people in the world are starving. Unless there has been a wedding reception or a funeral in the meetinghouse during the past week, or a ward member has brought a floral arrangement from his own garden, live flowers just aren't part of the budget. But in nearly every meetinghouse some compassionate soul usually buys a silk flower arrangement or two to add a little beauty to the surroundings. Some of them even look almost real, especially if you squint.

If the concept of silk flowers in a house of worship drives you crazy, here are a couple of options for you. First, you can grow your own garden and bring live flowers to replace those dusty silk ones. Everyone will think you're a hero. But if you're not a gardener, you can look upon those silk flowers as an object lesson. President Gordon B. Hinckley has compared silk flowers to some people—pretty, but without life or purpose. He councils Church members to develop spiritual roots that will allow them to weather the storms of life. From now on when you look at the silk flowers, remind yourself that you don't want to be a "silk flower" Church member, but a living, vital member of the community.

3

WHAT EXACTLY IS THIS CALLING THING?

If you've already attended a Sunday service in the LDS Church, you've probably noticed how many different people participated. In sacrament meeting, you probably saw ushers who greeted you, music people who accompanied and directed the congregational singing, and young boys who prepared and distributed the sacrament to the congregation. The music and talks that followed the sacrament were probably also presented by members of the ward.

Throughout Sunday School and Primary, Young Men and Young Women, Relief Society and priesthood meetings, the same thing happened. The meetings were kept moving by the members of the ward, each of them filling roles that had been previously assigned.

As you learned in the previous chapter, there are a large number of organizations within each ward that are designed to meet the needs of its various members. These organizations do not run themselves but require dozens of people to serve as leaders, teachers, and secretaries. When you start adding up all these numbers, you start to wonder. How did they rope all these people into doing all this work? How much are they paid for all they do?

A Lay Ministry

Although most churches have paid ministers who serve the congregation on a full-time or part-time basis, the LDS Church uses a lay ministry and expects the members of each ward to provide the needed leadership and service without financial compensation. Even the bishop, who devotes countless hours of time each week to the ward, receives no salary for his efforts.

The Church does employ some full-time administrative staff, but most of these people work at the headquarters offices of the Church in Salt Lake City, Utah. A few people in your local area are also employed to perform maintenance and cleaning services for Church buildings, although even there the local members are expected to do their part in keeping the building clean and maintained. But for the most part, the vast majority of service provided in the Church is donated by the individual members. They do this with no expectation of financial reward. Rather, they show their love of the Lord by serving their brothers and sisters in their wards and communities.

When a Church member gives time to serve others in the Church, that service performs a dual purpose. Not only is the ward enriched by the talents of the one who works, but the worker himself is also blessed because he grows socially and spiritually. Think of the way a flower gives beauty to those around it. At the same time its blossom and fragrance delight us, the flower is attracting the bees that will pollinate it and offer renewed life to the plant. The rewards for such service are spiritual in nature, and Church members who serve consider themselves richly blessed.

The remainder of this chapter will describe the procedure used by your bishop to fill the various service positions in your ward and will also describe what you should expect as a new member in terms of the service that you will probably be asked to provide. The next chapter will provide descriptions of the various positions for service in a typical ward.

The Proper Order of Things

Before proceeding further, we should probably add another

word to that list of words that seem to be unique to the
Mormon faith and culture (by now you probably have a
growing list of such words). The various service positions that
exist in the Church are referred to as "callings." You might hear
someone say, "I am so excited about my new ward calling," or,
less optimistically, "That new ward calling of mine has me
scared to death." Sometimes the word *job* is used, as in "What
is your church job?" However, *calling* is more common and
more proper.

The term *calling* is used because it emphasizes the divine
nature of the assignment. Just as God called Moses and
Abraham to be prophets in ancient times, so He calls Saints to
build His kingdom in the latter-day Church. The procedure
used to place people in callings is quite formal. It follows the
same protocol in all locations of the world and in all callings in
the Church. The woman who is called as a new Primary president in Eugene, Oregon, for example, would have been placed
in that position by means of the same procedure as the man
called to be a new Young Men president in London, England.
One reason for this is to ensure a consistency of Church operation in all areas of the world.

Some non-LDS denominations vary greatly from congregation to congregation, even within the same city. The members
of these denominations may profess to belong to the same
church, but there is great diversity both in the day-to-day operation of their individual congregations and also in the doctrines
they profess to believe. Members of the LDS Church are often
amused to read accounts of how some denominations have
voted to accept certain doctrines during their conferences while
other congregations have dissented and announced that they
will not accept those teachings. Such a concept is foreign to
Latter-day Saints. Although each ward and branch in the
Church will have its own local color and distinct personality,
you will find a remarkable consistency in the way the Church
works in all parts of the world. This degree of consistency is
comforting. It is part of the reason you will immediately feel at
home when visiting any Mormon congregation anywhere in the
on earth.

A more important reason for the consistency you will find
in the Church is that the Lord himself has commanded that it

should be thus. As recorded in Doctrine and Covenants 132:8: "Behold, mine house is a house of order, saith the Lord God, and not a house of confusion." Revelation has told us that the proper order of the Church comes through obedience to prophets who are inspired by God to guide and direct Church members in their worship. No Saint who is in harmony with the Spirit of God would presume to override decisions that have been made by the true and living prophet.

The process of calling members to serve in the Church is done as three distinct and separate events—the calling, the sustaining, and the setting apart. Each of these will now be explained in detail.

The Calling

Only those who have the proper authority may issue callings in the Church. In most cases, this will be your bishop or one of his counselors. The Lord has given the bishop the responsibility to oversee the spiritual progress of the members in your ward, which also gives him the authority (in the name of the Lord) to call people to assist him in accomplishing that charge. When the bishop asks you to accept a calling in the ward, you should treat that with the same reverence as if Jesus Christ Himself had called you. This doesn't mean that you are bound by an ironclad edict to accept all callings that are issued to you, but it does mean that you should consider each request as though it were the Lord Himself issuing the calling.

Although the bishop has a sacred responsibility, or stewardship, to guide and direct his ward members, some callings in the Church are issued by other authorities. If you are a man who holds the priesthood, your priesthood leaders may issue callings relating to the operation of their quorums. Also, you will learn in chapter 5 about callings in the stake. These callings are issued by stake authorities. In both cases, callings are made after consultation with the bishop, who is ultimately responsible for the members of his ward.

Another word you will often hear in the Church is delegation. This refers to a case where someone with authority will delegate, or assign, part of his authority to somebody else.

There are some duties that a bishop must always do himself, and some that can be delegated to his counselors or to organization leaders. The issuing of callings is one duty that can be delegated, at least for many callings. As counselors are often asked by the bishop to oversee certain auxiliaries in the ward, it is also common for the bishop to delegate the issuing of callings in that organization. For example, the bishopric counselor assigned to oversee the Primary organization will often issue the callings within the Primary, or the Relief Society president may call a member of the Relief Society to a particular position, such as visiting teacher. This does not mean the bishop is unaware of the callings. The bishop is involved in all ward callings and must approve each one, even if he delegates to others the actual task of issuing the call to the member.

When issuing the actual calling, the bishop or other authority will have a private meeting with the person to be called. There are probably as many different ways to issue callings as there are leaders in the Church. Some leaders will jump right into it, spare you the suspense, and just say, "Brother Jones, the Lord wants you to serve in this ward as first counselor in the Sunday School presidency." Others will prefer to visit for a while and help you feel a bit more comfortable before asking the big question. They will ask about your life, your family, your work, your testimony, and your general impressions of the ward. They may even explore certain organizations or callings in the ward, and you might start to get a general feeling about the calling that is about to be issued. Some leaders are very open about this, and will even say something to the effect of, "We need a new Young Women president in the ward, and I would like to hear your feelings about that calling." You should be honest and open during this discussion, as the leader probably wants to verify that you are in a position to accept the calling he is about to offer you and that you would feel comfortable in serving in that calling. You should feel free to ask questions during this part of the interview. If he is discussing a position in one of the auxiliary organizations, you might ask, "Who are the other people in that organization, and what would they expect of someone in that position?"

After some period of discussion, the bishop or other leader may decide that you are not in a position to accept the calling.

In that case, the calling will not be issued, and the interview will be concluded. If the bishop is satisfied that you would accept the calling and that you are the right person for the job, he will do so by saying something like "Sister Jones, I feel that the Lord wants me to extend to you a calling to be the Young Women president in our ward."

Before you give an answer, it is still appropriate to ask more questions if you have them. A common question is, "Why me?" (The common answer to that question is the less-than-helpful, "Why *not* you?") Or you might have more specific concerns about what would be involved. Or you may have reservations or concerns that you think might affect your ability to carry out the calling. All of these should be discussed with the leader before giving an answer.

When you are comfortable that all your questions have been answered, the time has come to accept the calling or refuse it. As a general rule, most callings are accepted (you can read more about this in the questions at the end of this chapter). Remember that the person issuing the calling is your spiritual adviser and would not issue a calling unless he thought it was in your best interest and the best interest of those whom you will serve.

Sometimes you may be intimidated by the time commitment a new calling will entail. The bishop will completely understand this, because no matter what calling he extends to you it won't take nearly the time as his own calling does! Other times you may feel inadequate to the job. Some Church callings can be mighty intimidating. There's a saying in the Church: "Whom the Lord calls, He qualifies." That little homily is a great comfort to people who feel inadequate in a new calling, because as trite as it is, it seems to be true.

The bishop realizes that it may be a sacrifice at times for you to serve and that you may be haunted by feelings of inadequacy. Yet with that understanding, he or his delegated representative has still been impressed to issue the calling to you. Here's your opportunity to show a little faith and accept it.

If you decline a calling, it is appropriate to tell the person who issued the calling why you cannot accept. Sometimes, especially if the bishop has felt strongly inspired to issue the call, he may hear your concerns and ask you if you will accept the calling anyway. Bishops are well aware that people who accept callings are often blessed in many ways. In all likelihood, even a calling that seems unsuited to your talents can bless your life in ways you cannot yet fathom. If you listen to what the bishop or his representative has to say and still believe it would be in your best interests to decline the calling, the bishop will accept your decision and offer the calling to somebody else. If you accept the calling, however, the next step will be to get you sustained.

The Sustaining

One thing unique about The Church of Jesus Christ of Latter-days Saints is that every member serving in a calling must be approved by the other members with whom they will serve. This is known as the law of common consent and is described in Doctrine and Covenants 26:2: "And all things shall be done by common consent in the church, by much prayer and faith, for all things you shall receive by faith."

Before you can serve in your new calling, you must be sustained by those members you will serve with or preside over. In most cases, this will be the members of your ward. For brethren called to serve in priesthood callings, it will be their priesthood quorum. For stake callings, the sustaining must take place in a meeting of the entire stake or in separate meetings in each ward in the stake.

Assume that you have accepted a calling in your ward. After you accepted, the bishop probably said, "We will sustain you next Sunday," or "We will sustain you in two weeks." This is a gentle reminder that you should plan to be present in sacrament meeting on that day so your name can be presented to the body of the congregation.

When the sustaining occurs, the person who is conducting the meeting will ask you to stand up, usually from the audience where you are sitting. He will then say, "We have called Brother John Jones to serve as the Scoutmaster (or Young Men president, or whatever) in the ward, and he has accepted. All those who can sustain Brother Jones in that calling, please manifest it." The audience will all raise their right hands—

including you, who will raise your own hand to vote for yourself! He will then say, "Anyone opposed may also manifest it." At this point, you hold your breath and hope no one votes against you. Don't worry, the odds are in your favor. After the vote, the bishop will thank the audience, and you may sit down.

Occasionally, the person conducting your sacrament meeting will turn the meeting over to an authority from the stake, such as a member of the high council. The visitor will then proceed to read a sustaining list of people who have been called to serve in stake callings. Because those who have stake callings serve all the wards in that stake, the ward members from each ward are called upon to sustain them. You are also given the opportunity to sustain other changes in the ward, such as the dividing of a ward or the changing of ward boundaries. And at least once a year, you will be given the opportunity to sustain all the leaders of the Church, including the President of the Church and those who serve with him.

Sustaining is not the same as voting for a person. Church callings are not popularity contests where the person with the most votes wins. The Church is a theocracy, not a democracy. What a sustaining represents is that you approve, or sustain, an action that your designated leaders have proposed. When the bishop asks for the congregation's sustaining vote, he is saying, "I have felt impressed that the Lord wants this person to serve in this calling. Will you support that decision?" It is only in the very rarest of circumstances that anyone votes negatively in a sustaining.

But the process of sustaining is more than a one-time hand raising. Sustaining a ward or stake member in a calling is a process that continues throughout the life of that calling. When you raise your hand to sustain someone, you are pledging to the Lord and to the person who has accepted the calling that you will sustain him, or support him, as he fulfills his obligations.

If you sustain Brother Jones as the Gospel Doctrine teacher in Sunday School, your job doesn't end when you raise your hand to sustain him. It is your responsibility to attend the class rather than to stand in the hall outside the class, visiting with your friends. Brother Jones may turn out to be a natural teacher, in which case all he may need is an appreciative audience and somebody to close the meeting with prayer when called upon to do so. But if Brother Jones doesn't have that natural aptitude, and if sitting through his lessons is a trial and a tribulation, he needs the class members to sustain him even more by participating in the class in a positive way, by reading the assignment or answering questions in class, or perhaps by asking questions in class to stimulate discussion. It's not always fun to sustain a person in his ward calling, but it's our obligation—just as it is the obligation of others to sustain you in the callings you hold.

You can—and should—sustain ward members even when their calling doesn't affect you in any way. A man can sustain the Relief Society homemaking leader by helping his wife on homemaking nights so she can attend the meeting without having to worry about what's going on at home. The childless couple can sustain the ward nursery leader by expressing appreciation to her for giving the little children a good start in the Church, or they may perform an even more active role by volunteering to substitute occasionally when the teacher is ill. Ward members can sustain the bishop and his clerical staff by taking food in for them to eat during the marathon days of tithing settlement. And any ward member can write a note of appreciation to someone who has given a talk in church or who has otherwise performed a service, just as we can sustain ward members with an encouraging word during times of trouble.

There are as many ways to sustain a person in a calling as there are people in the ward to observe that person in his calling. As someone who has sustained a ward member, you also have the right to ask the Lord to prompt you with ways you can help that person when he needs to be lifted up.

The Setting Apart

Once you have been called and sustained to a particular position, the last step of the process is to get you set apart. In the setting apart, the bishop actually gives you the authority to perform your calling, along with other spiritual gifts that will allow you to succeed in the work you have been called to do.

When Joseph Smith founded the Church, he was visited by a number of heavenly messengers who laid their hands on his head and gave him various keys, or rights, needed to administer the affairs of God's earthly kingdom. These keys passed from Joseph Smith to the Quorum of the Twelve Apostles, and from there down through all the leaders of the Church to the current prophet. Although only the prophet has all the keys necessary to govern the Church, other leaders are given the keys they need to carry out their callings. After the bishop of your ward was called and sustained by the members of the ward, someone having authority (probably the stake president) placed his hands on the bishop's head and set him apart to be the bishop of your ward. That means he has the spiritual authority from the Lord to carry out all the duties related to the members of your ward. Unlike the President of the Church, his keys are limited in that he has no jurisdiction over members in any other ward.

Similarly, when you are set apart, someone with authority, such as your bishop or one of his counselors, will place his hands on your head and give you the authority necessary to perform your new calling. He will lay his hands upon your head to do this, just as he or someone else laid hands upon your head when you were confirmed a member of the Church. Another similarity to your confirmation is that other worthy priesthood holders may be asked to lay their hands upon your head to participate in the setting apart. Other ward members may also be present, including your family and friends, as well as those who have been called to serve with you.

The first part of the setting apart is when you are actually given the authority to perform your calling. The person in charge will say words that are similar to these: "Mary Elizabeth Jones, by the authority of the Melchizedek Priesthood and in the name of Jesus Christ I set you apart to be the Young Women president in the Jackson Hole First Ward of the Jackson Wyoming Stake. I confer upon you all the rights, responsibilities, and duties associated with this calling."

Notice the words that were spoken in this example. (1) You are singled out by name, (2) told by what authority this setting apart was taking place, and then (3) reminded that the leader who has singled you out is serving as an agent of Jesus Christ and that you are (4) called and set apart to fulfill a position in His Church. (5) You are then given a specific assignment (Young Women president) but (6) told that your responsibilities will be performed within a certain scope (only in your own ward). (7) You are then given all the rights and responsibilities associated with that calling.

Usually the second part of the setting apart will be a general blessing related to the calling, as the person speaking is moved upon by the Holy Ghost. It is difficult to say what counsel this blessing will contain because every situation is different. In most cases you are promised certain spiritual gifts that will help you succeed in the calling. Occasionally you are encouraged to pay particular attention to certain aspects of your calling for a reason that may or may not be mentioned in the text of the blessing. Sometimes you are promised certain blessings that will be yours if you carry out your calling well.

Just as the bishop's authority is limited in scope to the members of his ward, your authority will be limited to those you have been called to serve. If you are called to be a Sunday School teacher, you will be assigned to teach a specific class. Being set apart as a Sunday School teacher does not give you the authority to teach a Primary class or to give unsolicited criticism or advice to members who have been called to teach other classes in the ward. Nor does your call to teach a Sunday School class in your ward allow you to teach the same class in a different ward.

Occasionally you will start serving in a calling before you have been formally set apart. Do not worry if this happens. Occasionally, overworked bishops may go for many months before a ward member is set apart for a particular calling, although this isn't an ideal situation. In fact, your bishop may have so many other things on his mind that he may forget to set you apart altogether. Be of good cheer: the calling is no less valid if you are never set apart for it. But if you want the comfort that a priesthood blessing can give, you should not be shy about reminding the bishop that you would still like to be set apart—even if months have passed in the interim.

What might appear as a formality to some is really a critical part of the process. Being set apart will give you certain blessings to help you perform that calling to the best of your ability. You may do a fine job in your calling if you're never set apart, just as a car can get from point A to point B with a cylinder missing. But there's no denying that you can do an even better job with the Lord more closely at your side than you can if you muddle through alone. This assurance is what a setting apart gives to you.

Kathy once served as a Relief Society teacher for more than a year and during the life of the calling was never set apart for that position. Although women told her they enjoyed her lessons, it was only after she was released from the calling that she realized she hadn't been seeking the Lord's help as she prepared her lessons every month. She had taught adequate lessons—perhaps some of them were excellent lessons—but it was only years later that she began to wonder if she had taught the things the Lord wanted the women in her ward to hear. If she had been set apart for that Church calling, the blessing she would have received might have reminded her to pray for guidance instead of relying on her own intellect, and it could have set her on a course that would have been entirely different from the one she took. She still wonders if she might have approached her calling differently had she not lacked the courage to remind her bishop to set her apart.

Your First Calling

If you've been counting on your status as a newly baptized member of the Church to exempt you from Church callings, you're in for a big surprise. It's common for bishops to have callings picked out for new members before they've even dried out from their baptism. Perhaps you feel inadequate to serve or to teach people who have been Church members all their lives, but service is only part of the reason we accept callings. Getting you immediately involved in serving other ward members will accelerate your growth and show you how to apply the principles the missionaries taught you. In fact, many times Church service provides more benefit to those providing the service than to the people they are serving.

If you doubt your ability to make a meaningful contribution to the structure of your ward, take consolation from the fact that your bishop will be sensitive to your feelings of inadequacy and will not ask you to do anything that would exceed your capabilities. In fact, he may have a better grasp of your capabilities than you do because he realizes that when you were confirmed a member of the Church you were given certain spiritual tools that will help you succeed in any Church responsibility. In addition to the blessing you were given at your confirmation, your setting apart for whatever new calling you receive will provide strength and inspiration for whatever task you are called upon to do.

Because this will be your first calling as a member of the Church, your bishop will probably be the one to issue the call, and he will probably take a little more time than usual to make you feel comfortable. He has no intention of scaring you away from Church service before you have even begun! In fact, despite any feelings of inadequacy that may possess you, your first calling will probably be a richly satisfying experience.

Keep in mind that although most ward callings follow the pattern of calling, sustaining, and setting apart, there are a few callings that do not require you to be sustained or set apart. Some other callings require that you be set apart but not sustained. If you have any question about a particular calling you receive, make sure to ask the person who issued the calling. Nobody expects you to know everything at the beginning, and your Church leaders should always be willing to answer your questions.

After you are set apart for your first calling, your first impulse may be to sit around and wait for somebody to train you. You may have a long wait. People are so busy running around performing their own callings that they don't even think about staying behind to show the new person what to do. Unless someone has volunteered to show you the ropes, it's up to you to put forth some initiative to learn your duties and start performing them. As Doctrine and Covenants 107:99 reminds us, "Wherefore, now let every man learn his duty, and to act in the office in which he is appointed, in all diligence."

Even if someone has volunteered to train you, it is likely that he won't think about giving you some training until you remind him. You need to be a self-starter if you're going to learn the information necessary to perform your calling well.

Consider one or more of the following sources:

- Contact the person in charge of the organization where you will be working. For example, if you are called to be a teacher in the Sunday School, you can talk to the Sunday School president. In some cases, you will report to the bishop directly; in that case, he or one of his counselors can help you.

- Find out the name of the person who was just released from the calling you now hold. Contact him or her and ask to meet together to learn your duties. There may also be some materials that need to be turned over to you. If the person who previously held your calling is no longer in the ward, contact the head of your organization to see if there are any such materials.

- For some callings, the Church publishes training manuals that outline your responsibilities. See if a manual is available; if so, request a copy.

- Contact the person who issued you the calling. Even if he will not be working directly with you, he can point you toward the proper people and offer some suggestions.

- In some areas, the stake offers training sessions for certain callings. Not only do you learn new things at these sessions, but you will also have the opportunity to meet other people who might have your same calling in another ward. Some of these folks with more experience can be a great resource.

- Ask anyone within your ward or stake that you feel close to. This could be a friend or neighbor, a priesthood leader (for the men) or Relief Society president (for the women), your home teacher, or your visiting teacher. Even if the person you contact doesn't know the specific duties of your calling, he will be glad to push you in the right direction or send you to the proper person.

Because the Church is strictly a volunteer organization, some people believe they should just give a Church calling their "leftover" time and everyone will excuse them if they only make a half-hearted attempt to perform their duties. But although it is true that your spouse, your family, your career, and even your leisure pursuits cry out for your time, Church

callings are serious undertakings that should be performed to
the best of your ability. Failure to do so will deprive those
people you are called to serve, and it will also stunt your spiritual growth in the kingdom of God.

Many times in the Church you will be encouraged to "magnify" your calling. As the phrase implies, magnifying a calling
may mean to (1) enlarge your influence on those you serve and
(2) focus intently on seeing your calling and those whom you
serve as through a magnifying glass. It means going the extra
mile, or expending extra effort to serve as the Lord would have
us do it. As we are admonished in Doctrine and Covenants
58:27, "Verily I say, men should be anxiously engaged in a good
cause, and do many things of their own free will, and bring to
pass much righteousness."

As you carry out your first calling, you should strive to
learn your duty, then do all that is expected of you, plus additional things that will benefit those you serve. As you do your
best to magnify your first calling, you will grow in the kingdom
and learn to serve others as Jesus Christ would serve them.
And as you grow in service in the Church, remember that how
you serve is far more important than what calling you receive.
In the Lord's eyes, the calling of a home teacher is as important
as that of a mission president.

The End of Your First Calling

No matter how long you serve in your first calling, the time
will eventually come that you will be asked to no longer perform that calling. This is known as being "released from your
calling" or, more commonly, just being "released." When being
asked to accept a challenging calling in the Church, we can
always take consolation from the fact that all callings eventually come to an end. In one of the questions at the end of this
chapter, we will describe the various reasons why you might be
released from a calling.

When the release does occur, a member of the bishopric (or
the leader of the organization where you served) will meet with
you privately, inform you that you are being released, and
thank you for your efforts in performing that calling. He may

also ask you to share some of your experiences (positive and negative) associated with the calling, along with suggestions you might have to make the calling more effective and enjoyable for the person taking your place.

Just as you were formally sustained in a public meeting when you were called, you should also be formally released in public. The person conducting the meeting will announce that you are being released from a certain calling and ask those in the audience to thank you by raising their right hands. If the person replacing you has already been called, it is quite common that you will be released and your replacement will be sustained during the same meeting. You will first be released, and then your replacement will be sustained.

As you will learn in the next chapter, your bishopric has an incredible number of duties to perform in the ward. As a result, they may not be as good about doing releases as they should be. The interview during your release may be short, or your release might even occur as part of a phone call rather than a personal interview. On occasion, people have arrived at sacrament meeting only to hear the announcement of their release, with no prior notification that this was going to occur. If any of these things happen, please forgive your leaders, realize that they are busy, and understand that the Lord and those you served with appreciated your work on their behalf.

Types of Callings

The next few chapters will provide detailed descriptions for most of the callings you will encounter during your Church experience. But before doing that, we would like to provide a summary of the three major types of callings you will find in the Church. Most callings can be grouped into one of three categories:

- **Leadership** callings provide the opportunity to inspire and lead others, encouraging them to keep the commandments and grow in the gospel. Your bishop has the primary leadership calling in your ward, as he has the responsibility to coordinate the efforts of other ward leaders and to oversee the spiritual progress of all ward members. Others in leadership callings include the counselors in the bishopric, priesthood quorum leaders, and presidencies of auxiliaries, such as the Primary, Relief Society, and Young Men and Young Women programs.

- **Administrative** callings are those where members work behind the scenes to make sure everything is running smoothly in the ward. These include the various clerks and secretaries. Some of these work directly with the bishop, attending to details at the ward level, while others serve as secretaries for the various auxiliary organizations. If those people with administrative callings do their jobs correctly, there will be more time for those in leadership callings to actually be leading the people rather than being bogged down by administrative details.

- Members with **teaching** callings are expected to prepare and teach regular gospel principles to other members within the ward. These callings are usually associated with auxiliary organizations, such as the Primary or the Sunday School. Teachers are generally given an instruction manual each year and are expected to prepare a lesson each week as directed by the manual. Of course, effective teachers will supplement the basic ideas in each lesson with their own experiences and ideas, as the manual suggests.

A Convert's Questions

How long does a calling last?

A bishop of ours used to say that as soon as he saw a ward member start to feel comfortable in a calling, he started looking for that person's replacement. Although Kathy once thought of herself as Relief Society homemaking leader-for-life, and Clark has spent virtually his whole Church career bouncing from one clerical job to another, the truth is that nobody owns a particular calling. If you're too attached to a calling, you need to prepare yourself for losing it. And if a calling seems interminable, you can be comforted with the knowledge that one day it will eventually end.

Your release date for any calling will depend on your own circumstances or on the needs of the ward. Generally, you will be released when one of the following occurs:

- **You Have Served a Specified Length of Time**

    Especially for demanding callings, there is usually a suggested length of time for the calling. For example, most bishops serve in their callings for about five years, and most stake presidents serve for about seven to ten years.

- **You Have Served Whatever Purpose the Lord Had in Mind for You in This Particular Calling**

    Recently, our ward sustained a new Relief Society president only three months after another woman had been given the calling. It was hard for the first woman to understand why she had been released so quickly—until several previously inactive women announced that because of her they had started coming back to church. This Relief Society president had fulfilled her purpose in months instead of years. Then she was released to make room for a new president whose different strengths would allow her to serve the Relief Society in different ways.

- **You Are Called to Another Position**

    If you have served well in your calling, it is not uncommon for you to be given a different assignment with other responsibilities. Then someone else who needs the experience of serving in that position (perhaps even a newer convert!) will be moved into your old job. It could be that the bishop believes you would be the best candidate to fill another calling where your particular skills can help meet a need in the ward.

- **Your Organization Gets Reorganized**

    If you are working in an auxiliary when the president is released, there is a chance that you will be released also. New presidents will sometimes keep one or more of the previous counselors, but more often they like to start with their own team. There is also a chance that

you will be reassigned from second counselor to first
counselor, or from first counselor to the new president.

- **You Move Out of the Ward**

  If you physically move out of the ward, or if the
  boundaries are changed to put you into another ward,
  you will obviously be released from any callings you
  may hold in your old ward. One of the major upheavals
  of any ward boundary realignment is the domino effect
  it produces in terms of staffing.

- **You Ask to Be Released**

  Asking to be released from a calling isn't usually the
  preferred way to escape your responsibilities, but it can
  be done. This isn't something you should do at the first
  sign of frustration, but it may be a legitimate course of
  action if you have a sudden change in your life (health,
  job status, financial) that would keep you from serving
  in an honorable manner. It is often better to be released
  than to just go through the motions of holding a calling
  but not fulfilling it. That situation doesn't help you
  grow, and it might even harm those you should be
  serving.

Can I ever refuse to accept a calling?

There are some people who, as a matter of policy, make it a
point never to refuse a calling. There are others who will pick
and choose, only accepting the callings that sound fun or easy
or even prestigious. The best course of action is probably to
take just about any calling that is extended, allowing yourself
the latitude to turn down a calling in rare circumstances.

There are definitely individual circumstances that may be
legitimate reasons for refusing a Church calling. If you're a
painful introvert who can't even say hello to strangers, the idea
of being a stake missionary may be too much for you to overcome. If you faint in the heat, it could be a good idea to decline
any callings related to summer camp. If you loathe any form of
organized sports and know you couldn't hide that animosity, it
wouldn't be good for the ward basketball team if you took the
job of coaching them. Discuss your situation with the person
who issues your calling. If your circumstances would prohibit

you from serving in a way that would help the ward, it may be in the ward's best interests for you to decline.

But perhaps the most common reason why people refuse a calling isn't a valid reason at all. That reason is inadequacy. If you're tempted to refuse a calling because "I can't teach (even though I've never tried it)," or "I can't lead (nobody would follow me)," or "I can't be compassionate service leader because I'm not compassionate," you're tying the Lord's hands and thwarting His purpose in your life.

Just remember the saying we quoted earlier: "Whom the Lord calls, He qualifies." This will happen time and time again during the course of your Church career. The Lord is able to do miracles on our behalf. Usually the only thing that prevents Him from doing so is our lack of faith. Miracles can happen in your callings if you do two things. You must act in faith, taking the calling despite your feelings of inadequacy. And you must do everything in your power to overcome your weaknesses by studying or preparing or doing whatever else is needed to allow you to succeed in the calling you have accepted.

If you do these things, the sky's the limit. There have been cases where people who can't read music have been called as a ward organist and have learned to play the organ in an amount of time that indicated divine intervention had taken place. There have been instances where people who could barely speak English have gone on a foreign-speaking mission and have almost immediately served as mouthpiece to the Lord in that unknown tongue. Don't shut doors by refusing a calling where a miracle could happen to you, if only you had the faith to let God do His work.

It is human nature to experience moments of inadequacy. It is only natural to be nervous when a calling comes to you that would force you to grow and change. It is the nature of a good calling to make you stretch a little as you grow within it, just as a new shoe stretches when it becomes accustomed to a human foot.

Is it possible to have more than one calling simultaneously?

Having multiple Church callings is probably the rule rather than the exception. It is the common practice to have a ward calling issued by the bishop, but other organizations to which you belong, such as priesthood quorums and the Relief Society, will also give you callings. Those in leadership positions will try to balance your callings so that you are not overworked and so that you have no more than one "major" calling. It is also possible to have multiple ward callings if none of them requires a great deal of your time. Thus, having several "small" callings will not take any more of your time than having one major calling.

One place where you will often see people with many callings is if you belong to a small ward or branch. When there are not a lot of hands carrying the load, it is not uncommon to find a handful of people who literally seem to be running the branch. You have to wonder if maybe you've found a branch of twins or triplets as the same people seem to be in two or three places at once.

Why would anyone vote against a sustaining?

Voting against a sustaining is such a rare occurrence that many Church members never see it happen. The reason for this is that most members realize that they are not casting a vote when they raise their hands to sustain a member for a particular position. Instead, they are being asked to ratify or sustain a decision that has already been made by those in authority. Thus, it is only under extreme and unusual circumstances that anyone in the congregation would ever oppose a sustaining.

One valid reason for opposition might be if a member of the congregation knows something about the proposed person, such as a serious unknown and unconfessed sin. Any objections that are raised should be based on personal experience, and never based on rumor or gossip.

Nobody should ever raise a hand against a fellow ward member strictly because of personality issues. Church members are human and fallible. Wards are composed of human beings, and it is only natural that you will love some members of your ward while others will drive you crazy. Just because you're not fond of someone is not a valid reason to oppose that person's calling. Indeed, it is our responsibility as servants of

Christ to sustain all ward members in their callings, despite personal preferences.

By the same token, it is not appropriate to object to a calling because you've had what you considered to be personal revelation that this calling was supposed to go to someone else. It is the bishop who has stewardship over the ward and who is entitled to receive revelation concerning the placement of individuals within the ward's structure. If the calling disagrees with what you perceived should happen, your perceptions may have been wrong—or they may have been premature. Perhaps the person you believed was being groomed for a particular position will serve there the next time around.

If an opposing vote is received in a meeting, the person who presides over the meeting will wait until after the meeting and then speak with the person or persons who opposed a particular sustaining. If the issue can be resolved to the satisfaction of the leader, the calling will proceed as planned and the person who was called to that position will be set apart. If the leader does find circumstances that would disqualify the candidate, the calling will be withdrawn. In any case, the leader will try to resolve the conflict so that all parties are satisfied.

Sometimes a Church member will not oppose a calling but will not raise his hand to sustain it either. If the person conducting the meeting notices the abstention he will usually try to meet with the person who abstained to determine why he was unable to support the person in the proposed calling.

Every effort is made to ensure that every member of the congregation supports everyone else in their Church callings. In a literal sense, all callings in the Church really are performed under the law of common consent.

Which callings are the most important?

One side effect of having to live in the real world is that we try to apply worldly principles to the kingdom of God. Thus, we treat the Church like a business and associate certain levels of status with certain callings. Then we tend to rank people based on their perceived spiritual status. No one can deny that the calling of bishop requires more energy and time than the

calling of a Primary teacher. Yet, is the reward for serving in
the Primary any less grand?

Although there will always be those in the Church who will
try to climb spiritual career ladders, you should just concentrate at being the very best at whatever you're called upon to
do. Your reward will be as great as the reward given to the
President of the Church if you have fulfilled your calling as
well.

*I'd feel better about callings if I were asked to serve in a ward
job that only lasted for a few months. Any chance of that?*

There certainly are a few short-term callings in the
Church. Most of them are related to the youth programs. There
are some youth camp directors who usually serve for only one
summer. Sometimes wards will also call advisers to plan and
participate in a one-time event, such as a youth conference or a
ward preparedness fair. There are also callings within athletic
programs, such as coaching, that are often extended for just
one season. Or a couple can be asked to be in charge of a ward
Christmas party, or a ward dinner, or another one-time event.

There is a fine line between an assignment and a calling,
but that doesn't really matter. Even just a one-time assignment
should give you a pretty good idea of what a calling would
involve.

If you really are concerned about not being able to handle a
calling, ask your bishop if he can give you a one-time assignment. That will give you some experience and confidence so
that you can handle a more formal calling.

Is the bishop always inspired when he issues a calling?

Sometimes you will hear someone say, "Brother Jones has
done so well in that job. It truly was an inspired calling." Or
you may hear, "I have been so frustrated trying to perform this
calling—I'm sure there was no inspiration when the bishop
thought of me."

Although we would like to think the Lord is always
standing behind the bishop, whispering in his ear and governing every aspect of the ward, we must also realize that the
Lord wants the bishop to grow in his calling also and will some-

times leave decisions to that bishop's best judgment. However, the Lord will certainly let the bishop know if he is about to make an incorrect decision if it is a decision of significant consequence.

When Kathy was called as Relief Society homemaking leader-for-life, her bishop confided that this was one of those instances where he hadn't seen a neon sign pointing to Kathy as the candidate for the calling. He said he knew that Kathy would do a good job in the calling, but he hadn't received any spiritual promptings to tell him she was the person for the job. In fact, he said that any number of women in the ward could have served as Relief Society homemaking leader and done a good job of it; Kathy's name just happened to be at the top of the list.

This bishop is not an incompetent man. At the time he called Kathy to work in Relief Society homemaking, he had been sustained as a bishop or branch president on four separate occasions, and he has subsequently served a fifth time. People often say that he was born to be a bishop. But he says that he didn't always feel a definite spiritual prompting every time he issued a calling. Sometimes, he relied on his knowledge of the people in the ward and his own common sense to determine who should serve in what position.

It should also be kept in mind that when it comes to deciding on callings the bishop is not an island. In arriving at these decisions he usually consults with his two counselors and receives input from those in leadership positions over the various ward organizations. The involvement of these other people leaves room for both inspiration and good judgment to play a part in the issuing of any call.

Each calling we receive will give us opportunities for spiritual growth. If a calling doesn't suit us, we can adapt ourselves to suit the calling. We can discern the Lord's needs for the members of the ward through study and prayer, and we can endeavor to fill those needs through our service. We can be a blessing in the lives of others, if we choose to do so. Instead of wasting valuable time trying to determine if a new calling is inspired, we should just get busy learning and magnifying the assignment we have been chosen to do.

4

THE BISHOPRIC
AND OTHER
WARD CALLINGS

The last chapter introduced you to callings and showed you why the Church could not operate without them. Every activity that occurs within your ward or branch happens because someone with a calling has been doing his duty. If you have not already received it, you should be anticipating your first calling. Your ward assignment will give you an opportunity to learn, grow, help your fellow Saints, and help move the work of the Lord forward.

Much as a corporation is made up of many workers with different jobs and job descriptions, each ward organization is composed of similar "jobs," each with its own responsibilities and duties. You will find quite a bit of similarity between the Church and the business world, but there is a danger in carrying this analogy too far. The similarities in structure are outweighed by vast differences in the way leaders are selected and in the way they execute their responsibilities. Trying to run a ward the way you run a business would result in disaster because the elements that comprise an effective leader in the business world are far different from the attributes of an effective ward leader (although it is unfortunate that businesses aren't conducted in a more Christlike manner).

Because all Church members deal with the bishop and his staff time and time again, this chapter will give you a brief overview of the various assignments that are performed by the bishop and his staff on your behalf. Once you know what the bishop's role is, you'll understand his place in your life as a Latter-day Saint. You'll know when to use him and, just as important, you'll know when you should leave him alone.

There's another reason we're telling you about the bishop's duties. Once you know how much he and his staff do for you—all without pay, and all in their allegedly "free" time—two things will happen. First, you'll develop a respect for the bishop and his staff and an appreciation for the countless hours they spend in your service. Second, you'll be absolutely convinced that you would never, never want to be a bishop.

We will also give you a short summary of the other more common organizations and callings found within a typical ward. It is beyond the scope of this book to describe all these callings in detail (that would be a separate book in itself!), but we will try to at least give you an idea of all the various opportunities for service in a typical ward.

The Bishopric

The bishop and his two counselors are known as the bishopric, and they have the primary leadership responsibility for your ward. Once you see them in action, you'll wonder how they have time to carry out all their Church responsibilities and still manage to earn a living and preside over their families. Being a bishop is equivalent to having an additional full-time job—one where you're on call twenty-four hours a day. Being a counselor in a bishopric is roughly equivalent to taking on a part-time job. In reading through the rest of this section, you will be amazed at all the different responsibilities that are given to the bishop and his counselors. You'll also see why men who really understand what is involved in being a bishop would never aspire to be called to that position.

The Bishop

In the New Testament, there are many parables about shepherds and their sheep. Christ Himself is often referred to as the Good Shepherd because of His role in guiding us back to our Father in Heaven. In a similar way, the bishop is truly the shepherd over your ward. He is assigned the ultimate responsibility for the physical and spiritual welfare for all the Saints within your ward boundaries.

In the previous chapter, you learned about the principle of delegation, where a leader can assign part of his authority and responsibility to others. There are some duties the bishop can delegate to his counselors and other leaders, but there are some that he must do himself. In the remainder of this section, when we refer to the "bishop doing so-and-so . . . ," it means that the bishop must do this task and not delegate it to a counselor. If we refer to the "bishopric doing so-and-so . . . ," that means that either the bishop or a counselor may assume the duty, as determined by the bishop. But even if a duty is delegated to others, the ultimate responsibility will fall back on the bishop for all things related to the ward. As President Harry Truman said, "The Buck Stops Here." In your ward, the buck stops with your bishop. If you fall down in your calling as Scoutmaster or Primary president, for example, the inefficiency that will result in the ward will reflect on the bishop almost as much as it does on you.

A bishop wears five different hats as he goes about providing leadership for your ward:

- **President of the Aaronic Priesthood.**

In chapter 2 you were introduced to the two priesthoods within the Church—the Aaronic, or lesser, Priesthood, and the Melchizedek Priesthood. In chapter 8, you'll learn about the priesthood in greater detail. Those who hold the Aaronic Priesthood are usually young men 12–18 years of age; the others are adult male converts who have recently been baptized. One of the primary responsibilities of the bishop is to oversee the youth in this age group. He is assisted in this calling by his counselors and the leaders of the Young Men and Young Women organizations, whose responsibilities also deal with this same age group.

The bishop must hold regular, individual interviews with each priest and Laurel (ages 16–18). He should regularly attend the priests quorum during priesthood meeting each Sunday. The bishop serves as president of the priests quorum, but he should call two priests to be his assistants. The bishop will preside at all of the meetings he attends, but one of the assistants will usually conduct.

These terms *preside* and *conduct* may be new to you, but they are often used in the Church. The person who presides in any Church meeting is the person with the most authority or jurisdiction over that group. For example, you could say that the president of the United States presides over the U.S. military. Even though he does not usually involve himself in military affairs, his title of commander in chief puts him at the top of the command chain and gives him the authority to make decisions related to the military. Similarly, the person who presides over a Church meeting has the most jurisdiction in that meeting and is the ultimate authority for any decisions that need to be made. The place the analogy falls down is that the president of the United States is always commander in chief, even when he's not present at the meetings of the joint chiefs of staff, but the person who presides over a Church meeting must attend the meeting. Thus, the bishop usually presides over sacrament meeting, but when the bishop is out of town, the bishop's first counselor presides in his stead.

The person who conducts the meeting is the one who stands behind the microphone and starts the meeting, welcomes people, makes announcements, and outlines the program. In some cases the same person will preside and conduct (such as when your bishop conducts sacrament meeting), but more often the person presiding won't say a word or leave his seat during the course of the meeting.

The bishop must also nominate worthy young men to be advanced through the offices of the Aaronic Priesthood. After a deacon reaches a certain age (usually 14) and remains worthy and faithful, the bishop should nominate him to become a teacher. Similarly, worthy teachers who reach a certain age (usually 16) should be nominated to become priests. The bishop also interviews young women as they advance through the various classes in the Young Women program.

All youth aged 12–18 must be interviewed on a regular basis. The bishop must interview the priests and Laurels (age 16-18), but the younger youth may be interviewed by any member of the bishopric.

Just as the bishop is required to preside over the priests quorum, his counselors should regularly preside over the other Aaronic Priesthood quorums and the Young Women classes. Bishopric members assigned to Aaronic Priesthood quorums or Young Women classes should also have periodic leadership training meetings with the youth leaders in those quorums or classes. Bishopric members should participate in all youth activities, including activities on week nights and special youth conferences and youth trips. They should always be an example to the youth, encouraging them to live the commandments and set worthy goals in their lives.

- **Presiding High Priest in the Ward**

The bishop holds the Melchizedek Priesthood and has been ordained to the office of a high priest within that priesthood. Because he holds jurisdiction over all other priesthood holders, he is known as the presiding high priest in the ward. This means he presides over all ward members, priesthood quorums, auxiliary organizations, and programs. Unless there is a higher official visiting from outside the ward, the bishop presides over all ward meetings he attends.

The bishop must regularly interview Melchizedek Priesthood quorum leaders and other auxiliary leaders who are accountable to him, recommending worthy men to receive the Melchizedek Priesthood or be advanced in the priesthood. When one of his counselors in the bishopric needs to be replaced, it is the bishop's responsibility to recommend the replacement counselor. He is also responsible for approving all callings that are issued within the ward. Even though auxiliary presidents may suggest names, and even though others may be delegated to issue the call and set apart the new candidate, the bishop must still approve each name before a calling is issued. He must also meet regularly with Church leaders outside the ward level (see chapters 5 and 6), coordinating ward activities and assignments with them.

Just as clergymen in other denominations are authorized to perform marriages, the bishop can perform marriages that do not take place in the temple. Even if these marriages take place inside the ward meetinghouse, they are referred to in the Church as civil marriages. (Marriages that take place inside the temple are referred to as sealings and are performed by men who are called as sealers.) Marriage is not the only ordinance that comes under the bishop's jurisdiction, however. The bishop has the task of making sure that every ordinance that is performed in the ward is performed properly.

Have you ever noticed that the priests at the sacrament table look over toward the bishop after saying the sacrament prayers? They are checking with the bishop to see if the prayer was said correctly. If the bishop indicates by a shake of his head that the prayer was not said perfectly, the prayer must be repeated. But there is more to the proper performance of an ordinance than just saying the words correctly. The bishop must also verify that the person performing the ordinance is worthy and has the proper authority, and he must verify that the ordinance is performed properly and then properly recorded in the records of the ward.

There will be a more complete description of ordinances in chapter 9. Right now, the only thing you need to know about ordinances is that the bishop is responsible to see that all ordinances that are performed in his ward are performed correctly.

The bishopric plan and conduct each sacrament meeting, and they also conduct the opening exercises in the Sunday priesthood meeting. The bishopric also hold regular bishopric meetings to conduct the business of the ward. Actually, the bishopric meeting is only one of a host of Church meetings for the bishopric. Meetings that are held regularly include the priesthood executive committee (PEC) meeting, the ward council, and the welfare committee meeting. Also, the bishop should meet at least quarterly with his Melchizedek Priesthood quorum leaders to review their home teaching activities.

Each auxiliary president should have regular meetings with a member of the bishopric. Typically, the bishop works with the youth and the Melchizedek Priesthood quorums and assigns the ward auxiliaries to his counselors. Each counselor will typically be assigned to several auxiliaries and will meet with them regularly to discuss staffing and other issues. The Relief Society may be assigned to a counselor, but the bishop must work directly with the Relief Society president when dealing with welfare issues.

As if all these assignments weren't enough, the members of the bishopric must also be responsible for the spiritual growth and development of each member of the ward. They need to prepare young men and couples to serve missions, attend to the needs of single members, and teach the gospel to the Saints through their words and actions.

- **Common Judge**

Just as King Solomon was often called upon to make judgments concerning his people, the bishop is called to be the common judge over the members of your ward. He will decide issues such as worthiness and the completeness of repentance. He will decide if and when official Church discipline is necessary, including the severity of that discipline. Lest you worry that the bishop will abuse this power, most bishops in our acquaintance report that this is the most difficult task of being a bishop, and the one that inspires the most prayers for heavenly guidance. Bishops realize the effect of their actions on the lives of ward members and try hard to discern the Lord's wishes in these areas.

The bishop regularly holds worthiness interviews to determine if members of his ward are worthy to attend the temple for the first time or to go on a mission. The purpose of these interviews is twofold—the bishop will need to decide whether the member understands the significance of the action he is about to take, and he must also determine whether the member is morally clean and is obeying the laws of the gospel. The bishop should also interview young men considered for Aaronic Priesthood ordination or advancement, adult men considered for Melchizedek Priesthood ordination, prospective missionaries (including couples), candidates for seminary and institute graduation, and single members within the ward, as needed. There are other interviews, too—so many of them that it would wear you out just to read about them. When one of those interviews pertains to you, you'll be called and asked to visit the bishop or one of those counselors.

The bishopric will also be involved in formal disciplinary proceedings, and the bishop must preside and conduct at those proceedings. This type of proceeding is called a disciplinary council and is called when a member of the ward has committed a serious transgression. These councils are not held for the day-to-day sins that are committed by most Church members but are reserved for serious sins that put the person's status in the Church in danger. Examples of this would be criminal activity, apostasy, or serious moral transgressions. The decision of these councils may be to take no action, to put the member on probation, to disfellowship the member, or excommunicate the member in question. Disciplinary councils are also held when a former disciplinary action was taken, but the member has repented and desires to be a member again with full privileges. If repentance is complete, even excommunicated members can be baptized again and have their full blessings restored.

It should be noted that there are great differences between a civil court and a disciplinary council. The entire purpose of the disciplinary council is to help a member correct his life and get back on the proper path. When making decisions regarding a man or woman's membership status, the bishopric focuses more on repentance than on punishment.

- **Directing Care for the Poor and the Needy**

The Church has always placed emphasis on both physical and spiritual care. While most Church meetings are designed to cause spiritual growth, there are also a number of programs in place to teach members the principles that will help provide a comfortable physical environment as well. This welfare arm of the Church will be covered more fully in chapters 7 and 10.

As chairman of the ward welfare committee, the bishop should preside at the monthly committee meetings. He will also meet at least monthly with the Relief Society president to discuss welfare needs, but his responsibility doesn't end there. It is his job as bishop to search out everyone in the ward who has physical needs and see that those needs are somehow addressed.

It's obvious that the bishop can't be everywhere. As often as not, he'll learn of a ward member's needs through other ward members, priesthood quorum leaders, or auxiliary presidents. These people serve as the bishop's eyes and ears. But although others may tell the bishop a need exists, it is the bishop who must follow up on these leads and make sure that nobody falls through the cracks.

In addition, the bishopric has the responsibility of teaching correct welfare principles to the members of the ward. This is usually done through the welfare committee in ways that will be explained in greater detail in chapter 7.

• **Administering Finances and Records**

The Church takes record keeping seriously. Indeed, the scriptures tell us that record keeping is so important that what is recorded on earth will be recorded in heaven, and what isn't recorded on earth won't be recorded in heaven (see Doctrine & Covenants 128:8). Because there is such a heavy emphasis placed on accurate record keeping, it is ultimately the bishop's responsibility to see that accurate records are kept by the clerical staff of his ward. The bishop must attend and approve regular audits that take place to ensure that all records are being kept in the proper order. The bishop must also review and sign most reports, even the ones prepared by his clerks and counselors.

Although many churches feature the passing of the collection plate as a prominent part of the Sunday service, no plate is passed around during LDS meetings for contributions. Somewhere near the bishop's office you should find a supply of small envelopes and contribution slips. Members are expected to place their donations and a completed donation slip in the envelope, seal it, and give it to a member of the bishopric. One of the weekly activities of the bishopric is to meet in a group of at least two persons to open the envelopes, make sure the contributions are credited to each member, prepare a bank deposit, make sure the contribution total balances with the deposit total, and then make the bank deposit.

Each ward is also allocated a yearly ward budget, used to pay for utilities (phone, power), ward activities (dinners, parties, youth activities), and other similar expenses that occur at the ward level. The bishopric must prepare the yearly budget, approve expenditures during the year, and make sure the ward and all the groups stay within their budgets for the year.

The bishop must also meet with each member of the ward near the end of the year for tithing settlement (read more about tithing in chapter 8). During this meeting, he will review your financial contributions for the year and make sure the Church's records balance with yours. He will also ask you to declare your tithing status (whether you pay a full 10 percent tithing, or a partial tithing, or no tithing at all). This is done partially for financial reasons, because it is important to close the books for the year. It is also an opportunity to meet with the bishop annually to touch base with him and meet privately for just a few minutes.

Even if you haven't paid tithing, it's important for you to go to tithing settlement and to take your whole family with you. Don't worry—you will not be facing an inquisition. In case you haven't learned this yet, bishops work mainly through encouragement and not through threats. You have no reason to fear tithing settlement, even if your financial contributions have been less than you hoped to give.

Bishopric Counselor

Each bishop calls two counselors to assist him. These men are referred to as the first and second counselors in the bishopric. Although the name is always the same, there's no telling what a bishopric counselor may be assigned to do. Every bishop has latitude in the way he'll use his counselors, and the result is that every bishopric counselor in the Church probably has a different job description.

The bishop *must* assume certain duties, he *may* assume other duties, and the rest he will assign to his two counselors. So you may have one ward where the bishop does all the temple recommend interviews, and another ward where the bishop interviews just those who are attending the temple for the first time, letting his counselors handle the renewal interviews. Or you may have one ward where the bishop conducts every sacrament meeting, and another where he alternates with his counselors. If you have not already done so, read through the previous section where we described the duties of the bishop. We tried to list all the duties that a bishop has, making a distinction between duties that have to be done by the bishop and those that can be delegated to his counselors. So, any duty described in that section where we refer to "the bishopric" (as opposed to "the bishop") could be something delegated to one or both of the counselors.

There is usually no automatic assignment of duties based on the position of the counselor (first or second). For example, in one ward the first counselor may be assigned to oversee the Primary, while in another ward it may be the second counselor. The assignment of duties will often depend on how the counselor is called. If the entire bishopric is changed and both counselors are new, the bishop will assign duties as he sees fit, often asking his new counselors for their preferences. If one of the counselors is released and replaced with someone else, the new candidate will probably inherit most of the duties of his predecessor, although even then bishops will sometimes make adjustments. The bishop and ward members will usually regard the two counselors as being equals, but the first counselor will be the one to preside at meetings if the bishop is unavailable.

This would be a good time to mention another bit of Mormon culture. When the first counselor in a bishopric (or any church presidency) is released, it is quite common to release both counselors, move the second counselor to first counselor position, and call a new second counselor. This does not always happen, but often does. The duties of the counselor usually will not change because of the change. Instead, this is primarily done as a courtesy so that the counselor who has served the longest will be closest to the head of the organization. Although it doesn't happen as often, when the bishop (or president) is released, you will sometimes see one of the counselors made the new bishop (or president).

Although every ward is different, you will usually find bishopric counselors doing the following:

- Doing youth interviews with the younger Aaronic Priesthood boys and the girls in the same age group.
- Supervising one or more of the ward auxiliaries (Primary, Sunday School, etc.).
- Extending ward callings as approved by the bishop (usually within the auxiliaries they supervise).
- Serving as the ward representative to the local Scout district or council (in wards that participate in the Scouting program).
- Setting apart members who have accepted ward callings.
- Conducting meetings.
- Preparing the weekly bank deposit of contributions.
- Presiding when the bishop is not present.

This last one is interesting. When the bishop is out of town, his first counselor will preside in his absence and will assume many of the duties of the bishop. If both the bishop and first counselor are unable to be present, the second counselor will preside. In the rare event that all three members of the bishopric are absent, there will be some degree of panic behind the scenes but have no fear. Arrangements will be made for your Sunday meetings to proceed as scheduled.

The Ward Clerical Staff

Executive Secretary

The ward executive secretary is a man who is called to provide administrative support for the bishop in running the ward. While not technically a member of the bishopric, the executive secretary usually attends the same meetings as the bishopric and has a pretty good idea of all that's going on within the ward. A friend of ours whose husband used to be an executive secretary would often call him "the fourth member of the bishopric." He certainly put in the time to earn that nickname.

As with any ward calling, the bishop will determine the exact duties of the executive secretary. But in most wards, his duties will include the following:

- Schedule the bishop's appointments. This would include appointments for youth interviews, appointments to extend callings, temple recommend interviews, priesthood interviews with other priesthood leaders, and appointments to meet with ward members who need counsel or comfort. If you want to schedule a personal meeting with the bishop, this is the person you should call first.
- Schedule appointments for the bishopric. It is common for the entire bishopric to visit ward members—to visit the sick or to welcome a new family that has moved into the ward. The executive secretary will usually schedule these visits as well.
- Assist during ward meetings. The bishop will preside and conduct most ward meetings, but the executive secretary will be at work to make sure the meeting is effective. This includes the preparing of agendas and other written materials and communicating with other ward

leaders to remind them of meetings or notify them of schedule changes.

- Maintain the bishop's calendar. As the executive secretary probably knows more about the bishop's schedule than even the bishop himself, it is quite common for the executive secretary to provide the bishop with a daily or weekly calendar. This will include all of his appointments, meetings, and family obligations. We suspect that a good deal of the money spent on appointment books and calendar software comes from executive secretaries trying to keep track of their bishops!

- Attend all meetings where the bishopric is present, often taking notes and following up when assignments are given. Based on the decisions made in some meetings, the executive secretary may be asked to convey information to other ward leaders. For example, the bishopric may decide that the Relief Society president should speak at a future sacrament meeting on a specific topic, and the executive secretary might be asked to call her and extend an invitation on behalf of the bishop. The giving of assignments should not be confused with the extending of callings.

- Offer advice, when asked by the bishop. Because the executive secretary will be present at all bishopric meetings, he will hear many discussions related to callings and other issues in the ward. Some bishops really consider their clerical staff to be an extension of their counselors, and they will solicit advice from them on occasion. If asked, you should be honest and helpful in the opinions you give. But you must remember that the bishop is the leader of the ward, so you need to sustain and support whatever decision is made.

- Monitor new ward callings. As we described in the last chapter, it is a regular occurrence for ward members to be called and released from callings. Releasing one person will often cause a "domino effect," where an entire chain of people will be released and called to something else. Given the nature of change, and the number of different jobs in a ward, it becomes a major effort to keep track of all these changes and make sure the callings and releases are done according to proper procedure. The executive secretary may be asked to monitor the progress of all callings and releases and make sure these are done correctly, including the releasing, calling the new individuals, and making sure they are sustained and then set apart.

- Assume other duties as assigned by the bishop. The executive secretary could be thought of as the "grease" that keeps a well-oiled ward moving correctly. While the bishopric is involved in the spiritual aspects of running the ward, the executive secretary is the guy behind the scenes that makes sure everything is moving smoothly and nothing is being overlooked. As such, he will often have a wide variety of assignments—anything the bishop can think of that will help the ward run more efficiently and be more effective in the lives of the Saints.

If he performs his calling correctly, a man called to be an executive secretary can do much good in the ward and will indirectly shape the opinion of the ward related to the effectiveness of the bishopric. Our experience in the Church has shown that bishops are often called because of their love, compassion, righteousness, and ability to serve the members of the ward. Although it's considered a plus to have a bishop who is organized, finding a bishop with good organizational skills seems to take a back seat to getting a bishop who is spiritual and who can work well with people. As a result, you sometimes get bishops who are wonderful and gifted leaders but who don't have the ability to balance a checkbook or find their keys. A bishop in this latter category can overcome this deficiency by calling an efficient executive secretary who does have the skills to deal with details.

Being an executive secretary can be one of the most enjoyable callings in a ward. The executive secretary knows virtually everything that happens in a ward, but none of the major decisions are his responsibility. The buck doesn't stop with him as it does with the bishop. In fact, the executive secretary doesn't hold the buck for a minute, as the counselors may do. The executive secretary is in the position of privileged observer, and this can be a fascinating place to be.

However, being executive secretary isn't all gravy. You'll be absolutely amazed how hard it is to keep a bishop's schedule. You'll get telephone calls at odd hours (specifically during dinner times when you're trying to relax). You'll have people make and break appointments time and time again, until you may want to do bodily harm to some of the members of your ward. It's important to remember that although you may often be tempted to lose your temper, your behavior reflects on the bishop. Bite your tongue and treat the members of the ward with unfailing kindness, no matter how thoughtless or even inconsiderate they may be.

A final point to make is perhaps one of the most important. An executive secretary must be able to keep confidences. He is never, under any circumstances, to discuss sensitive items that are brought up in bishopric meetings, not even with his wife or other family members. Nothing will erode the spirituality of a ward faster than having confidences broken, resulting in rumors circulating throughout the ward.

Assistant Executive Secretary

A bishop may occasionally call someone to be an assistant executive secretary. This may be done if you live in a large ward or if the responsibilities of executive secretary are too great for the person serving in the calling (because of health problems, time constraints, etc.).

If you are asked to serve in this calling, the bishop and the executive secretary will determine which portions of the calling you will be asked to assume. For example, you could be asked to help schedule appointments for the bishopric counselors, while the executive secretary handles only those for the bishop. As with many other callings, there is much discretion here, depending on the needs of the ward. You should be prepared to serve as best determined by the bishop.

Ward Clerk

Although the bishop has the ultimate responsibility for administering the finances and records of the ward, this duty is usually delegated to one or more clerks. The primary clerk is known as the ward clerk, who oversees all record keeping in the ward. The duties assigned to the ward clerk are usually as follows:

- Oversee the processing of member financial donations. Each week, ward members will mail contribution envelopes to the bishop or will give them to a member of the bishopric during Sunday meetings. After the block of Sunday meetings, the clerk and one or more bishopric members will open the envelopes, prepare a bank deposit, make sure the contributions are in balance and credited to the proper member's account, and deposit the funds at a local bank. Contributions can be made to several categories, such as tithing, fast offering, and missionary fund, and the clerk must also ensure the proper ward account is credited with the funds (we will talk more about the categories of contributions in chapter 8). At the end of each year, the clerk will participate with the bishop in tithing settlement, where all members visit with the bishop to declare their tithing status and to make sure the Church records agree with their own records of contributions.

- Oversee the spending of ward funds. Each ward will have a local checking account, and the bishopric and clerk will be authorized to write checks against the account. The clerk will usually write the checks to pay expenses, and then a member of the bishopric will approve the expenditure and add their signature to the check. Expenditures will include the normal expenses of operating a ward (utility bills, office supplies) and payments to ward members to reimburse them for expenses related to ward activities. As part of the bishop's role in caring for the needy of the ward, he may also approve checks to be written to pay for expenses incurred by needy members. In addition to just writing the checks and balancing the checking account, the clerk must make sure that all expenditures are credited against the proper budget category, as described next.

- Manage the ward budget. While some checks are written against accounts created through member contributions (fast offering, missionary fund), the majority of checks probably are written against the ward budget. Each year the stake (you will learn more about the stake in chapter 5), gives each ward funds to be used for running the ward and all its programs. The bishopric, with the assistance of the clerk, will establish a yearly budget for the ward. This will include expenses for running the ward itself, plus a budget amount for each ward auxiliary or group. The clerk will then reimburse organization leaders for their expenses and reduce their budget accordingly. For example, the Primary president may buy cookies for a Primary party. She will then submit the receipt to the clerk, who will issue her a check for that amount and also reduce the Primary's budget by the same amount. Thus, the clerk usually assists in preparing the budget, making sure all checks are taken from the proper budget account, and regularly updating each organization as to the balance remaining in their account. It is almost as if the clerk were running his own small business!

- Maintain membership records. When you were baptized a member of the Church, a membership record was created for you. This contains basic information about you, such as your name, address, and birthday. But it also contains important information about your life in the Church, such as the dates you were baptized, confirmed, and ordained (for men). The clerk is responsible for making sure the information on the membership records is accurate. This includes updating your record when important events occur in your life. When members move out of the ward, the clerk must obtain their new address and forward their membership records to their new ward. Similarly, as members move into your ward, the clerk in their previous ward will forward their records to your ward. Your ward clerk will then notify the bishopric and other ward leaders so that they may contact these people, welcome them into the ward, and see if they need any assistance in getting moved and settled. Sometimes a clerk has to be a little bit of a private detective to track down members that move from the ward, particularly when those members are not as active as they should be and want to become lost.

- Provide rosters, reports, and rolls. Using the information from the membership records, the clerk can provide the bishopric and other ward leaders with class rolls, rosters of members in specific organizations, and other reports. These reports are useful in helping these leaders perform their jobs as the reports identify those for whom they have responsibility. As part of their duties, it is also important that ward leaders notify the clerk of any errors or omissions in those reports, so that the clerk can change the membership records to reflect the correct information. Although the clerk is the one who actually makes the membership changes, it is the duty of all ward leaders to make sure the ward membership records are accurate. For wards that use computerized membership systems, organizations can often use the computer to generate their own rolls and reports and do not have to request them from the clerk.

- Complete and submit reports. In addition to providing useful reports to ward leaders, the ward clerk must regularly prepare certain reports for Church headquarters and for the stake (see chapter 5). These reports provide ways for Church and stake leaders to monitor the performance and needs of the ward.

- Prepare certificates. After important ordinances, the ward clerk will prepare a certificate to give to the member involved. For example, certificates are prepared after baptism, confirmation, and Aaronic Priesthood ordinations. Certificates are also prepared for Melchizedek Priesthood ordinations, but that is done at the stake level (see chapter 5). When you receive a certificate, you should keep it with your important records. Not only is this important for your own family history, but it serves as proof that the ordinance occurred in case your membership record does not get updated.

- Take minutes. The ward clerk will take minutes during important meetings, such as sacrament meeting. The clerk may also take minutes in other meetings, as directed by the bishop. The ward clerk will usually be expected to attend most of the same meetings as the bishopric.

- Attend disciplinary councils. The ward clerk will be involved with many aspects of the council, such as sending notifications and letters to the member involved, attending the council and taking notes, submitting paperwork to Church headquarters, and updating the member's membership record with the results of the council.

- Train other secretaries. Most priesthood and auxiliary organizations have secretaries who keep rolls and statistics for their organizations. One of the duties of the ward clerk is to train these other secretaries.

- Participate in audits. The ward clerk must regularly meet with stake auditors to review the accuracy of ward records and make sure that correct policies are being followed. These audits will usually concentrate on specific areas, such as financial records or membership records. Audits also occur frequently after major leadership changes, such as after a new bishop is called. The Church takes the accuracy of records very seriously, especially financial records, and there are many checks and balances in place to protect the ward from accidental or deliberate errors.

- Assist in ward boundary changes. When you live in an area that is experiencing rapid growth or other demographic changes, it will occasionally be necessary to divide wards, create new wards, or change the boundaries of existing wards. When this occurs, the ward clerks of the affected wards will often be asked to meet with other leaders to determine where the new boundaries should be. This is done by analyzing where the current families live within the ward, proposing new boundaries, and then analyzing the effect of those boundaries on the composition of the new wards. This process may be repeated several times until the best boundaries are determined.

- Give advice to the bishopric. As with the executive secretary, some bishops include the ward clerk in bishopric discussions and solicit their advice. Remember to give your opinions honestly, but sustain whatever decision is made by the bishop.

The ward clerk and the ward executive secretary are really the two primary administrative positions in the ward. Their effectiveness—or lack of same—can determine whether a ward will operate smoothly or be chaotic. Although the administrative staff may not provide the same level of spiritual support as do people who hold some other callings, they can improve the running of the ward to such an extent that they have a great effect on the success and even the spirituality of the ward.

Like the executive secretary, a ward clerk is in a position that requires the absolute keeping of confidences. No mention should be made of the things that occur in the ward, except to those who have been determined by the bishop as having a need to know.

Finance Clerk

Usually only a branch or a small ward will expect one ward clerk to do all of the functions just described. In many wards, especially the larger ones, assistant clerks will be called to help the ward clerk perform certain ward functions. These clerks will report to the ward clerk but will be assigned specific duties. One type of assistant clerk that is often found is a finance clerk, also known as a financial clerk.

The ward finance clerk is usually assigned all the ward clerical duties related to financial matters. This would include processing member donations, writing checks, managing the ward budget, and participating in tithing settlement.

In many parts of the world, specific Church computer software is used to help manage the finances of the ward. If you live in a ward that has a computer and has this software installed, it will make it much easier to manage ward finances.

Membership Clerk

The membership clerk is an assistant clerk called to assist the ward clerk with the clerical duties related to the ward membership records. These duties would include creating and updating membership records, moving records in and out of the ward, creating reports related to membership records, and supporting other ward leaders who need rolls, rosters, or reports derived from the membership records.

In many parts of the world, specific Church computer software is used to help manage the membership records of the ward. If you live in a ward that has a computer and has this software installed, it will make it much easier to update and move membership records and to generate meaningful reports.

To give you an idea of how much of a difference a good membership clerk can make, here's a personal example. Once, Kathy was called to serve as secretary to her ward Relief Society. This was a big ward, and there were many women who attended Relief Society—so many that quite often women filled the room to capacity and had to stand in the back. Nevertheless, this ward was considered to have the worst Relief Society of all the wards in the stake—at least statistically speaking—because such a small percentage of the women attended Sunday meetings or were visited by their visiting teachers. Much effort was expended by the stake Relief Society presidency in trying to get the ward Relief Society presidency to improve things, but the president and her counselors were doing the best they knew how to do.

It didn't take Kathy long to see that the Relief Society rolls were a mess. There were many women who were still being counted as Relief Society members several years after they had left the ward one way or another. It's hard to make a monthly visiting teaching visit to a woman who has moved five hundred miles away. It's even harder to plan homemaking meetings that will attract the interest of women who died nearly a decade ago. But as long as those dead or missing women continued to be listed on the rolls of the ward, Kathy had to count them as being legitimate Relief Society members who were available to attend church but just weren't interested in doing so.

About this time, Clark was called as ward membership clerk. He immediately started purging the rolls of people who had moved away or died or otherwise disappeared. After the next reporting period, just three months later, our Relief Society had gone from being considered the worst Relief Society organization in the stake to being considered the best. Our attendance and visiting teaching statistics were far higher than those of any of the other wards. The stake leaders were so impressed that they asked the Relief Society presidency to speak at a training meeting to tell what they had done. They couldn't speak at the meeting because they hadn't done anything. The Relief Society was moving along just as it always had. The only difference between a Relief Society that was considered to be the worst in the stake and a Relief Society that was considered to be the best in the stake was that a new membership clerk had given the Relief Society an accurate roll to work with.

Assistant Clerk

This is an alternate title for one of the secondary clerks called to assist the ward clerk in managing the clerical duties of the ward. Membership clerks and financial clerks really are just assistant clerks who are assigned specific duties. But sometimes a bishop will call a man to be an assistant clerk without specifying in his title what his job description involves. This gives the clerk more latitude as to the types of assignments he can perform. He might do membership work, financial work, or other duties as assigned by the ward clerk. For a small ward, one assistant ward clerk might be called to handle both membership and finance so the ward clerk can cover everything else.

The Elders Quorum Presidency and Staff

All adult males within a ward belong to one of two groups, called quorums, that meet and serve together. But these are more than just social groups because the brethren in each of these quorums hold the same office in the Melchizedek Priesthood. For a more complete explanation of the meaning and importance of both the Aaronic and Melchizedek Priesthoods, see chapter 8. For now, just remember that there are two Melchizedek Priesthood quorums in a typical ward—elders and high priests—and all priesthood quorums exist to perfect the lives of their members and to provide opportunities for members to render service.

When a young man advances out of the Aaronic Priesthood into the Melchizedek Priesthood, he is first given the office of an elder. These are men who are usually college age or perhaps just married and in the process of starting families. Young men called to serve as full-time missionaries are also made elders before they leave on their missions.

Those men in the ward who hold the office of elder are members of the elders quorum and are presided over by an elders quorum presidency that consists of a president and his two counselors. These callings are unusual because they are issued by the stake president rather than by the bishop. The presidency will certainly cooperate with the bishop and coordinate all their activities with him, but they also report their activities to the stake presidency and are accountable to them. This is because the bishop is the president of the Aaronic Priesthood, while the stake president oversees the Melchizedek Priesthood in the stake. Thus, the stake president must issue the calling for elders quorum president and will also set him apart and give him certain spiritual keys associated with the execution of his calling. Counselors in the quorum presidency do not need to be called by the stake president but are usually called and set apart by another stake authority, such as a high counselor or a member of the stake presidency.

Other callings within the elders quorum include a secretary (who performs clerical functions) and an instructor (who teaches many of the Sunday quorum lessons).

The elders quorum presidency should also organize three committees within the quorum to help carry out the three areas of the mission of the Church (see chapter 7). The three members of the quorum presidency should each be assigned to oversee one of these committees. Members of the quorum are called to serve on each of the three committees.

High Priests Group Leadership and Staff

Men who hold the Melchizedek Priesthood and do not hold the office of an elder are called high priests. The office of high priest is required for many leadership offices in the Church. Before a man can serve in a bishopric, a stake presidency, on a high council, or in certain other leadership callings, he must first be ordained a high priest. Even after he is released from that calling he will remain in the office of high priest rather than moving back to the elders quorum. You will learn more about Melchizedek Priesthood offices in chapter 8.

If your ward is typical, the elders quorum will consist of young men in college or just recently married, while the high priests quorum consists of older men whose children are mostly grown, and who have served (or are serving) as leaders of the Church. Of course, there are exceptions to this general rule. Some wards have young men who are high priests because they were called to serve in bishoprics at an early age. Similarly, older men who are very faithful in the Church but have never had higher-level priesthood leadership callings may remain with the elders.

Although the structure and function of a high priests group is similar to that of an elders quorum, there is one difference that should be explained. Each ward in your stake should have an elders quorum, presided over by a president. In contrast, there is only one high priests quorum in the stake. This quorum is presided over by the stake president, who holds the spiritual keys as the presiding high priest in the stake. His counselors in the stake presidency also serve as the counselors to the stake high priests quorum.

Most stakes will have one or more high priest quorum meetings per year, where all the high priests in the stake will attend and the stake president will preside. But on most Sundays, the high priests are expected to meet at the ward level, much as they do in an elders quorum. But because the high priests in just one ward do not constitute a quorum, they are known as a high priests group. To supervise the high priests in each ward, the stake presidency will call a high priests group leader, who will then request two assistants along with some other staff positions. Thus, the head of the group is called a leader instead of a president, and those who help him are called assistants rather than counselors. Other than those titles, and the keys associated with the callings, you will find that the day-to-day duties of the elders quorum leaders and the high priests group leaders are pretty similar.

As with leadership callings in the elders quorum, calls to

serve in the high priests group leadership come from the stake presidency rather than from the bishop. The group leader does not have to be called and set apart by the stake president and may be called by a member of the stake presidency or the high council instead (although the stake president may do it in some stakes). As with the elders quorum presidency, the high priests group leadership is expected to work with the bishop and coordinate their activities with him, even though they report to the stake presidency and are accountable to them.

Similar to the structure of the elders quorum, other callings within the high priests group include a secretary, a quorum instructor, and committee chairmen and members for the three quorum committees.

Relief Society

The Relief Society is the Church organization that was specifically designed for women. It doesn't matter whether you've worked in Primary for twenty-seven years and have never darkened the door of the Relief Society room. It doesn't matter if you never go to meetings at all. If you're a female Church member who resides within the boundaries of the ward, the Relief Society considers you a member—and considers itself to be at least partially responsible for your welfare. Just as the Savior never gives up on one of His lost sheep, the Relief Society never gives up on one of its lost members. Thus you'll occasionally see a woman return to full activity because the Relief Society never gave up on her, even after an absence of many years.

Because Church activity in the wife and mother is often reflected in the Church activity of the rest of her family, the Relief Society program is an extensive one. Many women attend Relief Society for the simple reason that they're supposed to do so, but other women must be enticed. If a woman isn't lured by a sense of duty, perhaps she'll be drawn by the lessons. If the lessons don't attract her, maybe she'd like to learn homemaking skills or crafts. If she isn't interested in that sort of thing, perhaps the social activity will be a draw for her. And if all that fails, she may be loyal to the organization because of the service it has given her family—or the service it has allowed her to give to others. Naturally, there are Relief Society staff members who work in all these areas. From the president on down to the visiting teacher, everyone who works in Relief Society is an integral cog in the machinery. If somebody falls down on the job, the whole organization suffers. But it's amazing how often a spirit of mutual cooperation pervades the Relief Society, so that at least from the outside, the women's organization seems to be a smoothly running clock.

The Relief Society is presided over by a president and her two counselors. The education counselor (first counselor) supervises the teachers and the content of the Sunday lessons. The homemaking counselor (second counselor) is responsible for making sure women are attracted to the homemaking program of the ward—specifically, to homemaking meeting.

The compassionate service leader has the assignment of coordinating acts of service that are performed through the Relief Society for ward members in need.

The homemaking leader works with the homemaking counselor to plan and publicize homemaking meetings. Because the typical Relief Society is composed of women with many interests, one homemaking meeting may offer several different classes being taught on the same night. These might include things such as cooking classes, craft classes, financial workshops, and spiritual lessons.

The home management teacher is responsible for teaching a fifteen-minute lesson in homemaking meeting every month, taken from the Relief Society personal study guide.

The Relief Society single adult representative serves women who are young single adults (ages 18-30) or single adults (ages 31 and older). In a ward where there are fewer single women, she may serve all single women, regardless of age. But no matter which age group she serves, it's her job to be a liaison between single women and the rest of the ward. The primary way she is expected to do this is to serve on the single adult committee of the ward, which is under the direction of a bishopric member.

Depending on the size of your ward, you may have one woman who is set apart to teach the Sunday Relief Society lessons, or you can have several of them. Up until the beginning of 1998, it was customary to have up to four Relief Society teachers. Now, under an updated Church curriculum, most Relief Society organizations have three or fewer women who are sustained to teach the Sunday lessons.

The Relief Society president is also assisted by a visiting teaching board member, whose primary job is to gather the visiting teaching statistics every month and perhaps help compile the monthly report. She may also help the Relief Society president assign visiting teaching routes and otherwise ensure that the ward will have a thriving visiting teaching program. In larger wards, the visiting teaching board member is assisted by one or more visiting teaching supervisors, who help collect monthly visiting teaching statistics. Usually this means a telephone call to each visiting teaching companionship, to see who was visited and to determine which women in the ward have needs that should be reported to the Relief Society presidency. Because the calling requires telephone calls rather than personal visits, the job of visiting teaching supervisor is a good calling for shut-ins or for women who stay at home with young children. You'll learn more about visiting teaching in chapter 8.

Other callings in the Relief Society include that of the chorister and pianist, who help with the music, and a secretary who performs clerical functions for the presidency.

Young Men and Young Women

The Young Men and Young Women programs work in tandem to support, encourage, strengthen, and train the youth of the ward. The Church places a great deal of emphasis on the youth because these young men and women will be the future leaders of the Church. In most wards, the more skilled ward members are usually called to work with the youth, and it is a good bet that the lion's share of most ward budgets is probably directed towards youth programs and activities.

Young Men

The Young Men program can best be understood if it is

viewed as two different programs operating together in cooperation:

1. Because all worthy young men in the ward should hold the Aaronic Priesthood (see chapter 8), a good portion of the Young Men program is designed to teach these young priesthood holders about the duties and responsibilities associated with that priesthood. This type of instruction is typically received during the Sunday priesthood meetings but should also be reinforced by all other youth activities throughout the week.

2. One night during the week (never Sunday or Monday) should be set aside by each ward for Mutual. This is an activity night for the youth, designed to expand their knowledge, broaden their interests, and improve their social skills. This activity typically is not as spiritually oriented as the Sunday lessons, but gospel and Aaronic Priesthood principles should be the basis of all activities. The Young Men and Young Women usually meet separately, but they occasionally have joint activities, typically monthly.

For many wards in the Church, Mutual night activities for the Young Men relate to Scouting. The Church has been affiliated with the Boy Scouts of America since 1913, and the Scout program is used in conjunction with the Aaronic Priesthood program in many wards.

If your ward participates in the Scouting program, Scouting activities start when boys are still in the Primary organization and then continue through their years in the Aaronic Priesthood and the Young Men program. During the years that boys are part of the Young Men program (ages 12–18), they may participate in up to three different Scouting programs—Boy Scout troops (age 12–13), Varsity Scout teams (age 14–15), and Venturing Crews (age 16–18). Your bishopric and stake leaders decide which of these programs will operate in your ward. Many young men have lost interest in Scouting by the time they get older, so in some cases the Varsity Scout or Explorer programs will not be implemented. When this happens, these programs will be replaced with other programs that are designed to train young men of that age.

Another level of complexity is added by the fact that the Aaronic Priesthood-age boys meet together in three different groups—both on Sunday and during Mutual:

- **Deacons and Scouts**
  Young men age 12–13 meet together in the deacons
  quorum. These are boys who have been ordained to the
  office of deacon in the Aaronic Priesthood. If the
  Scouting program has been implemented in the ward,
  these boys will also be members of a Scout troop.
- **Teachers and Varsity Scouts**
  Young men age 14–15 meet together in the teachers
  quorum. These are boys who have been ordained to the
  office of teacher in the Aaronic Priesthood. If the
  Scouting program has been implemented in the ward,
  these young men may also be members of a Varsity
  Scout team.
- **Priests and Venturers**
  Young men age 16–18 meet together in the priests
  quorum. These are young men who have been ordained
  to the office of priest in the Aaronic Priesthood. If the
  Scouting program has been implemented in the ward,
  these youths may also be members of a Venturing
  Crew.

If you'll remember from earlier in this chapter, the bishop
is president of the Aaronic Priesthood in the ward. All callings
that are issued in the Young Men program of a ward will
operate under the direction of the bishopric, who administers
the program. Whenever possible, the bishopric may attend
Young Men–Young Women meetings, including those on Sundays and on Mutual night. Whenever possible on Sunday, the
bishop should meet with the priests or the Laurels, one bishopric counselor should meet with the teachers or Mia Maids,
and the other counselor should meet with the deacons or Beehives. Remember that each member of the bishopric should
also be interviewing each of the youth regularly.

An adult male is called in each ward to be the Young Men
president. He serves with two counselors, and they form a
Young Men presidency. These men act as a liaison between the
bishop and the young men, serving with the bishopric and supporting them in carrying out their responsibilities to the youth.
However, they do not give priesthood assignments, call quorum
meetings, or do anything to imply that their callings put them
in a position to preside over the Aaronic Priesthood.

These three men collectively are known as the Young Men presidency, but they also serve individually as quorum advisers. The president is the quorum adviser to the priests. The main function of the quorum adviser is to prepare and teach the lesson each Sunday in the quorum meeting. A quorum adviser should meet together often with the youth in all their meetings, both on Sunday and on Mutual night.

Like the president, the Young Men counselors serve as quorum advisers, with the first counselor usually assigned to the teachers and the second counselor usually assigned to the deacons. Their role as quorum advisers is to usually teach the Sunday lesson and to support the youth in all their activities, both on Sunday and throughout the week.

In wards where the Scouting program is active, the Young Men presidency may also have secondary roles as leaders in that program. The president may be called as the Venturing Crew adult leader, while the first counselor serves as the Varsity Scout coach, and the second counselor serves as Scoutmaster. If these callings are too much work for the presidency, secondary advisers may be called to help with the Scouting functions. When multiple advisers are used, however, they should attend all Sunday meetings and all Mutual meetings.

The Young Men president calls a secretary to work with the presidency. The secretary performs such duties as keeping attendance rolls and working with the ward clerk to prepare monthly reports related to the attendance and activity of the youth.

As president of the Aaronic Priesthood in the ward, the bishop also serves as the priests quorum president. The bishop will select two assistants, plus a secretary, from the quorum membership. This group will serve to provide leadership and direction to the entire quorum.

From the ranks of the teachers quorum, the bishopric calls a teachers quorum president and two counselors to provide leadership for the quorum. Unlike the priests quorum (where the bishop is the president), all of the members of the teachers quorum presidency come from the teachers quorum itself. The presidency consists of a president and his two counselors. A quorum secretary should also be called.

The bishopric also calls a presidency of young men to

provide leadership for the deacons quorum. Like the teachers quorum, all of the leaders in the deacons quorum leadership come from the deacons quorum itself. The presidency consists of a president and his two counselors. A quorum secretary should also be called.

When the Scouting program is implemented in a ward, youth from the various Scouting organizations should be called to provide leadership. Each Scout troop should have a senior patrol leader to govern the troop. Similarly, each Varsity Scout team should be led by a Varsity team captain, and each Venturing Crew should be led by a Venturing Crew president.

In wards where Scouting is implemented, the bishopric should form one or more Scouting committees. These are composed of adults, including nonmembers of the Church who have an interest in Scouting. One member should be called as the Scouting committee chairman, while the others serve as Scouting committee members.

Young Women

The Young Women organization complements the Young Men program in that there are spiritual lessons on Sunday and Mutual activities during the week. Although the Young Women are not involved in Priesthood or Scouting, the training they get is analogous to that of the Young Men. Their goals are to help the young women grow spiritually and to help strengthen their families—both the families they have now and the ones they will have in the future. Young Women participate in the Personal Progress program and in Young Women in Excellence—two programs that allow achievements for the individual young woman that are similar to the achievements attained by boys who advance toward Eagle Scout.

Young Women are divided into three classes by age groups. Laurels are girls age 16–18; Mia Maids are girls age 14–16, and Beehives are girls age 12–14. The "Mia" in Mia Maid comes from the initials of an obsolete name for Mutual— Mutual Improvement Association.

An adult female serves as the ward Young Women president. She serves with two counselors who are chosen by the bishop after hearing her recommendations. A secretary also serves, who can be a great resource if the president needs help.

The president is responsible for the Laurels, while the first counselor is responsible for the Mia Maids, and the second counselor is in charge of the Beehives.

In wards that have a large number of young women, the presidency may choose to call advisers to assist them. They have the opposite function as advisers in the Young Men program. In the Young Men program, it's the advisers who coordinate the Mutual activities, leaving the presidency to give the spiritual lesson on Sunday. With the Young Women program, however, the advisers are customarily the ones who teach the Sunday lessons. However, wards and stakes may adapt the advisers' assignments to fit local needs.

Each of the three Young Women classes are presided over by a presidency, composed of the class members. Thus, a typical ward will have a Laurel president, a Mia Maid president, and a Beehive president. Each president will be called by the bishopric and will be asked to choose two counselors. A secretary should also be called. In addition, the Laurel class presidency is in charge of conducting meetings of the girls when all the classes meet together.

Another office in the Young Women organization is that of camp director. This hardy soul organizes, plans, and conducts the annual camp program under the direction of the Young Women presidency. If the camp is held on a stakewide basis, the ward camp director may primarily serve as a cheerleader who will encourage the girls to go to camp and help them succeed once they're there.

Sunday School

Although various aspects of the gospel are taught in all Church meetings, the Sunday School is the auxiliary specifically tasked with the responsibility of helping Church members become familiar with the scriptures. Sunday School is a 40-minute portion of the Sunday three-hour meeting block, usually occurring right in the middle between sacrament meeting and priesthood meeting or Relief Society. There are classes geared to all age groups, 12 and older. Those younger than 12 spend the Sunday School time attending Primary.

One man is called as president of the Sunday School organization, and he should recommend the names of two other men to assist him as counselors. They may also call a secretary, if desired. The main duty of the presidency is to make sure the organization is fully staffed and that the teachers are being effective.

The most common calling in the Sunday School organization is that of a teacher. A typical Sunday School curriculum will consist of two classes for adults, six classes for the youth, and other special classes being taught occasionally. Each of these courses requires a teacher.

The study material for most courses centers around the standard works, which are the books considered by the Church to be scripture.

The Gospel Principles class is designed for those investigating the Church, new members, and others who may want to know more about the basic principles of the gospel. (As a convert, you should continue attending this class until you're familiar enough with the lessons taught there that you want to move on.) The Gospel Doctrine class is the one that will be attended by the majority of the adults in the ward. The lessons are based on the scriptures and will try to provide a deeper understanding of the scriptures, combined with an understanding of how the scriptures complement the principles of the gospel. Course 12 through Course 17 are the classes for the youth, where the course number corresponds to the age of the students. Special classes that may be taught on an occasional basis include a Teacher Development Basic Course and a family history class.

Each Sunday School teacher is encouraged to have one member of the class serve as the class president. This person is called by the Sunday School president but is not set apart. The class president should conduct every class. This consists of arranging for an opening prayer, introducing visitors and new members to the class, turning the time over to the teacher for the lesson, and then asking someone to give the closing prayer.

Primary

The role of the Primary is to teach children the gospel of Jesus Christ so they will later live that gospel when they reach adulthood. Boys are prepared to receive the priesthood and to use it to benefit others, and girls are similarly prepared for lives of service.

Primary begins for children at the age of 18 months, when they enter the nursery. They remain in the nursery until they reach the age of three. (Primary children are always grouped according to their age as of December 31.) When they are 3 to 4 years old, they are classified as Sunbeams.

There are two other classifications of Primary children. From ages 4 to 7, they are known as CTRs. CTR stands for "Choose the Right," and the name is so popular that a big CTR industry has sprung up, providing jewelry for teenagers and adults that are emblazoned with those initials. After they reach age 8, and until they leave Primary on their twelfth birthdays, boys and girls are referred to as Valiants.

When boys reach age 12, they leave Primary and are ordained to the Aaronic Priesthood. When girls reach age 12, they go into the Young Women program. But Primary is an influence that can be felt throughout the life of a Latter-day Saint. After the child's own parents, a beloved Primary teacher may be the greatest influence in a young child's life.

Primary is held for one hour and forty minutes of the three-hour meeting block. Children who attend the nursery spend all their time in the nursery. Other children participate in opening or closing exercises, sharing time, and lessons geared to each age group. Opening exercises consist of a prayer, a recitation of scripture, and at least one talk, all of which are presented by the children. Sharing time is a general meeting where Primary children learn songs and do other community activities. Classroom lessons are geared around basic gospel principles for younger Primary children, but after they reach age 8, they are taught from manuals that correspond with manuals that are used in Sunday School.

In addition to the Sunday program, there are quarterly activity days that involve the whole Primary, weekly meetings for the boys who are Cubs, and bi-monthly achievement days for the older girls.

The Primary presidency consists of the president and her two counselors. A secretary should also be called. The presidency divides the responsibilities for the direction of the Primary, assigning different tasks according to the skills of each presidency member. They produce the annual Primary sacrament meeting program, plan and carry out activity days, coordinate achievement days, implement and supervise the Scouting aspect of Primary in areas where Scouting is part of the Church program, prepare children for baptism, and individually meet with children before they graduate from Primary at age 12.

Other callings in the Primary include the chorister and pianist, who assist with the music, and Primary teachers, who teach each of the classes.

The nursery leader supervises a flock of infants age 18 months to three years of age—those who are too young to attend the regular Primary classes but are too old to attend regular meetings with their parents without causing a major distraction. Some ward members are called as nursery leaders, with others called as assistant leaders. Assistants have it easy: they don't have to remember to coordinate the treat, the lesson, the wiggle time, or whichever program the nursery leader is trying to implement. Like the nursery leaders, assistants are primarily concerned with trying to impose order on free-spirited little hydrogen atoms that are accustomed to bouncing off the walls at will.

Cub Scouts

Cub Scouting supplements the regular Primary program for boys age eight and older. The purpose of Scouting is to build moral character in the boys who participate, so the earlier a child can have a Scout affiliation, the better it is for him. Boys progress from Wolf (age 8) to Bear (age 9) to Webelos (age 10) to 11-year-old Scouts as they age. At age 12, they graduate into the Boy Scout program that is administered by the Aaronic Priesthood.

The Cub program consists of activities once a week, following an outline that is in the Scout manual for each age group. Leaders help the Cubs pass off achievements, which are goals that must be completed before the Cub passes up to the next rank. In order to advance, the Cub must complete 12 achievements during the course of a year.

The Cub committees work under the direction of the ward Scout committee chairman. This committee addresses the needs of Cubs who have not yet reached age 11. Once a Cub has his eleventh birthday, he is represented by the committee that serves deacon-age Scouts.

The three Cub dens have similar programs, each geared to the Cub's age and skill level. Although the Wolves and Bears concentrate on miscellaneous subjects that are of interest to young boys, Webelos focus more on career-oriented interests.

In addition to helping the boys in their den complete their achievements, the adult den leaders serve as role models to the boys in their pack. During the course of the Cub experience, they teach boys to pray, keep journals, attend their church meetings regularly, search the scriptures for favorite stories, fill out a pedigree chart, and do many other tasks that will help them throughout their lives in the Church.

The den chief is a regular Scout who acts as an assistant to the Cub leaders. He will attend their weekly activity meetings and their pack meetings, serving as a resource to help the leaders plan and execute the Cub activities.

Ward Activities Committee

As a ward family, it is important that members are unified not just through worship, but through social, cultural, and athletic activities, as well as service projects. As a convert or investigator, you may have already attended at least one such activity in your ward. It may even be possible that such an activity was your first contact with the Church.

All ward activities should be coordinated through an organization known as the ward activities committee. This committee is composed of a chairman and several committee members who may be experienced in such areas as drama, dance, music, and athletics. The committee members may be called as either directors or specialists. In general, a director is someone who serves more or less permanently on the committee, while a specialist is called for a short time to help plan selected activities. All positions on the activities committee, including the chairman, may be filled by either men or women. The only exception is that coaches of athletic teams should be the same sex as the players. A secretary to the activities committee may also be called.

In general, the activities committee is most heavily involved in events that involve the entire ward or large portions of it. Examples of such activities would be ward dinners, summer parties, and ward camping trips. You will find that most wards have several activities that become traditional, such as a ward Christmas party.

The chairman supervises the other members of the activities committee. The committee should meet at least once a month, if not more often. Various subcommittees of the full committee may also meet as needed to plan their activities, and the chairman may attend those meetings also.

One or more cultural arts directors or specialists should be called to serve on the ward activities committee under the direction of the chairman. These persons assist when planning ward activities related to drama, dance, speech, music, or other cultural events. They should have experience that qualifies them to plan and present such activities, such as professional or amateur connections in these fields. As needed, other directors or specialists may be called to serve as dance directors, drama directors, and speech directors. Activities music directors may also be called to help provide the secular music associated with certain activities, such as music festivals and talent nights.

One or more physical activities directors or specialists should be called by the bishopric to serve on the ward activities committee under the direction of the chairman. These persons assist when planning ward activities related to sporting events and fitness. Although a physical activities director should have a general knowledge of all aspects of physical activities, other directors or specialists may be called who have a specific area of expertise. Examples of these callings would include male and female sports directors and coaches.

Single Adult Program

Although many Church programs focus on married couples with children, Church leaders realize that a surprisingly large percentage of most wards may consist of single members. In this context, the word *single* not only refers to unmarried members, but also to those members who are divorced or widowed. (Members in the process of being divorced should not participate in Church programs for singles until the divorce is final.) When considering the needs of single members, the Church provides separate programs for young single adults (unmarried members age 18-30) and single adults (unmarried members age 31 and over).

There are a number of programs for both groups at all levels of the Church (ward, stake, multistake) that may be in operation in your area. Whether you will find all of these programs in operation depends on the number of singles in the area and their interest in participating in such programs.

Some married members of your ward may not attend your ward but may be assigned to serve in young single adult wards or single adult wards. These are wards that are formed when there are so many single members within a stake that the stake presidency forms a ward or branch that is composed exclusively of single members. The bishopric of such wards should be composed of married men, drawn from other wards in the stake. Any single member within the stake who falls into the proper age group is invited to attend these wards, although members should also be given the choice of staying in their regular wards if they prefer.

The bishop should call one young single adult representative to represent all the young single adults in the ward. If there are a large number of young single adults living in the ward, multiple representatives may be called. Similarly, one or more single adults should be called to be the single adult representative for the ward. The term *single member representative* is used to refer to either of the above callings.

As directed by the bishop, single member representatives may be asked to participate in various ward and stake meetings. At those meetings, they should look for ways to get the singles involved.

Your bishop may organize a ward Committee for Single Members if he sees a need for it in your ward. It consists of a member of the bishopric (who leads the group), a member from each of the two Melchizedek priesthood quorums, a member from the Relief Society presidency, the ward single member representatives, and (optionally) a secretary.

So that singles have an opportunity to participate in family home evening, the bishop may organize one or more groups of singles that meet together on Monday evenings for family home evening activities. When these groups are formed, a family home evening group leader should be appointed to watch over the group, help plan the weekly lesson or activity, and make sure all members are invited and welcomed by the group. This leader should be a single male who holds the Melchizedek Priesthood.

The Ward Music Committee

Within a matter of months from the time the Prophet Joseph Smith founded the Church, his wife, Emma, was commanded in revelation to prepare a book of hymns to be used in worship services. Thus, ever since the origins of the Church, music has played an important part in the worship services of the Latter-day Saints. Congregational songs are sung in most Church meetings, and special musical numbers are often presented as part of sacrament meeting. All wards should have a choir, which provides music as part of sacrament meetings.

Just as the ward activities committee oversees all the secular music in a ward, the ward music committee is only concerned with worship music—music that is designed to glorify God and enhance the worship experience.

The ward music chairman must coordinate the presentation of all worship music within the ward. That person will work with a member of the bishopric, who serves as the music adviser. Once other people are called to be music officers, it will be the job of the ward music chairman to train them if training is required or requested. Most auxiliaries have music as part of their meetings, so there may be a fair number of choristers and pianists who need to be trained.

The ward chorister leads the congregational singing in sacrament meeting and occasionally at other ward meetings where the entire ward is invited.

The ward organist plays the organ or the piano for all worship meetings where the entire ward is invited.

The choir director leads the ward choir. He or she selects the music (always with the approval of the ward music chairman), schedules the rehearsals, works with choir members to improve their skills, and directs the final performances.

A separate calling may be made for someone to accompany the choir on either the organ or the piano. This choir accompanist will attend all the choir practices and performances and will work closely with the choir director to practice with the choir and then participate in the presentation.

In addition to the director and organist, there are other officers who may be called within the ward choir, depending on its size and activity. These might include a choir president, a choir librarian, a choir secretary, and choir section leaders.

During the Sunday priesthood meeting, all the Aaronic and Melchizedek priesthood brethren meet together for joint opening exercises before adjourning to their separate quorum meetings. As part of that joint meeting, an opening congregational song should be lead by the priesthood music director and accompanied by the priesthood pianist.

Just as individuals are needed to conduct and accompany the music for priesthood meeting, other ward auxiliaries need those with musical talents to assist them. The ward music chairman will work with the bishopric and the auxiliary leaders to call and train the auxiliary music staff. This may be composed of a Relief Society chorister, Relief Society pianist, Young Women chorister, Young Women pianist, Mutual chorister, Mutual pianist, Primary chorister, and a Primary pianist.

Ward Staff

Most of the callings in a ward are connected with a priesthood quorum or an auxiliary group, such as the elders quorum, the Young Women, or the Primary. But there are some ward callings that aren't connected with any of these groups. Those callings are usually grouped together under the generic term *ward staff,* and they will be described in this section.

With minor exceptions, all of the people holding callings described here will report to the bishopric directly, either through the bishop or one of his counselors.

Every meetinghouse will typically have a resource center containing items such as books, posters, and photographs. It will also have media material, such as filmstrips, sound recordings, video tapes, and the equipment necessary to play such material. A meetinghouse librarian may be called to work in the library and supervise the distribution and collection of library material. An older term for this calling that you will still hear is *ward librarian.* When there is more than one ward or branch meeting in a building, the agent ward should provide the meetinghouse librarian, and each of the other wards should call an associate librarian to work under the direction of the meetinghouse librarian. This spreads the work out more evenly across the wards, but also provides one focal point when decisions need to be made. Sometimes an assistant meetinghouse librarian will be called to help the meetinghouse or associate librarian serving in a ward. The assistant will work under the supervision of the other librarian and will probably perform similar duties.

In wards where there are printed Sunday programs, it is the job of the Sunday program editor to get the meeting agenda and then type the program, copy it, and arrange for its distribution to members on Sunday. The program may also include announcements and calendar items.

The ward mission leader is in charge of all missionary activities within the ward. He meets regularly with the stake mission presidency and the full-time missionaries to coordinate missionary efforts at the ward level. Even though most of the duties performed by the ward mission leader will occur right in your own ward, it is really a stake calling. As such, it will be described in greater detail in chapter 5.

The ward family history consultant is called to help members of the ward become more proficient in doing genealogy and family history work. Ward consultants may help members individually or in groups. If enough people in the ward want to learn a certain skill, the consultant can arrange for group classes to be taught. Under the direction of the bishopric, the ward family history consultant may regularly arrange for a family history class to be taught during Sunday School each week.

Much of the work done at family history centers relates to the discovery of one's own ancestors, with the ultimate goal of submitting those names for temple ordinance work. (This is explained in more detail in chapters 7 and 9.) But the Church also sponsors another program where groups of names are taken from vital records (census records, military records, birth certificates, etc.), and placed into a computerized database. The process of retrieving those names is known as the name extraction program and is performed by volunteer workers called home name extraction workers.

The teacher development coordinator works with a counselor in the bishopric to make sure all teachers in the ward receive ongoing training. The coordinator should be invited to attend the ward council meeting at least once per quarter. One responsibility of the coordinator is to teach a Teacher Development Basic Course occasionally during Sunday School time. Another duty of the coordinator is to organize quarterly teacher training meetings for all teachers within the ward.

Some wards publish a newsletter designed to keep ward members updated in terms of what is happening within the ward. If your bishop decides the ward should have a newsletter, he will issue a calling for someone to fill the position of ward newsletter editor. This person will have the responsibility of publishing the newsletter on whatever basis the bishop desires—once a month, once every other month, or whatever.

The seminary program is a daily gospel study program designed for youth of approximately high school age (grades 9 through 12). In areas with large LDS populations, full-time seminary teachers are used, and students meet in dedicated seminary buildings. In areas with smaller LDS populations, seminary is held in homes or meetinghouses, and ward members are called to be seminary teachers.

The institute program is another program administered by the Church Educational System (CES). It is similar to seminary but is designed for college-age members. As with seminary teachers, ward members may be called upon to serve as institute teachers. These members assist the full-time instructors assigned to the institute and may teach classes either during the day or at night.

The ward employment specialist is an expert in helping people find jobs or upgrade their current jobs. Ward members usually do not seek out this individual directly but are referred by ward leaders such as the bishop or the Relief Society president. There should be a ward employment specialist in each ward in the stake, and they should be able to trade notes about available jobs and candidates. There should also be a stake employment specialist. The Church also maintains a number of employment centers that serve as a clearinghouse for available jobs in the area.

Ward magazine representatives are called to help ward members subscribe to such Church publications as the four Church magazines or the weekly *Church News.* Magazine representatives know how to start or renew subscriptions to all the above sources and will do that for ward members as needed.

If your ward shares a meetinghouse with other wards, the bishop may call someone to be the ward building coordinator. This person should be a clearinghouse for everyone to call who wishes to reserve the building for an activity. The building coordinator will also have to meet regularly with the coordinators of the other wards that share the building. This meeting will reduce the conflicts that arise when different wards try to use the building on the same night.

There are few ward callings that offer more opportunities for creativity than that of a ward welfare specialist, and few areas where Church members need more help than in the area of self-reliance. Ward welfare specialists and other members of the welfare committee can implement programs to address some of the problems that may be prevalent in a ward community. This may include instruction in upgrading employment, avoiding excessive debt, preserving and storing food and other items, and obtaining and maintaining a year's supply of commodities.

A Convert's Questions

I was just asked to serve in a calling, but none of my friends have ever heard of it. Is the bishop trying to put one over on me? Should I accept the calling?

There are a number of legitimate reasons for declining a calling, but never because you could not find it in this book!

Church members believe that Christ stands at the head of His Church and takes an active role in governing it. As such, it is quite common for programs and procedures to change over time as the size of the Church increases and the needs of the members change. Programs that work well in leading a church of two million members may not work all that well in a church with ten million members and may have to be adapted or scrapped altogether. Similarly, policies that work fine in a Utah-based ward covering four square blocks may not work at all for a ward in Australia that covers hundreds of square miles.

That being the case, it's quite possible for you to be issued a calling that isn't described in this book, simply because the calling did not exist when this book was published. In writing this book, we found that information contained in Church publications just a few years old had been changed by later publications or bulletins. Since change is ongoing, some of the material in this book might be out of date within a month from publication. These changes are actually quite exciting, because they indicate you are a member of a church that is governed by revelation.

Another reason you might not find a calling here is because your bishop just made it up. This is not a joke. You will find that bishops have great latitude in asking ward members to do anything they think would be helpful to the ward or to individual members. If the bishop sees a need in the ward that cannot be fulfilled by an existing calling, he certainly has the freedom to create a new calling to address it. We once lived in a ward where Clark had the calling of ward photographer. The meetinghouse had a large bulletin board, and the bishop loved to display pictures there of ward members having fun at ward socials or youth activities. So Clark's job was to attend ward events, take pictures, and give them to someone else who would create the display. We have never seen the calling of ward photographer described in any Church publication, nor have we lived in any other ward with such a calling. Yet in that ward the bishop saw the need for it, and it did bring the members of the ward closer together.

Similarly, the bishop may devise a creative calling if he thinks it would take advantage of a particular member's talents or provide something that is missing in their lives. In a university ward that Kathy once attended, the bishop's son was almost the only child in the ward. In order to make the child feel as though he had a place in the ward, the bishop wisely created the calling of "assistant sacrament meeting hymnbook picker-upper." The calling was issued to help the boy, but the child was so diligent about his calling that he also performed a service to the ward.

One woman we know has a love for flowers and a talent for making attractive floral arrangements. Her bishop has asked her to supervise the spring planting of flowers outside the meetinghouse and to provide flower arrangements to be used in sacrament meetings during Easter, Christmas, and Mother's Day. This is an example of a calling that allows someone to exercise his talents and also lets other ward members benefit from those talents. It wouldn't be surprising to learn that every ward has at least one instance of a calling that was created to address a particular need or take advantage of a particular skill.

If you're issued a calling that is puzzling to you, remember that the bishop uses inspiration to give members callings that will benefit themselves, the ward, or (most often) both. If you don't understand what the calling involves, the bishop will certainly provide you with more information about what you would be expected to do. Make the decision a matter of prayer, then go forward with the knowledge that the Lord will help you in your service.

Wow! I've just found out about my new calling, and it sounds like a lot of work. Do I really have to do everything, or can I do the important stuff and let everything else slide?

As with everything in life, there is a difference between how something works in theory and how it is actually done. Probably with every calling in the Church, there is some variation between the textbook description of the calling and how it is actually performed. These variations are probably acceptable as long as the variations do not cause duties to be neglected.

We have a friend who accepted a job as president of the Young Men in his ward even though he was out of town nearly half the time, because the bishop assured him that he would have counselors who could take over while he was gone. Sure enough, the bishop called a counselor who was a firefighter and who was on call every other week. The Young Men president was able to schedule his out-of-town trips for the weeks when his counselor was available to take over, and he made sure he was in town when his counselor was on duty. The other counselor also filled in as needed. Although the presidency had to do a lot of juggling to make things work, they ultimately had a terrific program.

The person who issued your new calling should have taken the time to explain your duties, with particular emphasis on the ones that were the most important to your ward at this particular time. If this wasn't done for you, feel free to contact this person again and express any concerns you have. If there are some duties associated with the calling that you absolutely cannot perform, state that honestly and let the bishopric or the auxiliary leaders who called you decide whether they still want you to serve. It's much better to refuse a calling if you have a legitimate reason for doing so than to accept a calling you don't want and won't do, and then sit at home and do nothing.

With any calling, there is always a feeling that you should be doing more. But you have to balance the calling with all the other obligations in your life, some of which are equally or more important. If you have serious doubts about the quality of the service you are rendering, consider asking someone in authority if there's anything else you should be doing that you have forgotten, or if there's anything that you should be doing differently. If there is a need that should be addressed, your auxiliary leader will welcome an opportunity to talk with you about it and will probably be honest and helpful in answering your questions.

One bishop told us that he always debated whether he needed to attend certain Church activities. He knew he should attend many of the activities, but he also knew that some activities would carry on equally well without him. In those instances, he would rather spend that time with his family. He resolved these questions by asking himself, "Is this something the bishop should attend?" By taking himself out of the picture and pretending someone else was the bishop, he could objectively decide whether the bishop's presence was really needed. Perhaps an adaptation of this bishop's question could help you, too.

5

GOING TO THE
STAKE HOUSE

The title of this chapter comes from an old joke that went around the Church many years ago: "My Mormon neighbor invited me to go with him to his stake house, but they didn't feed me any steak. All I got was Jell-O, some cookies, and some red punch." Granted, it wasn't much of a joke, but LDS people who heard it laughed loud and long. The joke is still told occasionally by older Church members, even though the term *stake house* has been replaced by *stake center*. Those who tell the joke still expect everyone to chuckle at the pun.

As you start attending your ward, it won't be long until you start hearing phrases such as "stake president," "stake conference," and "stake missionary." This chapter will teach you a little about stakes, why they exist, and the type of support they can provide you as a new member.

What Is a Stake?

When you were baptized, you became a member of the Church and also a member of your particular ward. Although you may not have realized it, you also became a member of a stake. A stake is a collection of several wards or branches and is presided over by a stake presidency. (In areas where the Church is not as strong, you may belong to a district instead of a stake. Just as a branch is smaller than a ward, a district is smaller than a stake, with some of the minor functions reduced or eliminated.)

The number of wards or branches grouped into a stake will vary, although the average would probably be about eight. The term *stake* is taken from Isaiah 54:2, which says, "Enlarge the place of thy tent, and let them stretch forth the curtains of thine habitations: spare not, lengthen thy cords, and strengthen thy stakes." This scripture represents the kingdom of God symbolically as a great tent, strengthened and held in place by multiple stakes.

The remainder of this chapter will tell you why stakes are important and what they do. Armed with the information that follows, you'll be able to respond with an appropriately weak smile if anyone ever tries to pull the "stake house" joke on you.

Why Stakes Are Important

At first glance, you might think that everything you would ever need as a Church member would be contained within the confines of your own ward. You have a hardworking bishopric, plus priesthood quorum leaders, auxiliary presidents, home teachers, and visiting teachers. Why would anyone need more? Consider the following needs that are best met by a structure beyond the ward or branch:

Administration of the Church Within a Geographical Area

With thousands of wards throughout the Church, it would be difficult to administer them if they all reported directly to Church headquarters. For example, what happens when it is necessary to replace your bishop, either because he has filled his term or because he moves from the ward? Who will determine the best candidate to be his replacement? Who will set him apart and give him the keys and authority necessary to perform his calling?

In a church that grows as fast as ours does, it is unrealistic to expect Church headquarters to make hands-on decisions that affect individual congregations. Someone is needed as an intermediary between the ward and Church headquarters, and the stake organization provides part of that intermediary function. Dividing an area into smaller wards that are governed by larger stakes provides a good hierarchy that can move quickly to accomplish its goals. Members of other churches are often impressed at the speed with which the Church can organize its members and cause things to happen.

When we lived in Salt Lake City a few years ago, we got to experience a "hundred-year flood." Utah had received a large amount of snow that winter, and then spring arrived suddenly, with soaring temperatures. This sudden heat caused the snow to melt too quickly, and soon a wall of water was heading down the canyons to the city.

City officials, in desperation, turned to the Church for help in getting sandbags placed along the sidewalks of the downtown area. Stake presidents were called, who then called bishops, who then called priesthood leaders and auxiliary presidents, who then called home and visiting teachers, who then called individual Church members. Suddenly an army of Latter-day Saints descended on downtown Salt Lake, ready to divert the flood with sandbags and save the city.

City officials were amazed that thousands of Church members were stacking sandbags within hours of their call for help, but it was all in a day's work for the Church. This type of organization is not unique to Utah. Church members are often among the first to organize relief efforts for various natural disasters that affect regions of the world, and those outside the Church are amazed at an organization that can cause things to happen so quickly.

Consolidation of Church Callings

There are some Church callings that are better performed at the stake level because they can involve a larger number of people. For example, most stakes have a patriarch who has the assignment of giving patriarchal blessings to the members of the stake (you will learn more about these blessings later in this chapter and in chapter 8).

Because a person will receive only one patriarchal blessing during his lifetime, a patriarch called to serve at the ward level would probably have little to do other than to give an occasional blessing. But if you call a patriarch to serve an entire stake of up to a dozen wards, he will be kept pretty busy giving blessings to the people within his jurisdiction. Another advantage is that the office of patriarch is a hard calling to fill. If each ward were asked to call its own patriarch, some wards may not be able to find a worthy candidate for the calling. Filling the office of patriarch at the stake level ensures that the patriarch who is chosen is worthy to serve and that he has plenty to do once he is set apart for his calling.

Consolidation of Activities

Some activities are more effective if they involve several wards. During basketball season, for example, it is not uncommon for the stake to organize a tournament among the wards in the stake. Not having a stake organization would mean the ward would have to either organize competition with other wards or keep the activity just within the ward. But there are plenty of men within the boundaries of the stake who would be interested in scheduled basketball play.

Similarly, one of the major purposes of stake dances, stake youth conferences, and stake youth firesides is to bring together LDS young people from distant wards to meet one another in a Church-sponsored setting. Sometimes, ward demographics are skewed toward Primary-age children or Church members who are much older, leaving a ward short on teenagers. When that happens, stake-sponsored events are vital to allow young people who may not have friends in their ward to have the opportunity to associate with other LDS youths.

There are also other events, such as dramatic or musical productions, community service projects, or classes and instruction, which rely on a large pool of people who have diverse talents, both to produce them and to attend them. A stake provides that variety of warm bodies, allowing the Church to participate in programs and activities that would be unworkable on a ward level.

Training, Instruction, and Counsel

Another function of the stake is to train Church members in the wards to perform their callings better. This is done through stake auxiliaries, which are companion organizations to auxiliaries that are found in wards and branches.

For example, every ward has a ward Relief Society president, and every stake has a stake Relief Society president. Your ward Relief Society president will have stewardship over women in your ward, but the stake Relief Society president has stewardship over all the women in the entire stake.

In a practical sense, however, the stake Relief Society president is primarily concerned with teaching ward presidents to be more effective. She has a wealth of experience (she is probably a former ward Relief Society president herself) that she can share with the ward presidents, both in generalized training and in help with specific local problems. Although it isn't uncommon to see Relief Society events organized at the stake level (such as a fireside or seminar where all the women in the stake are invited), most of the efforts at the stake level— in the other stake auxiliaries as well as the Relief Society—are involved with teaching ward leaders to be more effective.

Where Stakes Meet

One of the buildings in your stake will generally be designated a stake center. To all appearances, this is a regular meetinghouse, but it includes a group of extra offices for the stake presidency and other stake officers. There are other changes, too. For example, the chapel and overflow area are larger in a stake center than they are in standard meetinghouses to accommodate large congregations when several wards meet together. Another difference is that although not every building in your stake will have a baptismal font, the stake center is likely to do so. Quite often, the stake center also houses the local family history center.

Stake centers are not reserved only for stake functions, however. One or more wards will share their building with the stake. It will not be uncommon to hear during your ward announcements that certain meetings will be held "at the stake center." When you hear this, you may need to ask someone in your ward for directions—unless your ward is lucky enough to meet in the building that the stake calls home.

Stake Leadership Callings

You may have overheard someone in your ward saying he doesn't have a ward job because he has a stake calling. Likely as not, the person you overheard was somebody you didn't know well because you didn't see him at many Sunday meetings.

A man or a woman who has a stake calling has been called to a position where he serves all the members in the stake rather than just the members of your ward. Bishops tend to think of the stake as somewhat of a two-edged sword. On one hand, wards draw support from the stake, so bishops realize that filling stake callings is important. There's a disadvantage, however, because the stake often taps some of the most reliable people in the ward so they cannot be used for ward callings. Yet most bishops are philosophical about this and realize that when the ward people are finally released from their stake callings, they will come back to the ward better equipped to serve there.

The remainder of this chapter will explain the various callings that exist at the stake level. As you'll see, the stake organization shadows the organization that exists in the individual wards, with a few major differences. When you study the functions of each stake official, you'll get a better appreciation of what that invisible entity, your stake, is actually doing for you.

Stake President

A stake president presides over a stake and is responsible for the physical and spiritual needs of all Saints within its boundaries. Typically, he is someone with a lot of experience in Church leadership. He usually has served in many of the major ward callings (bishop, bishopric, priesthood quorum leader). Although the stake president typically has limited personal contact with the members of his stake, he has much contact and influence over the leaders within the stake. The bishops and priesthood leaders who have stewardship over the members of your ward are in regular contact with your stake president and receive both training and counseling from him. In that sense, your stake president may have a great effect on your Church life, even if you don't know his name.

The stake president serves with two counselors, the three of whom comprise the stake presidency. Being the stake president or a counselor in the stake presidency involves as much time as being a bishop or a counselor in a bishopric. The difference is that the stake callings are more administrative in nature, with fewer opportunities to interact with individual members. This is not to say that members of the stake presidency are not aware of the problems of individual members. On the contrary, serious problems are often brought to the attention of the stake president as bishops seek advice and counsel.

The stake presidency is similar to a bishopric in the sense that certain duties must remain with the stake president and others can be delegated to his counselors. Listed below are the duties that the stake president must perform himself, although they may be temporarily delegated to a counselor if the president is absent or ill:

- The stake president is the main contact between the stake and Church officials beyond the stake level (see chapter 6).
- When a bishop needs to be released, the stake president will select a replacement, obtain First Presidency approval, call him to the office, sustain him in the ward, and set him apart. He is also responsible for training the new bishopric.
- The stake president calls members to the high council and directs them in their duties (this will be discussed later in this chapter).
- The stake presidency presides over the high priest group that exists in each ward. Although each ward group has a high priest group leader who directs day-to-day operations, the stake president presides over all high priests in the stake.
- The stake president recommends patriarchs, directs their activities, and reviews the blessings they give.
- The stake president must interview and set apart each full-time missionary who is called from the stake. He must also release full-time missionaries from their callings when they return from their missions.

- The stake president can perform marriages where legally authorized by local government.
- The stake president convenes and presides over stake disciplinary councils. These are similar to ward disciplinary councils (see chapter 4). Stake disciplinary councils are generally held for men who hold the Melchizedek Priesthood or for individuals who do not agree with the decision reached by a ward disciplinary council.
- The stake president verifies that stake records are kept properly, and reviews and signs all reports prepared at the stake level.
- Each stake receives a budget each year to cover stake costs, and the president is responsible for overseeing that budget.
- The stake president supervises the management of the physical buildings and property that are within the stake boundaries.
- The stake president calls and trains a person to perform public communications functions within the stake. This person is typically involved with the news media and will be involved with the publication and promotion of stake events and Church issues in general.

Stake Presidency Counselors

Just as in the case of a bishop and his counselors, the duties of stake presidency counselors will vary greatly depending on their own preferences and the needs of the stake president. The duties in the previous section will generally be performed by the stake president himself, rather than being delegated to his counselors, but the duties below may either be assumed by the stake president or assigned to a counselor:

- Set apart counselors in ward bishoprics as directed by the stake president.
- Suggest individuals to serve in stake assignments and make sure they are set apart. When their calling is completed, release them.
- Plan and conduct various stake meetings, including

stake conferences, general priesthood meetings, leadership training meetings, auxiliary training meetings, and other meetings that may be called by the stake president.

- Direct the training of bishoprics and Melchizedek Priesthood quorum leaders (elders quorum presidencies and high priest group leaderships).
- Call and set apart the officers in the stake mission, ward mission leaders, and stake missionaries.
- Approve and interview all brethren recommended to receive the Melchizedek Priesthood or be advanced to the office of high priest in that priesthood.
- Interview members who need to have their temple recommends renewed before attending the temple. The stake president should interview all those who are attending the temple for the first time, but the counselors usually handle recommend renewals for those who have been to the temple before.
- Counsel individual stake members who seek spiritual guidance.
- Hold a regular interview with each bishop and Melchizedek Priesthood leader. These should occur at least once per quarter.
- Oversee stake programs such as home teaching, member activation, family home evening, temple and family history work, missionary work, welfare services, teacher development, music, military relations, meetinghouse libraries, Church magazines, and public communications.
- Supervise the stake priesthood and auxiliary organizations.
- Recommend changes to stake units, such as creating new wards, dividing wards, or changing ward or stake boundaries.
- Supervise the auditing of stake and ward financial records.
- Encourage students to attend seminary and institute, and encourage all members to take advantage of educational opportunities.

Stake Administrative Staff

The stake presidency calls and works with several brethren who help administer the administrative affairs of the stake. This staff generally consists of the following offices:

- The **stake clerk** handles many of the clerical functions within the stake. He completes reports and forms, takes minutes of stake meetings, prepares Melchizedek Priesthood ordination certificates, handles the paperwork for stake disciplinary councils, and orders supplies from Church headquarters. He also is assigned the tasks of writing a yearly stake history, training ward clerks and ward auxiliary secretaries, and overseeing stake financial records.

- The **stake executive secretary** performs administrative and scheduling functions for the stake presidency. Duties typically include maintaining the schedules of the stake presidency, setting up appointments, preparing the agendas for meetings, notifying the wards of stake activities, writing letters for the stake presidency, and doing other tasks as assigned.

- Each stake may call one or more brethren to be **assistant stake clerks** or **assistant executive secretaries**. These brethren help perform the duties assigned to the primary stake clerk or stake executive secretary. It is not uncommon, for example, to call an assistant stake clerk who just deals with financial matters or to have an assistant executive secretary who just handles correspondence or scheduling. In some stakes, it is customary to have the stake president's schedule handled by the stake executive secretary, with an assistant stake executive secretary called to handle scheduling for each counselor.

The High Council

The high council is composed of twelve men who hold the office of high priest in the Melchizedek Priesthood. Like the members of the stake presidency, these men typically have much Church experience, and several of them probably have had previous callings as bishops. The duty of the high council is to advise the stake presidency and carry out assignments given by them.

Typical duties assigned to members of the high council are as follows:

- Review and approve the names of those individuals recommended for stake callings, as well as ward callings associated with the Melchizedek Priesthood (bishoprics, ward executive secretaries, ward clerks, ward Melchizedek Priesthood quorum and group leaders). Recommend the names of worthy brethren to serve in open positions for these same callings.
- Approve the names of brethren recommended to receive the Melchizedek Priesthood or to advance to a different office in that priesthood (such as ordaining an elder to be a high priest). Recommend the names of worthy brethren for priesthood advancements.
- Serve on stake disciplinary councils.
- Serve as stake presidency representatives to wards within the stake. The stake presidency will often appoint a different high councilor to be the ward adviser for each ward. The role of the adviser is to convey messages from the stake presidency, give advice, support the Melchizedek Priesthood quorums, and make sure proper procedures are followed in the running of the ward.
- Serve as members of the stake Aaronic Priesthood committee or the stake Melchizedek Priesthood committee. These committees address ways to strengthen each of these priesthood quorums within the wards.
- Encourage and support Church programs such as welfare services, home teaching, visiting teaching, member activation, family home evening, teacher development, temple and family history work, and family history records extraction.
- Serve as advisers to stake auxiliaries.
- Serve as advisers to stake programs, such as music, meetinghouse libraries, and public communications.
- Serve as advisers to stake councils, such as the young single adult council and the single adult council.

- One high councilor is usually selected to be the chairman of the stake activities committee.
- One high councilor is usually selected to be the physical facilities representative. This person coordinates repairs, cleaning, and maintenance for all the buildings in the stake.
- It is customary for the stake presidency to assign the high council to go out as sacrament meeting speakers to the wards in the stake, often accompanied by a youth speaker or a recently returned missionary. The speakers may deliver a topic of their own choosing or may convey a message selected by the stake presidency. Some stakes schedule these "high council Sundays" as often as once a month, giving you the opportunity of hearing the entire high council over the course of a year.

Although some high councilors are excellent speakers, high councilors are usually chosen for their administrative abilities rather than for their speaking ability. This gives rise to the quip you may hear in your ward that today is going to be a "dry council Sunday."

Stake Patriarch

A stake patriarch is called to give patriarchal blessings to the members of a stake. A patriarchal blessing is considered to be individual revelation from the Lord to each member as received through the stake patriarch. It declares the member's spiritual lineage through one of the twelve tribes of Israel, identifies certain spiritual and temporal blessings promised to the individual, and gives recommendations to be followed by the individual. As with any blessing, the person who receives a patriarchal blessing must live a worthy life in order for the blessings and promises to be realized. (See chapter 8 for more about patriarchal blessings.)

The calling of stake patriarch is probably one of the most spiritual callings within the Church. Men are called as patriarchs only after they have had a great deal of Church experience and have improved their lives to the point that they are very close to the Spirit of the Lord. They must also live harmonious lives that allow them to be receptive to the Holy Spirit as they give blessings. To ensure this harmony in their lives, patriarchs now must be at least 55 years of age, with no children living at home.

In some stakes, there are no men who are qualified to serve as patriarch. In those cases, Church members may be sent to adjacent stakes to receive their patriarchal blessings.

Public Communications Director

The stake public communications director serves as a liaison between the stake and the news media. For stake events that have community interest, he will create press releases, write articles, arrange interviews, and provide photos and other background information to the media. Men and women who are called to serve in this position typically have experience in media relations.

In larger stakes, or stakes where there is a pool of qualified individuals, the public communications director may call one or more specialists as assistants. These specialists typically develop relationships with the media (media relations specialist) or the community (community relations specialist).

Auxiliary and Other Stake Callings

The preceding long list of stake officers does not cover all the functions that are handled through the stake. In some cases, stake officers work through individual wards. In other cases, stake officers serve only those Church members who have specific interests. The following is a supplemental list of stake callings that will affect you through your ward or as your interests dictate:

Stake Auxiliaries

If asked to recall the various auxiliary organizations that exist within the ward, you should have named the Relief Society, Sunday School, Primary, Young Men, and Young Women. As previously mentioned, similarly named organizations also exist at the stake level.

Unlike the ward auxiliaries, which are designed to serve members directly, the main function of the stake auxiliaries is to provide training to the ward leaders. Thus, the stake Primary president should be in close contact with the ward Primary presidents and give them advice and training. This should occur through one-on-one contact and also through visits to the wards. As new programs and policies are introduced and implemented, they typically filter down from Church headquarters to the stake auxiliary leaders. Those stake leaders are then expected to train those in the wards regarding the new policies.

Another function of the stake auxiliaries is to plan multi-ward functions. A stake Relief Society may hold a yearly women's conference and invite all the Relief Society members in the stake. Similarly, the stake Young Men and Young Women organizations will often sponsor events such as stake dances, stake youth conferences, and stake service projects.

Stake Mission

As a convert, you were probably involved with the full-time missionaries, who taught you the missionary lessons and prepared you for baptism. In addition to the full-time missionaries, there are other Church members who are called to do missionary work in their local areas. These persons are organized around an organization known as the stake mission.

Although all Church members are expected to be involved in missionary activities, those assigned to the stake mission have specific callings related to missionary work. The officers in the stake mission will now be described:

- The stake mission is administered by a stake mission president, his two stake mission counselors, and the stake mission secretary. Those in the stake mission presidency call and train other mission leaders, coordinate with the full-time missionaries, and meet regularly with the stake presidency to report on missionary efforts within the stake.
- One priesthood holder from each ward is called to be the ward mission leader. He is in charge of all missionary efforts within that ward, meeting regularly with the

stake mission presidency and the full-time missionaries to coordinate all missionary efforts in the ward with them. Although the calling of ward mission leader is a stake calling, it is performed at the ward level by a person who lives within the ward boundaries. But the ward leader is called and approved through the stake mission. The ward mission leader is also involved with making sure that new converts are welcomed and involved in the ward. He makes sure new converts continue to receive instruction, receive callings, and make friends within the ward. He needs to make sure the new convert will make the sometimes difficult transition from investigator to convert to strong Latter-day Saint.

- In wards with a large amount of missionary activity, it becomes difficult for one person to coordinate all the activities. In these cases, an assistant ward mission leader is sometimes called to assist.
- One or more members of each ward are called to do missionary work within the ward. These are known as stake missionaries. Stake missionaries are initially called by a member of the stake mission presidency, but most of their missionary efforts in the ward are coordinated through the ward mission leader. They meet regularly with the ward mission leader and the full-time missionaries and are often involved in the teaching of potential converts or new converts.

Stake Activities Committee

The stake activities committee helps train the ward activities committees and also plans events to which all members of the stake are invited. The stake activities committee is usually composed of a chairman and one or more specialists. Each specialist may further be defined as a cultural arts specialist (musical or drama activities) or a physical activities specialist (athletic and recreational activities).

Examples of stakewide activities planned by the stake activities committee would include athletic tournaments, drama productions, musical productions, hikes, and camp outs.

Family History Center

One or more of the buildings in your stake may be designated as family history centers, where Church members and nonmembers alike may come to research their genealogy. These centers usually have computers, microfilm readers, and other tools to allow you to search for your ancestors.

If your stake has such a facility, it will be staffed by a family history center director and one or more family history center specialists. The director is in charge of the overall operation of the center, while the specialist assists the patrons that come to do research.

Director of Libraries

The stake director of libraries helps train the individual librarians assigned to the meetinghouse libraries throughout the stake. Most ward buildings include a library, which contains photos, books, and videos used for instruction by teachers and families. In wards where there is no library, these materials can be checked out through the stake director.

Music Chairman

The stake music chairman trains ward music chairmen and is also in charge of coordinating the music for stake meetings and stake activities that involve music. The director will choose appropriate music and will often organize and conduct stake choirs who provide inspirational music as needed.

Singles Councils

Each ward should contain a young single adult committee (for single men and women ages 18–30) and a single adult committee (for singles older than age 30). Similar singles groups are found at the stake level, but here they are known as the young single adult council and the single adult council. Their function is to train the ward committees and to plan stake activities for singles.

Although marriage and family life are heavily stressed

within the Church, there is a large percentage of adults who have either never married or who have lost a spouse through death, divorce, or separation. Singles councils provide a vital function in the stake as they determine the needs of these Church members and minister to those needs.

Stake Functions

With all those stake officers, it should be no surprise that they generate a lot of meetings and activities for the benefit of the people in the stake. This section will describe the different events or functions sponsored by the stake and which might involve a typical ward member during the course of a year. When you hear announcements about stake functions, refer to this section to determine exactly what will be presented and who should attend.

Ward Conference

Once a year, your regular ward meetings should be replaced by a ward conference. Despite the name, this is really a stake function, where stake leaders attend and instruct the members of the ward. There is much variation from stake to stake in terms of what is presented in ward conferences. It is common to have only one member of the stake presidency in attendance, but some stakes have the entire stake presidency there. Similarly, the stake officers only visit sacrament meeting in some stakes, while other stakes provide alternate programs for the Sunday school and other auxiliaries. You will just have to wait for your first conference to see how this is handled in your area.

Stake Conference

Twice per year, regular Sunday meetings are canceled and replaced by a stake conference. These conferences are typically held at the stake center or in some other large assembly hall, such as a school or tabernacle. It is not uncommon for a stake conference to feature meetings on both Saturday and Sunday.

Typically, the Saturday sessions will involve a leadership meeting for stake leaders only, followed by a leadership training session for all stake members who serve on ward councils. The Sunday meeting will typically last about two hours and will be open to all members of the stake—adults and children alike.

At a stake conference, instruction is provided by stake leaders and other members of the stake. Occasionally there may be a higher authority assigned to visit the conference and bring a message from Church headquarters. Stake conferences are conducted by the stake president and his counselors. In the absence of a visiting General or Area Authority, the stake officers choose a conference theme and plan the program.

High Council Sundays

As already described under the duties of the high council, certain Sundays throughout the year are reserved for speakers from the stake high council. During these weeks, a visiting high councilor will speak in your ward and will present a topic suggested by the stake president or by your bishop. It is not uncommon for the high councilor to arrange for other speakers, such as a youth or a recently returned missionary.

Every ward has a high councilor assigned to that ward as an adviser. Sometimes the stake adviser will be a member of the ward he advises, while other times he will be a member of another ward. Although there are few hard-and-fast rules about what a high councilor should do when he visits his assigned ward, many of them attend the entire three-hour block of meetings in an attempt to get to know the ward and its members. Visiting high councilors who are not assigned as advisers to a ward may also stay for the three-hour meeting block. There is no Churchwide rule about high council visits. Any customs in your stake have probably been established by the stake president, who knows the needs of the stake members.

Priesthood Meetings

Several times per year the stake will sponsor meetings to be attended by all brethren in the stake who hold either the

Aaronic or the Melchizedek Priesthood. A general priesthood meeting is open to all priesthood holders, while a priesthood leadership meeting is held specifically for those in leadership positions, such as bishops and priesthood quorum or group leaders.

Auxiliary Meetings

The stake auxiliaries may also hold several meetings during the year. As with the priesthood meetings, these may consist of general meetings open to all members of the organization and training meetings designed just to train ward leaders.

The general gatherings can often include more than simply meetings. For example, the youth organizations might sponsor stake dances and stake youth conferences. The Relief Society might hold stake education seminars and stake service projects. The Primary organization might organize a stake children's parade or a stake Primary talent show. The amount of stake auxiliary meetings depends on the stake itself, although it is refreshing to note that general Church leaders have been trying to cut back on these meetings in order for Church members to spend more time at home with their families.

Activities Committee Functions

Various stake-sponsored activities may be presented throughout the year through the stake activities committee. Because the committee may contain both cultural and physical activity specialists, there is a wide variety of events that are available.

Indeed, one of the challenges of stake activities committees is to strike a balance between doing nothing and doing too much. Sometimes Church members feel obligated to attend events out of loyalty to those who organized them. If the stake activities committee is too diligent, beleaguered families could find themselves attending stake-sponsored activities every weekend.

Remember—these activities are scheduled for your benefit, and you may find great satisfaction through them. But it's important to remember that these are extracurricular events, and attendance should be governed by whether it will be a good experience for your family.

Missionary Open Houses

The stake mission will often work with the full-time missionaries and the ward mission leaders to sponsor missionary open houses. These are designed so that you can bring along interested friends or neighbors who are not members of the Church and have them meet the missionaries, watch Church videos, or view exhibits. Sometimes the program will feature a satellite broadcast sent from Church headquarters, supplemented by music and exhibits in the local meetings. These programs provide a good way to introduce the Church to your nonmember friends.

Family History Events

The stake family history center will occasionally present programs designed to get both members and nonmembers excited about their family history. The idea is to teach these potential library patrons about the services that are provided by the library and get them started in researching their own family roots.

You don't need to have any knowledge of genealogy to participate in family history programs and events. The staff will be delighted to teach you anything you need to know. And they're equally happy to teach your non-LDS friends and family members, so you need feel no hesitation about inviting them to participate with you.

Preparedness Seminars

Welfare committees exist at both the stake and ward levels. In addition to providing for members in need, these committees are concerned with teaching each individual member to be more self-reliant. Because of this, seminars will often be presented that touch upon all aspects of being self-reliant. These may include instruction on such subjects as food storage, budgets, job interviews, wills and estate planning, and family health.

Singles Activities

The stake councils for single adults and young single adults may coordinate with the ward committees to provide stake activities for singles. These might include such activities as conferences, parties, dances, service projects, temple trips, and potluck dinners.

Although activities for single adults are extracurricular and attendance is optional, single adults who participate often get great satisfaction from doing so. Associating with other singles provides a feeling of community that can be vital in a stake that seems to be composed solely of married people and their children. In addition to being a great opportunity to meet new friends, singles' activities can focus on problems that are unique to single members of the Church and help those members find workable solutions.

A Convert's Questions

Is attendance optional at stake meetings?

There aren't any stake police who will knock on your door and arrest you if you miss a stake meeting, just as nobody from your ward will strong-arm you if you miss your regular Sunday ward meetings. However, these meetings have been organized for the benefit of stake members. Those who attend are usually glad they did so because they are usually enlightened spiritually, socially, and emotionally.

There's another reason for attending stake meetings, and that is to become acquainted with your Church community. This may not sound important, but we have personal experience to the contrary.

When we moved to Virginia after spending the first eleven years of our marriage in Salt Lake City, we were lost. The people in our new ward seemed strange and unfamiliar, and we didn't feel any ties to the area.

Our stake center was in Outer Mongolia—at least, that's how it seemed. We didn't know how to get there, and we weren't particularly interested in finding out. So when stake conferences arrived every six months or so, we used those Sundays as "free" weekends. Without any responsibilities on those Sundays, we visited many terrific places on the East Coast, and we had a lot of fun doing it. However, as much as we developed geographical ties to our adopted state, we didn't develop the close ties to the Mormon community that we so desperately needed.

All that came to a screeching halt after we'd been in Virginia for a few years. At that time, Clark was called to be an assistant stake executive secretary. This required weekly meetings at that stake center in Outer Mongolia, and trips to various wards throughout the stake. We had to get a map book and figure out where the stake center was. We also had to give up those two weekend vacations we'd been enjoying every year. But to our surprise, this wasn't a sacrifice. The friendships we forged by getting involved with other stake members meant far more to us than those occasional weekends of freedom.

Now, years later, that one stake has divided and Clark is now stake clerk of the new stake. These days, some of the wards he visits are so far from home that we occasionally have to spend the night in another town on Saturday night in order to attend a ward on Sunday. That old stake center, which we used to think of as impossibly far from our home, is laughably close to us in comparison to the distances we now travel. But we know Church members all over Northern Virginia, and we're so well acquainted with their wards that we could move to any one of them and immediately feel at home.

As you become involved in your ward, you will start to feel a kinship for the members of your ward and will be proud of the many good works accomplished by the members of your ward community. Similarly, as you participate in stakewide events, you will get to know the people in your stake and have a similar communal feeling about them. This will never happen if you stay home from stake meetings or activities; in order to forge feelings of kinship with your stake members, you have to rub elbows with them.

Both the ward and the stake represent groups of people who are trying to work together in doing good to others and in bringing the Lord's kingdom to the earth. As we can attest, associating with these people will be far more rewarding in the long run for you and your family than using the excuse of a stake meeting to take a night's, or a week's, vacation from church.

6

BEYOND THE STAKE LEVEL

The previous two chapters have introduced you to the organization of the Church at both the ward and the stake level. Although 95 percent of your Church involvement will be in either your ward or your stake, there are several organizations that exist beyond the stake level. It is the purpose of this chapter to briefly introduce you to those bodies. We will do this by starting with the President of the Church and then working along the hierarchy until we arrive back at the stake.

General Church Authorities

People who grew up in the gospel have a traditional view of the Church as being run from Salt Lake City, governed by a few dozen general Church leaders who live in Utah. As the Church grows, this traditional picture is changing. Church headquarters is still in Salt Lake City, but the body of leaders has grown and their responsibilities have expanded to accommodate a worldwide Church membership.

As you have already learned, stake and ward officials are local authorities or local leaders whose stewardships encompass a relatively narrow geographical area. In contrast, the men who serve in callings of general Church administration or leadership are known as General Authorities. These are men who help govern the Church at a general level rather than being involved directly with local congregations.

There are some common attributes of General Authorities. Their stewardship is global rather than regional, although they may be given temporary assignments over specific regions of the world. With some exceptions, which will be noted below, they are expected to give up any employment and be involved full-time in their Church callings. And traditionally, General Authorities have been expected to live (or move) near Church headquarters in Salt Lake City, Utah. But as we enter the 21st century, we are seeing more general Church leaders who did not grow up as lifelong Church members or come exclusively from the western regions of the United States. As the Church's membership becomes global, its leaders are also beginning to have a global flavor.

President and Prophet

Ever since Joseph Smith organized the Church in 1830, it has been governed by one man, known as the President and prophet. These titles are often used interchangeably, but the term *President* implies the one who presides over the organization of the Church, while the word *prophet* implies one directed by the Lord to spiritually lead the people (much like Moses in the Old Testament). Thus, there is only one President of the Church, but all the First Presidency and Quorum of the Twelve Apostles are considered prophets. The President of the Church is the only person on the earth who holds and is authorized to exercise all of the spiritual keys to govern the Lord's kingdom; he is also the only person entitled to receive spiritual direction for the entire body of the Church.

The man called to be the prophet and President of the Church will serve for life and is only replaced upon his death. His duties involve visiting with the members, counseling and warning members, dedicating temples, and making policy decisions that affect the daily operation of the Church.

First Presidency

The Church President calls two Counselors to assist him. This body of three men is known as the First Presidency and is the highest priesthood quorum in the Church. Similar to other

callings of counselor in the Church, the Counselors in the First
Presidency assist the President in governing the Church and
giving spiritual direction to the members. These Counselors, as
counselors in other Church capacities, are also authorized to
perform the duties of the President when he is not available
and when he has given them permission to do so. On rare occasions throughout the history of the Church, additional counselors have been called to serve in the First Presidency along-
side the standard two. This has been done when the President
was suffering the effects of illness or age and did not have the
physical stamina to do all that was required of him without
additional help.

Quorum of the Twelve Apostles

After the First Presidency, the next governing body of the
Church is the Quorum of the Twelve Apostles, more commonly
referred to as the Quorum of the Twelve. You will occasionally
hear of them being referred to as the Council of the Twelve.
Like the Apostles in the days of the New Testament, this body
is composed of twelve men called to be witnesses of Jesus
Christ to all the world. This quorum works with the First Presidency to help the kingdom of God roll forward on the earth.
The Apostles spend much of their time traveling all over the
world, meeting and counseling with members, participating in
conferences and temple dedications, and meeting with local,
national, and international governments to promote understanding and friendship.

Members of the Quorum of the Twelve are called for life.
The most senior member of the group (the one who has served
longest, excepting the President of the Church) is called to be
the President of the quorum. The exception to this is if the
senior member is serving as a counselor in the First Presidency. In that case, the next senior member of the group is
called to be the Acting President.

Quorums of the Seventy

As outlined in section 107 of the Doctrine and Covenants,
up to seven Quorums of the Seventy may be organized to tes-

tify of Jesus Christ, carry the gospel to all the world, and assist the Quorum of the Twelve in performing the administrative duties of the Church. Each of these quorums may consist of a maximum of seventy Brethren, so if all seven quorums were fully staffed, there would be 490 members. Regardless of the number of quorums in existence, seven Brethren are called to be the seven Presidents of the Seventy and to conduct the business of all the organized quorums.

For the majority of time since the Church was organized, there has only been one Quorum of the Seventy. About 25 years ago, a second quorum was formed. In April of 1997, it was announced that three additional quorums would be organized. These quorums are outlined under the heading "Area Authority Seventies." As of 1998, the First and Second Quorums of the Seventy are as follows:

- **First Quorum**
  The First Quorum of the Seventy consists of Brethren who are called to serve full time until they reach the age of seventy.
- **Second Quorum**
  The Second Quorum of the Seventy consists of Brethren who are called to serve full time for a period of 3 to 5 years.

The Presiding Bishopric

One man is called to be the Presiding Bishop of the Church. With his two counselors, these three Brethren form what is called the Presiding Bishopric. The duties of the Presiding Bishopric typically focus on the more temporal (physical) needs of the kingdom. For example, the Presiding Bishopric manages the property owned by the Church, such as welfare facilities and church buildings. They also oversee all purchasing, printing, and translation efforts of the Church, among many other duties.

Area Presidencies

Until recently, changes at the stake level were handled by members of the Quorum of the Twelve or members of a

Quorum of the Seventy. Thus, whenever a new stake was formed or a stake presidency was changed, one of those Brethren would have to travel from Church headquarters in Salt Lake City to make the change. As the Church grew to pass the 1,000-stake mark, this level of administration became impractical. The solution was to divide the world into a number of different areas, and name an Area Presidency to preside over each area.

The size of any area will vary according to the number of Church members who live within it. In locations with large numbers of Saints (such as Utah or California), an area may cover just a portion of one state. In other locations, a defined area may cover several states or even several nations.

Each area is governed by an Area President, who is assisted by two counselors. These three men form the Area Presidency, and they are stewards who attend to the needs of all the stakes within their area. They are authorized to visit the stakes as needed, counsel with stake presidents, make changes to stake boundaries and stake presidencies, and handle other administrative details as needed. Area Presidencies are formed using Brethren from one or more of the Quorums of Seventy. Members of an Area Presidency retain their status as General Authorities and as members of a specific Quorum of the Seventy. Being a member of an Area Presidency is just another one of their assignments.

Area Authority Seventies

Although the formation of Area Presidencies eased some of the burden of Church administration, it still did not solve all of the logistical problems of governing a worldwide church from a central location. This burden was eased by the creation of a new calling, an Area Authority Seventy. Brethren given this calling typically have much experience in Church leadership. Most of them are probably former stake presidents, bishops, and members of stake high councils. The three new Quorums of the Seventy are as follows:

- **Third Quorum**
  The Third Quorum of the Seventy consists of Area

Authority Seventies who are assigned the areas of Europe, Africa, Asia, Australia, and the Pacific. They serve for a period of 3 to 5 years.

- **Fourth Quorum**
  The Fourth Quorum of the Seventy consists of Area Authority Seventies who are assigned the areas of Mexico, Central America, and South America. They serve for a period of 3 to 5 years.

- **Fifth Quorum**
  The Fifth Quorum of the Seventy consists of Area Authority Seventies who are assigned to the United States and Canada. They serve for a period of 3 to 5 years.

Area Authority Seventies are different from General Authorities in a few respects. They have the following attributes:

- Multiple Brethren may be called in each area, and they report to the Area Presidency of that area.
- Under direction of the Area Presidency, they have authority to perform many of the administrative duties with the area, such as organizing new stakes or changing stake presidencies.
- Unlike other General Authorities, they only have authority to govern in the area to which they are assigned.
- They live in the areas where they are assigned, rather than living near Church headquarters.
- They are expected to continue their employment and perform their Church service on a part-time basis.
- Depending on the area in which they live and serve, they become members of the third, fourth, or fifth Quorums of the Seventy.
- They remain in their calling for a period of 3 to 5 years, depending on the desires of the Area Presidency and their own ability to serve.

Administrative Hierarchy

The combination of General Authorities plus local leaders

forms the following hierarchy of Church leadership and government:

> President / The First Presidency
> The Quorum of the Twelve Apostles
> The Quorums of the Seventy
> Area President / Area Presidency
> Area Authority Seventies
> Stake President / Stake Presidency
> Bishop / Bishopric
> Ward Priesthood and Auxiliary Leaders
> Head of Household
> Individual Member

As you can see from the above list, there are only nine degrees of separation between the President of the Church and the individual member. This simple line of authority provides the structure needed for a limited number of leaders to administer a large population of members.

This structure is not meant to imply that leadership has to always flow through the entire hierarchy. For example, bishops and stake presidents often receive letters and bulletins from the First Presidency or the Quorum of the Twelve directly, bypassing the levels that are in between.

Other General Leadership Positions

There are other general leadership positions where leaders serve the entire Church but are not considered General Authorities. The term *general Church officers* might be more appropriate for the members who serve in these callings. These positions will be examined briefly in this section.

General Auxiliary Presidencies

The Relief Society, Primary, and Young Women auxiliaries all have general presidencies that are based at Church headquarters and serve those organizations. These presidencies are composed of a president and two counselors. Although the general auxiliary presidencies have no direct hierarchical authority over groups at the local level, they do spend a good deal of time meeting with local leaders, revising instructional materials to meet the changing needs of the members, and preparing training programs.

Mission Presidencies

Although the full-time missionaries work closely with members, stake missionaries, and other local leaders, they are actually assigned to a mission that is presided over by a mission presidency. Like other presidencies in the Church, this one is composed of a mission president and his two counselors. The presidency has stewardship over all the missionaries in that mission and will decide where missionaries are assigned, which missionaries will be assigned as companions together, and when transfers and reassignments should occur.

Mission presidents are not considered to be General Authorities, but they are expected to devote their full time to the calling, which generally lasts about three years. When missionaries are called to full-time service, they are called to a specific mission and usually spend their entire time serving in that mission.

Missions cover specific geographical locations just as areas do, although there is usually no correlation between the mission boundaries and the area boundaries. So, two stakes could reside within the same area and yet be in a different mission (or vice versa). The size of the mission is probably more a function of how much missionary work is being done there. Where there is much interest and many baptisms, there will be more missionaries assigned, and the area encompassed by a single mission will tend to be smaller. The bounds of the mission can also change over time, if the mission president recommends changes.

Temple Presidencies

The Church has more than 50 functioning temples, and each one is governed by a temple presidency. These men serve with their wives, who are known as the temple matrons. These men and women are responsible for overseeing all the work that is done in their assigned temple, making sure it is done correctly. Members of the presidency also work with local leaders to encourage more temple participation by the members. This will often involve speaking in local meetings, such as stake conferences. It may also involve working with local leaders to coordinate ward and stake temple nights, where all members of a given ward or stake are encouraged to attend the temple on the same day.

As with a mission presidency, the temple presidency and matrons are expected to devote their full time to this calling, which typically lasts about three years.

Each part of the world is assigned to a different temple district, meaning that the members living within that district are encouraged to attend that temple. There is certainly nothing that will stop worthy Church members from attending any active temple in the world, but they are generally encouraged to usually attend the temple within their assigned district. There is no correlation between the size of the temple district and the size of specific missions or areas. The size of the temple district is generally determined based on the proximity to other temples and the number of temple-attending members within the district.

General Church Events and Programs

We started this chapter by stating that 95 percent of your Church involvement will be at the stake or the ward level. But what about the other 5 percent? This section will describe some of the events or resources that will bring you in contact with that level of the Church above the stake level.

General Conference

Twice each year (the first weekend in April and October), regular Sunday meetings will not be held, due to a general conference that is held at Church headquarters. (The April conference is officially referred to as the "annual" conference, and the October conference is referred to as the "semiannual" conference.) Many cable television systems and radio networks throughout the world transmit all or some of the conference sessions, allowing Church members to participate in conference from the comfort of home. Sessions are also transmitted over closed satellite systems to ward meetinghouses or stake centers that are equipped to receive these broadcasts.

If none of these means to participate in conference are available to you, the conference proceedings are published in the *Ensign* and the *Liahona* magazines. For Internet users, they are also posted on the official Church web site (www.lds.org), or the *Deseret News* web site (www.desnews.com) within several days of the final session of conference.

General conference usually consists of five different meetings, called sessions. Two general sessions are held during the day on Saturday, and two are held during the day on Sunday. In addition, there is a Saturday evening priesthood session, which all brethren holding either the Aaronic or Melchizedek Priesthood should attend. The priesthood session is not carried on radio or TV, so you should plan to attend a building in your stake that is equipped to receive satellite broadcasts.

The conference sessions consist of speakers, music, and Church business. The speakers are chosen from the General Authorities and general auxiliary presidencies of the Church. The First Presidency and the Quorum of the Twelve are always speakers, with the additional speakers being selected from the Quorums of the Seventy or from auxiliary presidencies.

Church business, which is conducted during the Saturday afternoon session, will often consist of sustaining or releasing general officers, announcing significant policy changes, and giving statistical information about Church membership.

Some members tend to think of general conference weekends as vacations from church. As a new convert, you should definitely *not* think this way. Participating in conference will give you a broader picture of how the Church operates, give you a better understanding of the doctrines of the Church, and increase your testimony of the Lord's kingdom. It will also give you an opportunity to listen to the Lord's prophet as he counsels members on specific improvements they need to make in their lives. General conferences are among the best spiritual opportunities of the year, and those who skip conference are poorer for having done so.

Regional Conferences

Once every few years, your normal Sunday meetings or one
of your stake conferences might be replaced by a regional conference. This is a special conference called for all Church members who live in a specific geographic region. The visitors at
these conferences will typically be selected members of the
First Presidency, the Quorum of the Twelve, the Quorums of
the Seventy, and the Area Presidency. The number of meetings
in the conference will vary, but they usually consist of a leadership training session, a general session for all members, and
often a youth session. These conferences are typically held in
large sports arenas or auditoriums, and the usual attendance
is from 5,000 to 30,000 members. The size of the specific region
invited to attend the conference will be determined by those
planning the conference, based on the number of members in
the area and the distances that will have to be traveled to
attend. In general, several stakes residing in a specific area are
invited.

The terms *region* or *regional* might be confusing to some
Church members. Prior to the implementation of areas and
Area Presidencies, the world was divided into regions that
were administered by Regional Representatives. Although you
still hear these terms today, they now tend to be used to represent stakes in a particular geographic area, rather than to
define formal entities governed by specific officers.

Stake Conference

You already learned about stake conferences in the previous chapter. They are held twice per year and are coordinated by the stake presidency and other stake leaders. Stake
conferences are mentioned in this chapter because general
Church officers often participate in stake conference. Usually,
one conference per year will have a General Authority visitor,
who is often the Area President or one of his Counselors but
who may occasionally be a member of the Quorum of the
Twelve.

Other general Church leaders are often asked to participate in stake conference. It is not unusual for a member of the

mission presidency to speak concerning missionary work in the stake, or for a member of the temple presidency to encourage temple worship.

Seminary and Institute Programs

You already learned about seminary and institute in chapters 2 and 4. These programs were mentioned in chapter 4 because ward members may receive callings to serve as part-time seminary and institute teachers.

Even though these teachers are members of your ward and were recommended by your bishop, they do not report to him. They were called by a representative of the Church Educational System (CES), which administers the seminary and institute programs. CES is administered from Church headquarters, through area offices located in different parts of the world. During the school year, the seminary and institute teachers will work closely with CES representatives to make sure the course material is being taught correctly.

If you are lucky enough to live in an area with a large population of Latter-day Saint students, there may be one or more full-time seminary or institute teachers. If so, they are actually CES employees paid a modest salary for their efforts.

When members of your family are making the decision of which college to attend, one factor to consider might be the availability of an institute program. Your bishop should be able to tell you the colleges in your area with active institute programs.

Temple Dedications

If you are lucky enough to be living in an area where a temple is being built, make plans to attend the dedication when the work is complete. Temple dedications are incredibly uplifting experiences. They feature messages from the First Presidency (often from the prophet himself) and several members of the Quorum of the Twelve. Similar experiences can be had when an existing temple is rededicated after undergoing extensive remodeling.

Prior to the formal dedication, new temples are usually

open for public tour. These open houses are good opportunities to do some missionary work, because your nonmember friends, neighbors, and family members are usually curious about what goes on inside a temple. Visitors to temples during this open house period often remark that the temple seems to have a feeling of peace and warmth that permeates the building. Missionary work greatly increases during these public tours, as men and women whose hearts were touched during the open house seek out more information about the Church.

Satellite Broadcasts

Just as satellites are used to broadcast sessions of general conference, other programs are broadcast regularly throughout the year. These broadcasts include events such as:

- General Women's Meeting (presented by the Relief Society general board and open to all women in the Church)
- General Young Women Meeting (presented by the Young Women presidency to girls of Young Women age)
- Singles Meeting (open to single adult members and presided over by General Authorities)
- Missionary Broadcast (open to Church members and their non-LDS friends and neighbors)
- CES Broadcast (presented by the Church Educational System) to young people who attend seminary and institute, as well as to the parents of seminary-age youth
- First Presidency Christmas Devotional (a Christmas program open to all)

All of these broadcasts should be announced in your ward as part of the weekly ward announcements.

General Church Resources

Church Magazines

The Church publishes four magazines, three of which are for different age groups, and the fourth being the international magazine, which you can order in English. The *Friend* is a publication for Primary-age children, the *New Era* is a magazine for teenagers, and the *Ensign* (pronounced N-sign, no matter what you may hear from Church members to the contrary!) appeals primarily to adults. The *Liahona* contains excerpts from these three along with news of international interest.

The annual subscription rates for these are modest (probably just enough to cover expenses). All four magazines contain news of the Church, faith-promoting stories, and messages from general Church leaders. The *Ensign* and the *Liahona* also contain the proceedings of the two general conferences held each year, although the conference issue for the *Liahona* is several months after the *Ensign's* conference issue.

There should be one person in your ward who is assigned as the magazine representative. He can help you subscribe to any of the magazines listed above. Your bishop or other ward leaders should be able to give you the name of this person.

Publications and Videos

Your meetinghouse library should have a collection of gospel-related publications, photographs, cassette tapes, and videotapes. Many of these are produced at Church headquarters for the benefit of Church members. Contact your meetinghouse librarian to see what is available and to determine which items may be checked out for home use.

Many of the same materials in the library are available for individual purchase from the Church Distribution Center for a nominal fee. Your meetinghouse librarian should be able to show you a catalog of available items and help you complete your order.

A Convert's Questions

What are the "keys" that are held by the President of the Church? Are they literal keys, or do they mean something else?

When the Lord first appeared to Joseph Smith, Joseph was told that he would be the instrument for restoring the Lord's kingdom to the earth. Various heavenly messengers appeared to Joseph and gave him certain keys, or rights and privileges, that were necessary for the restoration of all things to occur. (See sections 27 and 110 of the Doctrine and Covenants.) Joseph conferred these same keys upon the First Presidency and the Quorum of the Twelve. Even though Joseph was the only person authorized to exercise all of these keys, the same keys were held as a body by the members of the other two groups. Thus, when Joseph was martyred, the authority of the Church did not perish with him. The same keys were conferred upon Brigham Young by the Quorum of the Twelve, and he became the new prophet and President.

How is a new President selected?

When the prophet dies, the First Presidency is immediately dissolved and all the keys to govern the kingdom revert back collectively to the Quorum of the Twelve. Within a week of the death of the prophet, the Quorum of the Twelve meet in the Salt Lake Temple to select the new President of the Church.

Policy dictates that the senior member of the Quorum will become the new President. The Apostle second in seniority presents the senior Apostle's name to the Quorum, and they sustain him in his new calling. The members of the Quorum of the Twelve lay their hands upon the head of the new President, set him apart, and authorize the active use of all the keys that will allow him to function in his new calling. Later, the new President will select his counselors, they will be set apart, and the new First Presidency will begin its service. So while both the Quorum of the Twelve and the First Presidency hold all the necessary keys, they hold them as a group. The President of the Church is the only *individual* who is authorized to exercise or use all the keys.

How much are General Authorities paid?

Although General Authorities don't receive a salary as such, some do receive a stipend, or living allowance. Considering that many of them were quite successful in business, academics, or government service before becoming General Authorities, most of them probably suffer a sharp cut in income when they accept the call to serve. There is no fixed amount for this stipend; rather, it depends on the size of the General Authority's family, as well as other personal factors. Those General Authorities who qualify for a stipend include the First Presidency, the Quorum of the Twelve, and the First Quorum of the Seventy. As other General Authorities tend to serve for lesser periods of time, they are expected to pay their own way.

Some General Authorities receive small amounts of income from sources such as personal investments or royalties on books they have written which supplement their living allowances, but being a General Authority is certainly not a calling one should covet for the income. Considering the vast number of Church members who serve in their callings without pay, it would not be a boast to claim that the Church has the largest lay ministry of any church on the earth.

Can I ever receive revelation for the entire Church?

No, and if you ever hear anybody make that claim, you should run in the opposite direction, because he will either be mistaken or lying. Members of the Church are entitled to receive inspiration only for themselves and for those under their stewardship. Thus, a bishop can receive revelation for the members of his ward, and a teacher can receive revelation for the members of the class he teaches.

Although you as an individual member may occasionally get spiritual promptings about ward members, or even non-member strangers, that is not to be confused with the revelation of new doctrine for the members of the Church as a whole. Any direction the Lord decides to give to the Church will come through his designated prophet, and not through a bishop or stake president or your gospel doctrine teacher, no matter how righteous these leaders might seem to be.

How often do individual members hear from the General Authorities of the Church?

You can hear from the General Authorities every month if you read the Church magazines and watch general conference. Other than that, Church members will see General Authorities only occasionally, as those authorities attend regional conferences or temple dedications.

Members are strongly encouraged *not* to write to the General Authorities, as answering mail distracts them from the many tasks they are called upon to do. Most of the questions and concerns raised by Church members can generally be answered by leaders right within their own wards or stakes. Indeed, your local leaders are the ones who have immediate stewardship over you and your family and who should be your first resource when questions arise.

Why has there been so much change recently in the structure of the Quorums of the Seventy?

Recent changes in the Quorums of the Seventy reflect the tremendous growth of the Church over the past few years. It is comforting to realize the organization at the top (the First Presidency and the Quorum of the Twelve) and at the bottom (stake, ward) have not changed significantly since the Church was organized in 1830. It is even more reassuring to note that the original organization of the Church allowed for—and predicted—worldwide Church membership by providing for up to seven Quorums of the Seventy, even though there was only one quorum for more than a century and a half.

All of the recent changes in Church organization have occurred in the "middle" layers of general Church leadership and have been in response to the problem of a finite number of leaders governing an ever broader membership base. Thus, we have seen changes with regional representatives, Area Presidents, Area Authority Seventies, and the Quorums of the Seventy. We can anticipate that even more changes will occur as the Church continues to spread throughout the world.

Although a few members are troubled by these types of changes, most members realize this is evidence of the divine nature of Church leadership as programs are changed under inspiration to better suit the changing needs of the members.

Doesn't the structure of the Church above the stake level seem rather bureaucratic and rigid?

While the hierarchy of the Church may seem bureaucratic and rigid to some, others view the organizational structure as necessarily consistent. How else can we expect that the Church will be the same organization in Bangkok as it is in Salt Lake City?

There is a certain amount of comfort to know that the externals of the Church are the same throughout the world. When you take the sacrament in Spain, you can expect to see the ordinance performed just as it would be in your home ward in Alaska. When you are called to be a Primary president in Wyoming, your duties should parallel those of the president serving in New Zealand.

Critics outside the Church seem to view the tight organizational structure as being very "controlling." They fail to understand that such structure promotes unity and security among the members. It's important to remember that although the same rules and practices govern LDS wards throughout the world, members find they really have a refreshing amount of latitude in terms of how they live their lives and fulfill their callings.

It is also useful to remember that the structure is really just an outgrowth of the doctrines of Jesus Christ. He who taught clearly that the way is strait and the gate narrow could hardly be pleased with leaders who cared little about preserving the Master's Church and teachings as he revealed them.

Are the prophet and other General Authorities perfect?

Jesus Christ was the only person who ever lived a flawless life. Although the General Authorities possess a great deal of spirituality, they are still human and still make mistakes. Consider your own membership in the Church. Your baptism and confirmation were probably a good experience, but they didn't transform you into a perfect person. That is something you are trying to accomplish one day at a time.

It would be contrary to the Lord's plan if the Church leaders were always told exactly what to do—that would take away their agency and their ability to continue progressing through faith and experience. Early in the history of the Church, there was a man who left the Church because Joseph

Smith spelled his name wrong in a letter. We should never expect that level of perfection in our leaders. Despite being led by those with human frailties, we can take comfort from the fact that the Lord will never let the Church be led astray, and we will be blessed by following the counsel of our human leaders.

7

THE MISSION OF
THE CHURCH

You won't spend much time as a member of the LDS Church before you hear about the mission of the Church, which is to "invite all to come unto Christ" (D&C 20:59) "and be perfected in him" (Moroni 10:32). We do this in three major ways: proclaiming the gospel, perfecting the Saints, and redeeming the dead. Every Church-related meeting and activity is supposed to address one of these three areas of emphasis, although the tie to some social events may be tenuous. Virtually every program that is sponsored by the Church is centered on inviting "all to come unto Christ," frequently in one of these three ways, so an overview may be helpful to you as a new member.

Proclaim the Gospel

"Every Member a Missionary"

We are often reminded by our leaders that every Latter-day Saint is a missionary. In fact, that's a slogan you'll hear often. But you won't have to put on a missionary badge or ride a bicycle to be an example of the LDS Church. People will know who you are without your ever having to tell them. Some people will look toward you as an example of goodness and will be disappointed if you fail. Others will look at you as a member of a crazy fringe religion, and they'll be disappointed if you succeed!

When a nonmember commits a crime, his religion isn't blazoned across the newspapers in 72-point Railroad Gothic for all the world to see. You'll never see a headline that says, "Baptist Robs Bank" or "Presbyterian Involved in Shoot-Out." But if a member of the LDS Church gets into trouble, that's exactly what the headline is going to say. Over the years we've seen headlines that screamed, "Mormon Hijacks Plane," and "Mormon Congressman Arrested with Prostitute," and "Mormon Spy Sentenced." People expect law-abiding behavior from members of the Church. When an occasional Church member goes bad, it's headline news.

Like it or not, people are going to know your religion, and they're going to judge all Church members by the experience they have with you. Clark learned that firsthand when he was attending a computer convention in Florida several years ago.

Clark was an officer in this particular organization, so he had a high profile in the group. He worked for the Church in those days, and the name of his employer was printed on his name badge. Whenever the convention broke between sessions, men and women would gather around the refreshment tables for coffee or Cokes. At almost every break throughout the week, a total stranger would approach Clark with a Sprite in his hand. Invariably the person would say, "I know you're a Mormon and you can't drink coffee or Coke, so I found a Sprite for you."

This was not the place for Clark to give a lesson on the fine points of the Word of Wisdom, telling strangers that the Doctrine and Covenants says nothing about cola drinks and informing them that he could indeed drink a Coke if only he liked the taste of it. On the contrary, he realized—just as the Apostle Paul did in 1 Corinthians 8—that even though drinking Coke under ordinary circumstances may not have been a sin, consuming it in the presence of people who thought it would be a sin for him to do so would pose a significant problem. He thanked the Sprite-bearers for their kindness, and he was careful not to drink so much as a root beer out of a glass for the duration of conference, for fear that non-Mormons might think he was a Coke-drinking hypocrite.

It's probably not a wise idea to emblazon your car with those chipper little "Read the Book of Mormon" bumper stickers or personalized license tags if you drive like a maniac. If your computer online identity is "Mormon Guy," or "IMLDS2," remember the example you're setting whenever you're conversing with other computer users. As a member of the LDS Church, you wear your religion on your sleeve. Somebody is *always* watching you.

We were on a vacation once in a remote area of the United States, shopping in a tiny grocery store that was far away from prying eyes. As Clark walked down the aisle where the liquor was sold, he idly thought to himself that he was in a place where nobody would ever see him buy a bottle of wine if he wanted to do so. No sooner did he have that thought than he ran into a member of our ward. The first thing that came out of our friend's mouth was, "Gee, I'm glad I'm not carrying a six-pack of beer!"

It's important that we always remember we're under a magnifying glass, and act accordingly. You may live your whole life without being called or set apart as a missionary, but you're a missionary every day of your life. Just be sure that the gospel *you* proclaim is a gospel that brings honor to your religion rather than embarrassment or disgrace. The missionary work we do passively, through our example, may be the most important missionary work we ever do.

Informal Missionary Work

As important as it is to set a good example, example setting isn't the only missionary work that Church members are expected to do. Saints are expected to proclaim the gospel in an active sense as well as passively, doing their part to bring souls to the kingdom of God.

For many years, Church members were encouraged to ask people the Golden Questions: What do you know about the Mormon Church? Do you want to know more? The Golden Questions were such a popular missionary tool that some Church members used to wear pins or tie tacks in the form of a question mark, hoping to spark conversations with nonmembers. The Golden Questions are seldom talked about today, but the principle behind those questions is the same. Church members are encouraged to bring their religious affiliation into casual conversation with non-Mormons. The goal is not to ram religion down the throats of unwilling people but rather to give them an opening to ask questions about our faith if they are inspired to do so.

Church members who are attuned to bringing the Church into conversation with others can find unobtrusive ways to achieve their goal. "I'm sorry—I don't go to parties on Sunday," or "Thanks for the offer, but as a Latter-day Saint I don't drink coffee," or "I can't go out with you on Mondays because Mondays are family nights in our church," are good examples of sentences that might spark a gospel-related discussion, without being pushy or offensive.

Some Church members are even bolder, giving copies of the Book of Mormon to handymen or plumbers or anyone else who performs a service to them. We know one family who gives out dozens of copies of the Book of Mormon every year that way. They even give books to bank tellers, employees at the fast food drive-up window, and check-out clerks in the supermarket. Their missionary zeal is a family activity that draws the parents and children close together as they choose people they'd like to see join the Church and then figure out ways to present their gift.

Not everybody has the temperament to hand out copies of the Book of Mormon to used car salesmen. Fortunately, there are other options available. We once heard a General Authority say that people who didn't have the courage to start missionary conversations could pray for others to start missionary conversations with them, and we put that idea to the test. When we went to yet another of those Florida conventions, we decided ahead of time that while we wouldn't initiate any Church-related conversations, we'd be missionaries if the opportunity to do so was thrust upon us. Sure enough, we were stopped on the street by a total stranger, who, in the process of taking a tourist survey, found out we lived in Salt Lake City. She asked if we were Mormons, and when we answered in the affirmative she said she'd been wanting to be baptized for years but didn't know how to go about it. We sent her address to the local mission president, and she was baptized within six weeks. We had a similar experience in Salem, Massachusetts. No matter how shy you are about sharing the gospel, opportunities come if you're open to receive them and if you make the commitment to act on them when they come.

Just as the Golden Questions were essential missionary tools in past decades, current missionary efforts center around the family. Family home evening, which will be covered in more detail later in this chapter, is a fascinating concept to people who are not members of the Church. Nonmembers are also intrigued by the lower divorce rates within the Church and the concept of the eternal nature of the family unit. Families with young children may invite non-LDS families who also have young children to share a family home evening with them. This shared activity is a good way to inspire other families to have the blessings that your family enjoys.

The most important part of doing missionary work among your friends and neighbors is sincerity. If the only way you can see your next-door neighbor is as a non-Mormon who needs to be converted, you won't win any converts—or any friends— through your actions. Whether or not your neighbors are members of the Church, they are still valuable human beings in God's eyes, and they're worthy of your friendship. If your friendship is unconditional, and if your friends or neighbors or coworkers know you won't think any less of them or abandon them if they don't join the Church, you will have a better working relationship—and a better missionary relationship— with them.

Formal Missionary Work

There are three categories of missionary service beyond the informal level. Youths can be called on mini-missions to serve for a brief period. Adult Church members can be called as stake missionaries to serve in their home stakes, or they can be called as full-time missionaries to serve in an area that is determined by the Church Missionary Committee.

Mini-missions are a good preparation for full-time missionary service. The common practice is for a ward or a stake to have a youth mission day or week. The youths in the ward will be interviewed by the bishop, just as missionaries are, and set apart for missionary work. During the period of the mini-mission, boys and girls are asked to abide by mission rules, which means that among other things, they can't watch television or go to movies or listen to popular music.

During the period of the mini-mission, youths may go tracting from door to door in pairs. They may do some sort of service project that draws positive attention to the Church in the local community. Or they may work with the full-time missionaries who are assigned to the area, going tracting with them or otherwise working in ways that are assigned by the full-time missionaries. Mini-missions are occasionally wildly successful. More often, they open the eyes of the youth to the rigors of missionary service and provide an opportunity for boys and girls to share their testimonies with nonmembers of the Church.

Unlike full-time missionaries, who ask to be sent on full-time missions, stake missionaries are issued callings just as they would be called to fill any other position within the ward or stake. Although most Church callings are open ended, with a person serving as long as he is needed in a particular calling, stake missionaries are called to serve for a definite length of time. (This span is generally two years, but missionaries may be released early to take other callings.) Another difference between stake missionaries and people who hold other callings is that stake missionaries are expected to commit to serve a minimum number of hours every week. (Typically this is ten hours, but the time commitment can vary widely.)

Depending on the size of the geographical area, stake missionaries who live in a ward may serve throughout the stake, or they may administer to the needs of those who live inside the ward boundaries. Each ward should have a ward mission leader who coordinates ward missionary efforts between the stake missionaries and the full-time missionaries who are assigned to a particular ward. He reports to the stake mission presidency, a group of three priesthood holders who are responsible for coordinating missionary efforts on a stake level.

The work of stake missionaries is twofold: missionaries are called to seek out prospective members of the Church and work toward their baptism, and they are also charged with the responsibility of fellowshipping new members of the Church.

They may do this in a variety of ways which are limited only by the imagination of the stake missionaries in question.

Missionary discussions should be given by full-time missionaries who are assigned to the stake, but stake missionaries may assist as asked to do so by the full-time missionaries. Quite often, this consists of going tracting or teaching with the full-time missionaries. Frequently a missionary companionship will split up for the evening and team together with two men from the ward to form two companionships. This is referred to as going on missionary splits, and it is an excellent way for the full-time missionaries to be in two places at once, effectively doubling their efforts.

Preparing to Serve a Full-time Mission

The typical picture of a Mormon missionary is that of a pair of young men, wearing dark suits and white shirts and pedaling bicycles down a busy street. Indeed, the stereotype exists because a large percentage of LDS missionaries are young men, traveling in pairs, who wear business suits as they ride their bicycles to and fro. For many non-Mormons, this is the only image they have of the LDS missionary program, but it's not a complete picture. Mormon missionaries aren't always young, aren't always male, and don't always preach the gospel by traveling door to door.

As of 1998, some 19 percent of LDS missionaries were single women. Women aren't required to serve missions and aren't necessarily encouraged to do so. However, those who choose to serve missions often become effective missionaries and are responsible for a high number of convert baptisms. Unlike young men, who begin their missionary service at age 19, women are not accepted for missionary service until they reach their 21st birthday. This gives them ample time to decide whether missionary service is a course they want to pursue. Although the typical length of missionary service for a young man is two years, women serve for a period not to exceed eighteen months. The length of missionary service is determined by the age of the female missionary at the beginning of her mission, with younger women serving for longer time periods.

There is yet another category of missionaries, however.

Married couples who do not have children living at home may serve missions when they are financially able to do so. Generally these missionaries will not serve proselyting missions—which means that they, unlike the young men and young women who travel in pairs—will not be traveling from door to door trying to find converts. Instead they will be called to serve for either twelve or eighteen months and will serve the Lord in one of a variety of ways.

Missionary couples may be called on leadership training missions, serving in areas where the Church isn't as strong as it is in other areas. On these missions, couples will train local Church members to serve as leaders in their own wards. They may also work with Church members who have fallen away from the Church, hoping through their example to bring them back into the fold.

Couples and female missionaries also have other options. For example, they may be called to staff a mission office or to work at LDS visitors' centers. They may work in public communications, acting as liaison between the Church and the news media or between the Church and secular organizations. They may serve in temples as ordinance workers or in other capacities. They may work in family history centers or otherwise do genealogy-related work under the Family History Department. They may go on a welfare services mission, which can include anything from teaching personal hygiene in third-world countries to building chapels in places where architectural skills are limited. And finally, they can work in Church education, teaching seminary and institute classes when assigned to do so.

Just because there's a whole menu of options for couple missionaries and for some single women doesn't mean that missionaries can select their own form of service. Missionaries will fill out applications that detail their Church experience and other talents and limitations, but the type of missionary service—and the area where the missionaries will serve—will be determined by the First Presidency and the Missionary Department at Church headquarters.

After you have been a member of the Church for more than a year, you can request to serve a mission if missionary work interests you. Contact your bishop when the time is right, and he'll give you as much counsel and information as you need to make an informed decision. But before you contact your bishop, you should be preparing yourself for the rigors of full-time gospel service. There are three areas of preparation, and all the areas are equally important. Just as it would be folly to try to stand on a three-legged stool if one leg were broken or missing, it would be equally foolhardy to attempt to serve a full-time mission if any "leg" of missionary preparation had been neglected.

- **Intellectual Preparation**

It's hard to teach the gospel under any circumstances, but it's almost impossible to teach a gospel you don't know. Many of the men and women you'll be teaching will have spent years studying the Bible, so a familiarity with the Bible is an important tool. But the scriptural foundation of our church is the Book of Mormon, and missionaries should know and love that sacred book.

Scriptural preparation can come in a variety of ways. Seminary is an excellent tool for high school students; young adults can avail themselves of institute classes. Missionary preparation classes can teach prospective missionaries what they should know in a variety of areas too. The best way to prepare, however, is to read the scriptures, and then reread them. Daily scripture study will teach you the foundation of the gospel, and a knowledge of the scriptures will give you self-confidence that will be invaluable as you work in the mission field. But most important, daily scripture study—combined with daily prayer—will teach you to love the Lord. That love will be contagious. It is that love that will draw people to the Church, even more than your scripture mastery and gospel knowledge.

Another facet of intellectual preparation is the learning of a foreign language. Language training can be a big factor in serving a mission in a worldwide church. At this moment, there are LDS missionaries preaching the gospel in languages and dialects you don't even know exist. If you learn to speak a foreign language, it will give the Missionary Department a greater latitude in assigning you to your mission field.

Learning French does not guarantee that you'll go on a

French-speaking mission. If you spend years perfecting your German, you might easily be called to serve in Hong Kong or Peru. But the tools you use to acquire that first language will help you acquire another one. And even if you end up in an English-speaking mission and never use another language at all, learning a language teaches discipline and fosters a level of commitment that will help you in many ways.

- **Social Preparation**

It isn't enough to know the scriptures if you plan on serving a mission. There are practical and social skills that are equally important as scripture study, especially if the missionary plans on surviving his assigned length of service.

Don't even think of going on a mission until you've learned how to do your laundry and take care of yourself in a physical sense. Your clothes aren't going to wash themselves, and missionaries who represent the Church should always be clean and well-groomed. You can't carry Mom with you in a backpack to wash your dishes and iron your shirts and remind you to take a bath. It's your responsibility to do these things, and it's never too early to start learning how.

Cooking skills are equally important. Unless your mission companion is your husband or wife, the ideal situation is that you'll eat many of your meals as guests in the homes of ward members. But sometimes life doesn't live up to our expectations. We recently heard that the son of friends of ours, who was serving a mission in Washington, D.C., ate cold cereal for his Thanksgiving dinner because nobody invited him or his companion to share the holiday meal with them. Whatever cooking skills you acquire before you leave on your mission will serve you well as you labor in the mission field. Your cooking prowess may salvage an otherwise lonely holiday meal.

Don't think you're exempt from cooking or cleaning or laundry duty if you're a man who serves a full-time mission with his wife. Your wife will also be a missionary, and her work will be just as demanding as yours is. Cooking and cleaning and doing the laundry should be equally shared by husband and wife when they're serving in the mission field together. When you return home after your mission, there will be plenty of time for you to revert to whatever roles were traditional in your premission surroundings.

Potential missionaries should also prepare themselves for the physical rigors of serving a mission. Missionary service demands long hours and heavy physical exertion. If you are a young man who isn't accustomed to riding many miles on a bicycle or walking for great distances, and if your physical health allows you to do so, it would be far better for you to train now than to suffer later. Proselyting lady missionaries often walk great distances, too. And we can tell you from personal experience that even temple work can be as grueling as digging ditches. This is not to say that people who have physical limitations cannot serve a mission. However, while those who have legitimate physical handicaps may be accommodated, missionaries who are healthy but are simply out of shape will just be expected to measure up.

Finally, missionaries should prepare themselves for the hardest part of missionary work—the two years that will be spent with a companion who may not be of their choosing.

The missionary program is like "one size fits all" clothing. One size may indeed fit *most,* but not everybody is going to be able to squeeze into a "one size fits all" t-shirt. By the same token, the proselyting missionary program was designed to accommodate healthy, outgoing kids who are anxious to teach the gospel and are not intimidated at the prospect of spending 24 hours a day, seven days a week, in the company of at least one other person. Even if you've been married to your "companion" for 57 years, you have not spent every waking moment in the presence of your spouse. Adjusting to a mission may be as hard for you as it will be for a 19-year-old boy. If the idea of spending every waking moment in the company of somebody else sounds like a nightmare, you may want to prepare ahead of time to find ways to cope with the situation without doing bodily harm to yourself or your companion.

As you prepare to serve a mission, prepare to live with all kinds of people. Some of them may not be as clean as you

are. Some may not have the same commitment to serving a
mission as you do. Some may be so organized that they'll
drive you up a wall—or so disorganized that when you're
serving together you'll never arrive anywhere on time.
Some of them will be lazy. Others will be so energetic that
it will wear you out just to watch them. Some will be so
friendly they may smother you, and others will be openly
hostile. If you train yourself to adapt to different situations
before you leave on your mission, you'll be far better
equipped to succeed in the mission field than the person
who has no such training.

• **Spiritual Preparation**

No matter how good the apple looks, you can't eat it if
it's rotten inside. The same can be said for missionaries: all
the scriptural and temporal preparation in the world won't
do a bit of good unless the missionary is spiritually worthy
to serve.

Worthiness comes from a number of different things.
Prayer is essential, as are tithing and fasting. (Learn more
about tithing and fasting in chapter 8.) Priesthood blessings also fortify the spiritual armor of the missionary and
will give him comfort and strength as he goes about his
work. But the most important spiritual preparation a missionary can make is to be morally clean. Without this worthiness, a missionary is doomed to fail.

When your bishop interviews you to go on a mission, he
will ask you a number of questions to determine your moral
cleanliness. One of these questions concerns chastity. A
young man or woman can only be sent into the missionary
field if he or she has no unresolved moral issues. If there
are any transgressions in your past, be sure to clear them
up with your bishop and your stake president before you go.
Your mission may be deferred for weeks or months or even
years while you resolve these issues, but it's better to serve
a mission late than it is to serve one unworthily.

Yes, it is possible to lie to your bishop and your stake
president. It's even possible to get away with it. Your
Church leaders will probably know that you are lying, but
there isn't much they can do about it unless you confess.
People who lie to the bishop or the stake president may be

spared the embarrassment of leaving on a mission later than planned—but almost invariably, they suffer a far greater embarrassment when they are overcome by guilt in the mission field and are sent home early. Don't let this happen to you. Live your life in purity with an unshakable commitment to chastity. However, if you have any unresolved issues in your life—or even if you're just not sure something you did was wrong but suspect it may have been—it's far, far better to confess and repent now than it is to wait until later. Don't even think about going on a mission if you have to lie your way into the mission field. It's something you'll have to live with for the rest of your life.

Perfect the Saints

The concept of perfecting the Saints is a catch-all notion. Anything that isn't directly a function of proclaiming the gospel or redeeming the dead goes directly back to the perfection of the Saints. And this is as it should be—Jesus Himself told us that we must be perfect, even as He is. He didn't expect for His followers to become perfect immediately. Indeed, He knew that perfection would be a lifelong goal—and a lifelong struggle.

Perfect doesn't necessarily mean *flawless*. Living a flawless existence is beyond even the best of us. The prophets tell us that perfection is better described as being "whole" or "complete." Our goal should be to become fully developed in all areas, not picking and choosing our favorite commandments at the expense of the others, but striving to live all aspects of the gospel in goodness and in love.

The scriptures help us by pointing out ways in which we need to perfect ourselves, and the Church goes one step further by giving us programs that help us strive for perfection in one area at a time. We may not be able to be perfect in everything we do, but we can start by being perfect in obeying the Word of Wisdom as we understand it. We can be perfect in paying our tithing, too.

As a wise stake president once pointed out to us, we cannot be perfect in everything at once. There are seasons of our lives where our primary goal should be the perfection of the family or perhaps the attainment of the education that leads to a career. For those of us who go on missions, we have the opportunity to try to perfect ourselves in missionary service during the time allotted for that mission. We also have the opportunity to perfect ourselves in one Church calling after another, as we are given stewardship over those callings.

When we're in the midst of raising young families, we may not have the time to devote to temple work that we'll have later in our lives when our children are grown. When we're caring for an invalid parent, we may not have the resources to serve as Relief Society president. When we're studying toward a college degree and working full time, we may not have time to immerse ourselves in genealogy. But later in our lives, all these opportunities will present themselves when we'll be in a position to do them. At that time, we'll be able to perfect ourselves in those additional ways.

You don't need to do everything at once. As a human being, the best you can hope is to progress toward perfection one step at a time. When you climb a ladder, you start at the bottom rung and climb upward. So it is with perfection. Some people may climb faster than others, but all of us have started at the bottom rung and should be climbing steadily toward the top.

As you're ready to take additional responsibilities upon you, it's a comfort to know that the Church has developed programs to help you achieve your goal of perfection. The programs may change over the years, as the needs of the members and of the Church evolve. But you can be sure that whether you want to learn about food storage or genealogy, family home evening or temple work, the Church will not leave you stranded. There will always be guidelines to point you in the right direction, and resources that will help you succeed.

Family Home Evening and Other Family Activities

In quoting an American educator of days past, President David O. McKay once taught something that has had a profound influence on the Church: "No success in life can compensate for failure in the home." This statement is often repeated in the Church today, and many talks are given to remind men that they have no higher calling in life than to serve as husbands and fathers in their own families. Women too are taught the sanctity of the home and the worth of motherhood.

These admonitions are not just idle platitudes. A sound home environment is essential for raising healthy and happy children. Yes, your children can eventually be healthy and happy even if they were raised in a house of horrors, but life is hard enough without being saddled with that additional handicap. Being raised in a loving environment is more important than being raised in a wealthy one, or even a "comfortable" one. Your children can do without trips to Europe or home computers far more easily than they can do without the time spent with two parents who love each other and who love their children.

The family is so important that Church programs have been designed to foster a successful home environment. The most prominent family-oriented program goes by two names, family night and family home evening. This is a weekly event. Families are counseled to set aside one night per week—preferably Monday night—to be used exclusively for family activities. The Church is so serious about family home evening that no activities are scheduled in LDS meetinghouses on Monday nights, not even baptisms or wedding receptions or funerals. Indeed, Church members are often reminded not to call other LDS homes on the telephone on Monday nights so as not to disturb a family home evening in progress.

Family home evening manuals are available to serve as guidelines if you want to plan family home evenings for your own household. These thick books consist of lessons and activities that can be adapted to hold the interest of children of various ages. Although a typical family home evening might consist of an opening song, an opening prayer, a lesson, a closing song, a closing prayer, and the inevitable refreshments, there isn't anything carved in stone that tells families what they must do on family home evening nights. Some families may respond well to lessons (often given by the children themselves), while other families may respond better to activities such as a picnic or a family game night. The goal is that families spend that time together, fostering ties of love and friendship among family members. How families achieve this goal is up to the families in question.

One popular feature of family home evenings is the family council. This is a period that is set aside to discuss family business and to make decisions that affect the whole family. Fathers can give priesthood blessings to their children during family councils, a schedule of chores can be assigned, family vacations can be planned, or problems can be discussed. If matters are brought up for a vote, the father and mother should decide ahead of time how much weight will be given to their children's preferences. There's no sense in discussing the pros and cons of a particular matter if the parents have already decided ahead of time which action the family will take.

If you don't have children, you can celebrate family home evening by having a date with your spouse. If you don't have a spouse, you can set aside the evening to work on genealogy or to relax in some other way that will fortify you for the rest of the week. Once again, there are no hard and set rules. If not everyone in your family is a member of the Church, other considerations may have to be made. Experiment until you find something that works for you.

In some stakes, the Saturday before Fast Sunday is designated "family Saturday." This is a weekend day that is set aside for big family activities that supplement—not replace—family home evening. Once again, the point of the day is to spend time with the whole family together. How you choose to celebrate family Saturday is entirely up to your family.

Finally, families are encouraged to have daily family scripture study and daily family prayer. This is a hard thing to schedule, especially as children reach their teenage years and spend more time away from home. Many families arise early in the morning to accomplish these goals. Other families read scriptures when they're gathered at a family meal. Once again, there aren't any rules that tell people how they have to study scriptures: the Church makes recommendations, but it is up to the family to decide how to carry out the counsel of their Church leaders.

Home Teaching and Visiting Teaching

Home teachers and visiting teachers have been mentioned in passing throughout the text of this book. They are central characters in your life as a Church member, and you will find that during times of crisis they can be a great comfort and support to you and your family. Similarly, as an adult member of the Church you will also be expected to serve as a home teacher or a visiting teacher throughout your life. The dedication you should give to this calling cannot be overemphasized. Indeed, the prophets have repeatedly told us that being a good home teacher or visiting teacher should be one of our highest priorities.

In most cases, home teachers consist of two priesthood holders who travel together to visit their assigned families. These may be fathers who serve with their sons, or two unrelated priesthood holders who visit together by assignment as a home teaching companionship. There are also occasional exceptions made with husbands and wives who home teach together. This flexibility is allowed by some bishops because there are people in virtually every ward (including single women or part-member families) who might be intimidated by two men whereas they wouldn't be intimidated by a husband-and-wife team.

Although one set of home teachers serves an entire family, visiting teachers focus solely on women who are members of the Relief Society. In families where there is a mother and one or more single daughters of Relief Society age living under the same roof, the women in the family may have the same visiting teachers, but they are just as likely to have separate visiting teachers who are assigned according to the needs of each individual. Because visiting teaching is a program of the Relief Society, only women are visiting teachers. Ideally, they go visiting teaching in teams of two—but again, there are exceptions to this. Some women may feel less intimidated by a one-on-one relationship with a visiting teacher, and the rules may sometimes be bent to serve the member rather than members being bent to accommodate the rules.

Home teachers and visiting teachers cannot care for you and your family unless they are in regular contact with you. The Church asks that home teachers visit the home of every family in the Church at least once per month. Visiting teachers should also visit at least monthly, although in their case occasional telephone visits are permitted.

When you are called as a home teacher or visiting teacher, the best admonition is to remember the Golden Rule. Teach as you would be taught, concentrating on the person or the family you have been called to teach. Your priesthood leader or Relief Society president will try to assign a home teaching or visiting teaching companion to you who is personally compatible with you. This means the two of you may well form a strong friendship with one another, but that friendship should be strengthened outside the homes of the people you visit. When you cross those thresholds, you should concentrate on the individual or family inside that home. A visiting teaching visit is not the place for you and your companion to discuss your children with one another, leaving the childless woman you visit teach out of the conversation. Nor is a home teaching visit the place for you and your companion to talk about the big football game, while the family you're visiting waits with varying degrees of patience for you to say something to them. Instead your conversation should center around the interests of the person or family you're visiting. Get to know the people in that household. They are your stewardship, and you shoulder some of the responsibility for their well-being.

Although the typical home teaching or visiting teaching experience would include a lesson followed by a prayer, the people are more important than the program. (This is a phrase that has been used more than once in this book, but it's such an important concept that it bears repeating.) If a woman says she needs a friend more than she needs a lesson, jettison the lesson and concentrate on the friendship. If the head of a household you home teach wants your lessons to concentrate on his pre-teen children rather than his teenagers, plan your home teaching visit in response to that request. There is more than one way to home teach and visit teach, so don't be surprised if you find yourself doing a different thing in every home you visit. The key is to think of your families not as assignments, but as friends. Once you think of your families as friends, you will visit them with their interests and their needs in mind.

Remember that on each visit you're representing the Savior, acting as He would do if He were personally administering to that family. And you're also the eyes and ears of the quorum leader and bishop, with the stewardship to find needs of that individual or family that the ward may be able to fulfill and then to fill those needs as much as humanly possible.

The worst sentence that can come from the mouth of a home teacher or visiting teacher is this: "If there's anything I can ever do for you, let me know." This is the Mormon equivalent of, "We have to go to lunch sometime." Nobody who says, "We have to go to lunch sometime" is serious about it. People who are serious say, "When can we go to lunch?"—and then they follow through.

By the same token, home teachers and visiting teachers who really mean to be of service don't just give vague offers of help. They ask, "How can I help you?" and then don't accept, "We're okay" as an answer, or they anticipate the need and fill it without being asked.

Several years ago, a family in our area lost everything they had in a house fire. As the family watched their home burn to the ground, having no place to sleep that night and having saved nothing except the pajamas on their backs, a cheerful home teacher said, "If there's anything I can do to help, give me a call"—and then drove off into the night without doing a single thing to help. If Mormons believed in the traditional concept of hell, this home teacher would own a prime piece of real estate there. Hold the story of the house fire in your mind as an example of the kind of home teacher or visiting teacher you do not want to be.

Self-Reliance

For many years, members of the Church have been told to prepare themselves in a variety of ways. The obvious goal of this preparation is self-reliance that will shield Church members from many of the trials of life. For example, Church members are counseled to store a year's supply of food and clothing, and at least two weeks' supply of water. Storage of fuel is also recommended, if practical. Similar counsel is given for Church members to save enough money to provide for their family for a year in the event of some family or nationwide catastrophe.

But there's an equally important motivation for Church members to be self-reliant, and that is the spiritual reason. We are counseled to help people who are less fortunate than ourselves, and we can't give what we don't have. Church members who save their money or store their food and then hoard it, refusing to give it to those in need, are missing the point of self-reliance. Even if we worked to earn our money or labored to grow our food with our own hands, the things we possess are not ours but are gifts from God. We will be judged according to how we use the "talents" that are given us, whether those talents be skills or food storage or financial resources. If we bury our talents in the ground, we'll be under the same condemnation as the person in the parable who hoarded his own talent. But talents that are shared are multiplied many times, rewarding the giver as much as the recipient.

There are six areas where Church members are counseled to prepare themselves, and a welfare committee should function in every ward to provide counsel and training to ward members who need advice or encouragement in one area or another. If your family needs help getting started in any of these areas, don't hesitate to call a member of the welfare committee. You'll find there is information available that will help you and your family move toward self-reliance in any one of the six areas.

- **Literacy and Education**

Knowledge often leads to wisdom. The more knowledge we have, the better equipped we'll be to make the choices we need to make in our lives. Thus the Church encourages us to educate ourselves in a variety of ways. We are asked to make sure our reading and writing skills are adequate to serve us in our daily lives and to improve our proficiency in mathematics. We're counseled to study the scriptures and to read and ponder other good books. We're asked to learn the basics of effective communication with those around us. We're also counseled to be on the lookout to learn new things whenever the opportunity presents itself. You never know when something you learned just for fun can turn out to be a lifesaver.

As a journalism student in college, Kathy was forced to minor in sociology. She took what seemed like a hundred sociology courses, all of which she forgot as soon as she left the classroom. She rewarded herself for sitting through those sociology classes by taking classes in a variety of weird subjects, learning about farm animals and world religions and sanitation and public health. When she got a job as a newspaper reporter, she never needed a single thing she'd studied in sociology, but she ended up as agriculture editor and religion editor of the local newspaper. In her spare time, she covered a number of medical stories as well. The strange classes she'd taken just because they sounded interesting turned out to be just the classes she needed every day at work.

It's not uncommon for a class that is taught in Relief Society homemaking meeting to serve as a springboard for a lifelong interest or occupation. Sunday School lessons or sacrament meeting talks can give a glimpse of enlightenment that will change the listener's life. Church members who leave themselves open for any learning opportunity that comes will find themselves with greater success in the workforce, more self-confidence in their daily life, and a more solid spiritual foundation. You don't need to have a college degree to be a good Latter-day Saint, but you should strive to learn as much as you can during your lifetime. Our minds are designed for constant use. Don't let yours go to waste.

- **Employment and Career Development**

The goal of self-reliance includes employment in a field that will support you and your family. Women with young children are counseled to remain at home with those children if at all possible, relying on the husband and father to provide the family's temporal support. In today's economy, it may be difficult to survive on one income. This is an issue for which you should seek personal guidance from your Heavenly Father—and then follow that inspiration. Church members are counseled to forego expensive vacations and fancy cars and big houses, if doing so will keep the mother at home with her children.

Although women are encouraged to stay at home, unforeseen situations may force them into the workplace. Thus the admonition to prepare for gainful employment applies to women in the Church as well as to men. With that in mind, men and women alike are advised to prepare for a suitable occupation and then to seek training and experience that will allow them to thrive in their places of business. Even when a woman is staying at home and raising her family, she should keep her skills current in case something happens that would force her back into the workplace.

Although the ideal situation is to work at something you love, that isn't always possible. It's amazing how many people study things that are of absolutely no practical value to them. It makes no sense to prepare yourself for foreign service if you're unwilling to leave your home city. Unless you are going to inherit a huge amount of money, it's not a smart idea to major in a subject that can't possibly lead to job opportunities after you leave college. Make your career decisions with your head as well as your heart, and you'll be a lot better off in life than the person who left his head out of the equation.

If you find yourself out of work, or poorly suited for the employment you have, your ward employment specialist or your stake employment specialist may be able to help you. The job of these specialists is explained more fully in other chapters, but a brief explanation is that they can point you in the direction of job opportunities and can even offer training in a variety of skills that could make you more employable. If you aren't afraid of work, there's a job somewhere that you can do.

It isn't enough just to have a job. Church members are also counseled to give a full measure of work in return for each paycheck. Honesty in the workforce is as important as honesty anywhere else. Earn the trust of your employer and the respect of your fellow employees by working hard for the benefits you receive.

- **Financial and Resource Management**

The first rule of managing our resources is found in the law of tithing. Tithing will be more fully covered in chapter 8, so it is sufficient to say here that the payment of a full and honest tithe should be the foundation of any money management program.

Unfortunately, some Church members believe that if they pay an honest tithe, they'll be shielded from any financial hardship. This is not necessarily the case. Just as people who obey the Word of Wisdom will still get sick and eventually die, people who pay tithing may experience financial difficulties at some time during their lives. Church members who are not careful with their money will not end up with a surplus, tithing notwithstanding. And Church members who invest in shady moneymaking schemes are just as likely to get caught as are people who aren't covered by the tithing umbrella.

Since there is no guarantee that people who pay tithing will get rich, Church members are counseled to be prudent with what they have. We are told to live within our means and to avoid debt. We're counseled to save for the future. We are told to pay our bills and to be frugal with the resources we have. Being frugal and being cheap are two different things, however. We must always remember that the temporal resources we have are gifts from God and that it is up to us to freely help others who are worse off than we are.

Although money is the first thing that comes to mind when we think of our resources, our time is also a valuable commodity. Church members are counseled not to waste time. However, time spent in service is not time wasted. We should be willing to share our time and our talents with those in need, as well as sharing our financial resources.

If you need help learning how to balance a checkbook or manage your money, your ward welfare committee may be able to help you. Contact someone on the welfare committee. If you don't know who these people are, approach your Relief Society president or priesthood quorum leader.

• **Home Production and Storage**

In an ideal world, there will always be grocery stores full of healthy items to sustain our families. But anyone who has gone to the store to pick up a gallon of milk before a snowstorm or hurricane can attest to how quickly those shelves are emptied during times of emergency.

Just when you'll need a grocery store the most, grocery stores may be shut down or inaccessible. Thus Church members are counseled to have a year's supply of food and clothing on hand so that if the stores closed today, your family would be fed and clothed tomorrow.

During the ice storms of 1998, much of New England was without power for weeks on end during the dead of winter. Keeping a supply of fuel on hand may save your family's life, especially if you live in a cold area of the country. A year's supply of medicines and personal supplies is important, too. Another essential we take for granted is a clean supply of drinking water. Although it would be virtually impossible for most families to store a year's supply of water, Church leaders advise us to store two weeks' worth of water—just in case.

Once you've gone to all the trouble of learning to preserve your own food, you may find that it's cheaper to go to the discount food store and buy your food supply in bulk. But it gives you a certain peace of mind to know how to do these things, even if you may never use the skills again. After all, those discount stores may not always be among us. Your food preservation knowledge may one day be a lifeline for your family.

If you don't know how to plant a garden or preserve food, or if you need creative ideas for storing items in a small amount of space, you may try contacting your ward welfare committee. Your ward's welfare committee will also be aware of any local laws that may prohibit the storage of food in your area.

And finally, just because you've stored your food and clothing and all those other things, that doesn't mean you're the one who will consume the things you have stored. Your food storage could be wiped out in an earthquake or a flood. Or you could be asked to share your surplus with neighbors who, as nonmembers of the Church, have no supplies to sustain them in hard times. Just as you should be prepared for any emergency, you should also be prepared to share what you have.

- **Health**

God gave us the Word of Wisdom as a guideline toward good health, but the Word of Wisdom doesn't cover everything. Church members should strive to keep themselves healthy by exercising regularly and by keeping their surroundings clean and safe. Adequate medical and dental care should be available to every family member, and this includes having medical insurance to pay for those needs if it is at all possible to do so.

In addition, Church members are counseled to avoid things that abuse our minds or our bodies. This doesn't just apply to the substances that are mentioned in the Word of Wisdom, either. You don't have to be an alcoholic or a drug abuser to be an addict. If you find yourself unable to do without anything—whether it be a soft drink or a candy bar, computer games or television—you're a slave to it, just as much as is the cigarette smoker who is addicted to nicotine. Becoming too attached to the things of the world is a warning sign that should not be ignored. Physical or emotional addictions can be spiritual stumbling blocks. If you can't control your need for a particular substance or activity, it's better to do without it altogether. Joseph Smith taught that all commandments have both temporal and spiritual aspects. Giving in to addictions may often cause both physical and spiritual harm.

Similarly, something doesn't have to be bad for other people in order for it to be bad for you. If a certain grade of fuel is good for one Dodge Intrepid, it will probably be good for every Dodge Intrepid that rolls off the assembly line. But human beings are not automobiles. Each of us is different, and a diet that can nourish some of us, or even most of us, can be fatal for others. If you're allergic to fruit, you're violating the rules of common sense to eat fruit—no matter what the government guidelines say. If whole wheat causes you to break out in hives, eat something else and ignore the advice of the well-meaning teacher in homemaking meeting. If murder mysteries cause you to contemplate murder and mayhem, it's best that you find something else to read. Use a little common sense. Start with the Word of Wisdom as a guideline and go from there. Just remember that once you've made a decision to guide you in your own life, it is not your responsibility—or even your right—to try and force your guidelines on others.

- **Social, Emotional, and Spiritual Strength**

We should recognize that our social, emotional, and spiritual strength are our strongest resources. These areas of life should not be taken for granted. As part of the Churchwide program of self-reliance, Church members are told to study the scriptures, obey the commandments, develop faith and humility, and pray often. We should solidify our relationships with family members, friends, and neighbors, and we should always strive to improve ourselves in whatever ways we fall short.

Adaptability is a quality that will serve us well. This life is a rollercoaster of joys and misfortunes, and Church members who cannot adapt to the highs and lows of life will have a far rougher ride than will those who learn to take the bad as well as the good.

Lessons in priesthood quorums and Relief Society should give you many of the tools you'll need as you face the different trials of life. If you find yourself lacking direction in a particular area, ask your home teachers or visiting teachers to give you a lesson that will help you see things through a different perspective. And if you find yourself despondent for no apparent reason or over a long period of time, talk to your family doctor. You may be suffering from a treatable medical condition.

Other Church Programs and Opportunities

There are so many programs sponsored by the Church that are designed to perfect the Saints that it is impossible to list them here. Indeed, you'll hear so much about them as you attend church that you'll learn about them through osmosis.

Perfecting the Saints begins when children are tiny. Children are expected to give their first talks in Primary, and they read their first scriptures or say their first public prayers when they are barely able to speak. Children of any age are also welcome to bear their testimonies on Fast Sunday, although since a testimony is supposed to be a spontaneous expression from the heart, the act loses its meaning if parents whisper in their children's ears and tell them exactly what to say.

Primary children present programs in sacrament meeting, usually speaking from short memorized scripts. They also learn to perform in public when Primary children provide musical numbers in sacrament meeting. Children who are musically inclined may be asked to sing or to play a musical instrument in sacrament meeting when their families present the program, and indeed the children may prepare talks of their own on these occasions to present to the congregation. By the time a child who grows up in the Church reaches adulthood, he has generally lost all fear of public speaking. The poise that is gained through these public appearances will be a great asset to the LDS man or woman throughout life.

Young Women have a variety of programs that are developed specifically for them, designed to keep them strong in the faith during their teenage years. In fact, the Young Women program is so well focused in this regard that it is perhaps the best example in the Church for giving opportunities to its members.

Through its Personal Progress program, Young Women are given a variety of responsibilities and goals according to their age group. Young Women also learn to keep records and maintain personal journals. They're rewarded as they progress in this program, giving them ample opportunity to gauge their own progress. There is also an annual Young Women in Excellence event, which gives teenage girls the opportunity to complete projects that focus on one of the Young Women Values. These projects can involve art, music, poetry, speech or drama, photography, writing, or creative arts in a way that will portray the value each young woman has chosen to illustrate. There are also programs that continually remind the young women of the ward that their eyes should look toward an eternal perspective. These programs instill in young women the moral guidelines that should act as a beacon to them throughout their lives.

Young Men have the advantage of the Scouting program, with its merit badges and assorted awards, to give them incentives toward personal perfection. In addition, they must be found worthy by the bishop to advance from deacon to teacher, from teacher to priest, or from priest to elder. Young Men and Young Women should be given regular personal interviews by the bishop to determine how they're doing in a spiritual sense. If there are any problems in their lives, the bishop can suggest ways for them to improve and can schedule follow-up appointments to check their progress.

In addition to the classes that are found during Sunday Relief Society meetings and monthly homemaking meetings, women can improve themselves through a variety of cultural and educational programs. They may also participate in programs that are designed to help them set and keep goals, when such programs are sponsored by the ward Relief Society organization.

Those who are called to be teachers in the various ward organizations can attend training meetings to learn how to be more effective teachers. There are also teacher development classes in Sunday School that help develop teaching skills in ward members who haven't yet had the opportunity to teach.

If you're looking for a report card to tell you how you're doing in your Church membership, there are a couple of yardsticks that can give you a general idea. If you're a home teacher, you may be asked to attend regular priesthood interviews, which most people refer to as PPIs (see *priesthood interviews* in the glossary). A priesthood interview is an appointment you'll have with a member of your priesthood quorum leadership for the purpose of reviewing your home teaching assignment. If the priesthood leadership is doing its job, you'll have a monthly interview. In that interview, you'll be expected to give an update on what has happened in the life of every member of every family you home teach during the past month. As you discuss each family member, you and your priesthood leader can suggest ways for you to serve that person better during the coming month. Attending monthly priesthood interviews is an ideal way to get you out to do your home teaching because it's hard to report on the progress of people you haven't seen. It's also a good way to get you to go home teaching next month, so you can implement some of the suggestions that were discussed with your priesthood leader.

Visiting teachers have similar monthly reports with their visiting teaching supervisors. These are not as detailed as priesthood interviews, and they are usually done over the telephone rather than face to face. Nevertheless, a monthly accounting of the women you visit teach is an inspiration to do your visiting teaching. And problems you encounter as you do your visiting teaching can be reported to your supervisor, who in turn will relay your concerns to the Relief Society president.

The annual tithing settlement, which is mentioned elsewhere in this text, is a good way to reconcile your financial contributions to the Church. But the ultimate annual progress report comes when you have your annual temple recommend interview. These interviews, which will be covered in chapter 9, will gauge your spiritual steadfastness in a way that no other accounting can do. In fact, temple recommend interviews are so valuable to Church members that even members who can't get to a temple are often encouraged to have temple recommend interviews anyway, just to ensure themselves that they're temple worthy.

Redeem the Dead

All Christians, whatever their denomination, accept that we gain some form of eternal life through our faith in Christ. However, most Christians also believe that people who are born and die without ever hearing about the Savior are just out of luck. This is a major difference between Latter-day Saints and members of other churches, because we believe in the same doctrine of baptism for the dead that was mentioned in the New Testament by the Apostle Paul. You'll read more about ordinances for the dead in chapter 9, but here it's sufficient to say that temples provide a way to gain eternal life for those who passed through life without ever knowing of Christ. But we can't save those who have passed to the next world if we don't know their names or identities.

Church members are making every effort to identify every man, woman, and child who ever lived on the face of the earth so that baptisms and other ordinances can be performed on their behalf. We are undiscouraged by the sheer impossibility of this task. Indeed, we believe that the names we fail to uncover now will be uncovered during the Millennium and that saving ordinances will eventually be performed for everybody. Until the Millennium, we are seeking out the dead, one name at a time.

Under the four-generation program, every Church member is asked to complete a minimum of four generations of genealogy, starting with himself as the first generation and going back through the generations of his parents, grandparents, and great-grandparents. Although nobody is asked to do more than those four generations, the hope is that by the time a Church member has gone that far back, he will have developed a love for genealogy that will make family history a lifelong passion.

Doing genealogical work isn't as hard as it sounds. Each ward should have a family history consultant whose job it is to teach the basics of family history research. Occasionally classes are offered which are designed to show ward members how to search out family records and what to do with the information they find. If no classes are scheduled, your family history consultant will probably be delighted to give you personal instruction. There are few Church members who are as zealous about their callings as family history consultants. Generally, they're willing to spend as much time with ward members as the ward members could possibly need.

If your ward doesn't have a family history center, there should be one located in your stake or somewhere within a reasonable distance from your home. These centers are linked to the Church's vast store of genealogical records, which is located in Salt Lake City. They also feature microfilm readers, microfiche readers, reference books, and computers, all of which are available to be used free of charge. These centers are staffed by men and women whose enthusiasm for genealogical research is contagious. If you visit a family history center, you'll be given all the help you need to do your family history search.

If you're familiar with computers, there are several computer programs on the market that help genealogy buffs organize their family history records. These programs are so easy to use that they're close to being foolproof, but you can get instructed in the use of these programs by your local family history consultant. Everyone seems to have a favorite computer program to assist with genealogy. Virtually all these programs, even those that aren't published by the Church, are set up so that Church members can complete their genealogical work for submission to the temple.

In addition to getting the names of ancestors ready for temple work, Church members are asked to do other things to solidify their family ties. Journal keeping is encouraged. Many Church members also keep scrapbooks. Some ambitious souls even compile their family histories into books that are published for the benefit of other family members. Family reunions are common, with many families holding annual reunions that draw relatives from all over the continent—or even all over the world. And of course Church members take the names they've uncovered through genealogical research to the temple and perform temple work on their behalf.

It doesn't make much sense to tie your family together through temple work if you hate your family, so every effort is made to keep those family ties strong. If you're looking for ways to bring your extended family closer together, talk with ward members or get some ideas from your ward or stake family history specialist.

A Convert's Questions

I've heard that missionaries can't contact their families during the entire term of their missionary service. Is this true?

It's true that from the time a missionary leaves to serve a full-time mission, he will not return home until that mission is completed. If a family member dies while he is gone, he will not even be released long enough to attend the funeral. Unless a missionary is sent home early for misconduct, the only time a missionary may return home before the completion of his mission is for medical reasons. As soon as the medical condition is resolved, the missionary will return to the mission field and resume his missionary service.

By the same token, missionaries are not permitted to have telephone contact with those they left behind. There are two exceptions to this: missionaries are allowed to call their parents on Christmas and on Mother's Day. Missionary parents are normally not allowed to visit their children in the mission field until the mission has ended, either. We recently went to California with a friend, and as circumstances would have it we stayed in a hotel that was only a few miles from where the friend's son was serving on a mission. Although it just about killed that father to stay away, he did not contact his son during the week we were there.

Although telephone calls and personal visits are forbidden, missionaries are allowed to keep in touch with family and friends through the exchange of letters. Missionaries are allowed to receive packages, too, as long as the contents of the packages do not violate mission rules.

I'm confused. First we're told how much work we're expected to do in the Church, and then we're told that the home is more important than anything else. What am I supposed to do when church work conflicts with my job as a parent?

From time to time in the Church, a plain and precious idea becomes distorted by people so that it no longer means what the person who had the idea ever intended. The admonition championed by President David O. McKay that no success in life can compensate for failure in the home is an example of wise counsel that has been abused.

President McKay led the Church during a time when it was generally considered that raising children was women's work. Husbands and fathers were absent figures who brought in the paycheck but who were more interested in what happened at the office than they were in what happened at home. Church members were not immune from this. Some men were focused on getting ahead in the business world. Others, just as misguided, focused their energies on getting ahead in the Church hierarchy. In both cases, children suffered the absence of their fathers during those crucial formative years. President McKay's timely counsel reminded these men that no matter how far they rose in business, or even in the Church, their families were even more important.

Today there are many people who have adopted David O. McKay's counsel as a personal credo, using it as an excuse to stay home instead of carrying out their Church responsibilities. So many use President McKay's quote as an excuse to turn down Church callings and do a poor job on the callings they have that bishops have a hard time staffing positions in the ward, and ward leaders have an even harder time trying to convince members to carry out the assignments they've accepted.

These people misunderstand President McKay's counsel in two areas. First, they believe that if spending time with their children is good, then anything that takes them away from their children must be bad. Nothing could be further from the truth. Most of the choices we make in life are not between good and evil, but between good and better. It's good to spend time with our children; nobody disputes that. But occasionally, the better choice comes when a parent lets his children know how much he would like to stay home with them, and then goes off to fulfill his other responsibilities.

The second mistake these people make is that they believe that success as a parent can only be achieved by spending time with their children. "Quality time" has become a sacred phrase inside the Church as well as outside it. Parents believe that unless every spare minute is spent in the home, they're failing. They're wrong. A parent must spend time with his children in order to succeed, but that's only half the story. It is just as important to teach children by example—and this includes giving children an example of how a parent should dedicate his life to the Lord.

Sacrifice is one of the hallmarks of any religion, and Latter-day Saints are especially well acquainted with the concept. We are counseled to dedicate everything we have—our time, our talents, and everything else—to the kingdom of God. This means there will be many nights when we'll want to do something with our spouses, our friends, or our children but will have to postpone those joys to do the work of the Lord. This work may include home teaching visits, bishopric meetings, or compassionate service. If we do these things with a cheerful heart, ever mindful of the commitments we make as Latter-day Saints, we'll be teaching our children to live lives of integrity— and that's even more important than staying home to play basketball with them.

So if you're tempted to play with the kids instead of doing your home teaching; if you're tempted to skip church because the best soccer team for your daughter is one that plays on Sundays; if you're tempted to turn down a calling because it would require occasional or even numerous evenings spent away from home—don't use President McKay as your excuse. There's more than one way to be a failure in the home. A successful parent doesn't just spend time with his children: a truly successful parent teaches his children through his example how to live even after they've grown up and established homes of their own.

All my family's genealogy has been done. Does that mean I don't have to worry about family history?

There's a big difference between having your genealogy done and having it done right. There are many, many Church members who think their genealogy is done but who would be surprised to learn that the work is riddled with errors. Unfortunately, amateur genealogists often get huffy when their errors are pointed out to them. Pride prevents them from correcting mistakes that could topple their family trees.

Kathy was once hired to type a family history book for a woman who had spent a lifetime compiling her genealogy. The book was so badly flawed that Kathy wanted to stamp "fiction" on the cover. First, the author insisted that her family was entitled to use a particular family crest. The only claim she had on the crest was that her family's surname was the same as the family surname that had used the crest back in the Middle Ages. There was no evidence—no written evidence and even no family folklore—that connected the ancient family with the new one, other than that they shared a common surname. A *very* common surname. There were dozens and dozens of unrelated families who had this surname but were not entitled to use the crest, but the author of this family history insisted on putting the ancient family crest on the cover of her book.

But that was only the beginning. This sweet but misguided woman had done extensive research, looking for people who shared her family name. The first male she found who had the right last name and lived in the right state during a particular period would be identified as the father of the child who had been born in the same state 25 years later. Any children in the same geographical area who were born during the same decade or so were considered to be brothers and sisters. Generations upon generations of people were hooked up without anything more solid than the name they shared. Most of them probably weren't even related, but the author's descendants aren't going to know that. Unless they do original research, they're going to assume that Granny's work was valid, and they're going to send those names to the temple, causing all sorts of confusion.

Fortunately, the advent of computers has greatly simplified genealogical research. Name extraction workers are copying court records and other genealogical records into computer databases, which are being made available to Church members. These workers are not related to the people whose names they copy, so they have no incentive to beef up their work by making connections that don't exist. Plus, their work is verified by other unrelated workers before it is properly recorded. Family records that are compiled from these computerized records may be much more accurate than the records that Granny may have put together from her own failing memory. Before you accept Granny's records—no matter how sweet she may have been—do a little checking on your own. You and your ancestors may be eternally glad you did.

By the way, we know exactly what you're thinking, and the answer is no. Ancestors whose names aren't uncovered, or that are recorded incorrectly, aren't going to be denied the blessings of the gospel. Eventually everything will be straightened out, but it may not be for decades or even until the Millennium. You don't want your dead ancestors to have to twiddle their thumbs on the other side of the veil for all those years when they could have been reaping the blessings of the gospel, do you? In that case, you may want to think about verifying your family genealogical records—even if your relatives assure you that the work has already been done.

8

GROWTH AND PROGRESSION IN THE KINGDOM OF GOD

Nobody can wave a magic wand and turn a baby into a marathon runner. The baby must first learn to roll over. Then, in a slow progression, he learns to crawl, to creep, to stand, and to walk. Only years of practice and training and commitment will create a marathon runner from that helpless child.

So it is in the Church. If you read the previous chapter, you saw that a primary goal of the Church is to perfect the Saints. This is not an overnight process. Just as a baby becomes mature one step at a time, we Church members reach spiritual maturity through a series of steps. We can no more expect full spiritual maturity of a person who has just discovered the gospel than we can hope that a runner will win a race the first time he steps up to the starting line. There is hard work ahead—but just as a runner finds that running is something he grows to love, so you will find that growth in the gospel will be a rich and fulfilling experience.

The first step is to join the Church. No matter how you discovered the gospel—and there are as many stories as there are converts—the first common experience that all Church members have is baptism. This chapter will start you off at baptism and will let you know what you can expect as you grow and progress in the kingdom of God.

Becoming a New Member

Your Baptism

The hardest thing about your baptism will be deciding to do it. Baptism is a big step, and it should not be undertaken lightly. Only you can decide when you're ready for baptism. If you're ready, don't postpone it. If you're not ready, however, the world isn't going to end while you wait a week or two until you're confident you're taking the right step. Don't let anyone—except perhaps God, of course—coerce you into the waters of baptism until you're ready to take the plunge. Baptism is the beginning of a lifetime undertaking. On the other hand, there are people who have been waiting for years for "just the right time" to be baptized. Make sure you understand what you are undertaking, but then move forward without hesitation.

Keep in mind that minor children can't be baptized without parental consent, and a married person—male or female—shouldn't be baptized unless the spouse gives permission. There is a good reason for this. Church membership requires a vast commitment of time, talent, energy, and even money. The nonmember spouse should be made aware of this before giving consent for the baptism. If you are a new member with a nonmember spouse, you should make every effort to include your spouse in as much of your life as possible, in gratitude for the sacrifice he or she made to allow you to be baptized.

Once the commitment for baptism has been made, certain people will make all the arrangements for you. A priesthood leader (usually a missionary in the case of converts) will interview you to make sure you understand the ramifications of baptism and to ensure your worthiness to accept the ordinance. Others will reserve the baptismal font, arrange for baptismal clothing, and put together the program. The people who plan the program will probably consult with you to see if you have any favorite hymns, or if you know Saints who would be good speakers. After all, it's your baptism. If the people who plan the service don't contact you, speak up.

You are also free to choose the person who will baptize you and the person who will confirm you a member of the Church.

There are a few guidelines here. You can use the same person to do the baptism and the confirmation, but whoever baptizes you must hold the office of priest in the Aaronic Priesthood or be a holder of the Melchizedek Priesthood, and whoever confirms you must hold the Melchizedek Priesthood. If you were converted by missionaries, one of them can perform both ordinances, or one can perform each ordinance—or Church members who were instrumental in your conversion may be brought in to assist. If you have Latter-day Saint relatives who hold the required priesthood offices, they are also able to perform baptisms and would be delighted to do so on your behalf. But don't let people just assume they're going to have the honor. If somebody volunteers to perform the baptism for you, but you'd rather give the honor to somebody else, by all means do so.

The only other suggestion is that if you're a female convert who has a romantic attachment to the person who converted you, it's best to be baptized and confirmed by somebody else. It's fine to ask the person who converted you to speak or to offer a prayer, but you should ask a neutral party to perform the actual ordinances. That way you won't have painful memories of your baptism if your romance fades and you're embarrassed you ever loved old what's-his-name in the first place.

There aren't any absolute rules as far as the baptismal program is concerned. What usually happens is that there's an opening song and a prayer, followed by a couple of short talks that are related to baptism. At various spots during the program there may be a musical selection to set the tone of the baptismal service.

The baptism itself is short. You and the person who baptizes you will both be dressed in white clothing that does not become transparent when wet. (If you supply your own baptismal clothing, make certain this is the case!) You will enter the water, and the person doing the baptizing will take hold of your wrist with your left hand and will raise his right arm to the square. Then he will say the following words, after calling you by your full name: "Having been commissioned of Jesus Christ, I baptize you in the name of the Father, and of the Son, and of the Holy Ghost. Amen." You will then be fully immersed in the water.

You will be coached ahead of time as to how to hold your

hands and what you need to do, but basically your only responsibilities are to pinch your nose together with one hand and remember to take a big breath of air before you are immersed. Kathy neglected to do this, thinking she'd be underwater for such a short time that she didn't need any extra air. Then her long hair floated, and she was held underwater for an interminable breathless interval until her hair sank. She was flailing in the water, convinced she was drowning, by the time she was finally lifted out of it.

Because baptism is an ordinance, the words of the baptismal prayer must be said absolutely correctly. There will be two witnesses, one at either side of the baptismal font, who will make sure the proper words are said and the proper actions performed. If any word is missed, or if even a small bit of your body is not completely immersed when you are lowered under the water, the baptism will be immediately performed again. Remember, however, that if a baptism has to be repeated (which happens more often than you might think), the mistake wasn't your fault. These things happen.

Confirmation (Receiving the Holy Ghost)

Confirmation is a priesthood ordinance where hands are placed upon your head and a blessing is given to you. The primary purposes of this blessing are to confirm you a member of the Church and to confer the gift of the Holy Ghost upon you. Usually there will be other things said in the blessing that will offer personal counsel and direction to you as a new member of the Church. The words that are used in this blessing are given by the inspiration of God, and the counsel you receive in your confirmation blessing should be remembered and taken to heart.

You can be baptized by a priest, but you must be confirmed a member of the Church by a holder of the Melchizedek Priesthood. People consider it an honor to be asked to give a confirmation blessing, just as they consider it an honor to be asked to perform a baptism. If you would like to be confirmed by a specific member of the Church, make your wishes known. If you don't make your preferences known, someone will be chosen for you.

For many years, converts in the Church were confirmed just a few minutes after their baptism. However, in early 1998, the policy changed so that confirmation of new converts should now take place in sacrament meeting on a Sunday shortly after baptism. The reason for this is simple. If the confirmation takes place immediately following baptism, only the ward members who have attended the baptism will witness this important ordinance. But if confirmation takes place in sacrament meeting, every ward member can witness the confirmation and share the experience. This will perform the dual function of introducing the new convert to the ward community and giving the convert and the ward community a spiritual bond to share.

Home Teaching and Visiting Teaching

After you have joined the Church, your new ward shouldn't just leave you hanging. You will be assigned home teachers and visiting teachers who will help you adjust to your new life as a member of the Church.

If you don't hear from home teachers within a month of your baptism, ask your bishop to have home teachers assigned to you. If you're a woman who hasn't heard from your visiting teachers, talk to your Relief Society president. By the same token, if you are not given an assignment to home teach or to visit teach within a short period of your baptism, tell the bishop or the Relief Society president that you are ready to accept an assignment. You may think that as a new member you will have a "grace period" of several months before you are given any callings. This is usually not the case, and you should prepare to be put to work almost immediately. While this may seem scary, it is exactly what you need to start you down that road from new convert to involved member.

New Member Discussions and Gospel Essentials Classes

Just as you took missionary discussions before you joined the Church, the Church has prepared a series of new member discussions to help you make the transition to full Church membership. These six lessons should be given to you by your home teachers, with the help of the stake and full-time missionaries who are assigned to your ward. They consist of an overview of some of the things you learned in your missionary discussions, expanded just a little bit. There is also a Gospel Principles class in Sunday School that performs the same purpose of helping you get adjusted to life in your new church. Don't worry—you won't be hearing any drastic new doctrines in either the new member discussions or in your Gospel Principles class. These discussions and classes simply build upon what you already learned from the missionaries before your baptism, allowing you the opportunity to ask Church members questions that may have come up since you took the original missionary lessons.

Independent Gospel Study

If the only gospel study you ever receive is during forty minutes of Sunday School class every Sunday, your growth in the kingdom of God will be slow indeed. Converts are handicapped by growing up without childhood Primary lessons or the foundation of scripture study that is built in seminary and institute classes. You can make up that deficit through daily scripture study, and there are also other resources available that will teach you how to live as a strong Latter-day Saint. However, there are also materials that can distract from your spiritual progress and even cause you to question your testimony of the Church. Just as we choose television shows or movies by merit, we should also be scrupulous as we choose how to spend our time in gospel study.

- **Scriptures**
  If you were taught the gospel by a set of missionaries, they probably encouraged you to read the Book of Mormon. Perhaps you read the entire book by the time you were baptized, or you may still be wading through 2 Nephi. In any case, it's a good idea to read the Book of Mormon if you haven't already. The prophets have told us that this is the most truthful of all the books on the face of the earth, and that we'll come to God faster and surer through reading the Book of Mormon than through studying any other book.

That being the case, you may want to reread the book if you've already finished it. Every time you read it, you'll do so with a different perspective and will learn different things. But even if you've read the Book of Mormon a half dozen times, a lifetime of scripture study is still ahead of you.

When you purchase your permanent set of scriptures, you'll find that the Book of Mormon is bound together with two other books—the Doctrine and Covenants and the Pearl of Great Price. Together, these three works are referred to as the triple combination. Another name for them—and the Bible—is the standard works. The triple combination can also be bound with the Bible into a single, thick volume. When one large book is used, a common name for this bound volume is a "quad," probably because calling it a quadruple combination would be quite a mouthful.

We have been counseled to read the scriptures daily because they contain the word of God. Beyond that, it's up to the individual Church member to decide what scriptures will be read and how the reading will be done. There are differing theories about how we should study scriptures, but there isn't just one way to do it. Whether you read a chapter a day or even a verse a day; whether you ignore the footnotes or look them all up in a deeper study; whether you underline your scriptures and write in the margins or leave the pages spotless and pure—these things are up to you.

There are some, including some prophets, who have preached that our focus should be on the Book of Mormon. This is wise counsel, especially for new members of the Church. You have probably been exposed to the Bible throughout your life and have at least a fundamental grasp of that. It only makes sense to focus on the scriptures that are new to you—at least until you have an equal familiarity with them.

Once you have read the Book of Mormon and have acquainted yourself with the Doctrine and Covenants and the Pearl of Great Price, you may want to alternate your study of those books with readings from the Old and New Testaments, just as our Sunday School classes rotate among the different sets of scripture. Or you may want to read the Book of Mormon over and over again. The choice is yours. What is important is that scripture reading becomes a habit with you, and that you rely on the words contained therein to give you counsel and guidance.

- **The Articles of Faith**

If you're looking for a *Reader's Digest* condensed version of what members of the Church believe, the Articles of Faith are it. These thirteen statements of belief were written by the Prophet Joseph Smith in response to a question from a newspaper editor. They give a brief synopsis of who the Mormons are and what we believe. If you aren't already familiar with the Articles of Faith, they can be found at the end of the Pearl of Great Price.

- **Church-Related Magazines**

There are four magazines that are published by the Church for the edification of Church members of various ages. The *Ensign* (pronounced N-sign) is a magazine designed for adults, with the *New Era* appealing to youth, and the *Friend* reaching Primary-age children. The *Liahona* contains excerpts from all three magazines as well as news of international interest. Each of these magazines is a monthly publication, filled with articles and stories and artwork that are designed to bolster the faith of the members. These magazines are not required reading, although the November and May issues of the *Ensign* (the January and July issues of the *Liahona*) are particularly prized because they contain the texts of all the talks that were given in general conference during the April and October general conference sessions.

Church magazines are available by subscription for a nominal cost and can be obtained through your ward magazine representative. If the subscription price is prohibitive for you, you can check out the magazines from your local meetinghouse library for no charge. If you live in a non-English-speaking country or simply read another language better than you do English, check with your magazine representative to see if the *Liahona* is available in your language.

There are other magazines available to Church members, which are published through unofficial sources. These magazines will not be named here, because the titles come and go. Like all publications, they range in content and professionalism. Some are slick magazines that adhere to the traditional beliefs of the Church but may have little in the way of substance. Others are chock-full of substance, but they may also espouse fringe doctrines. Be careful in choosing among these magazines, just as you would in selecting any other publication. Some of them are worthwhile, but others are less so.

• Church Distribution Center

A wide variety of Church-related materials can be found at the Church Distribution Center, which is located in Salt Lake City. If you're looking for the scriptures on audiotape, lesson manuals for Sunday School, copies of the Book of Mormon in Korean, hymnbooks for home use, or artwork with a religious theme, this is a good place to go.

A current catalog of materials that are available through the Church Distribution Center can be found in your meetinghouse library, or you can order one by calling directly. At the time of publication, their toll-free number for calls within the United States was 800-537-5949.

• Church Bookstores

Church members are hungry for Church-related doodads, and they can be found in any one of a number of bookstores that have sprung up across the United States and elsewhere. You'd be amazed at the scope of supplies that are available through these bookstores—from cheap plastic trinkets to children's toys to neckties to expensive artwork to fiction with an LDS theme. Some bookstores are larger than others. Deseret Book owns a chain of bookstores, with outlets throughout the United States. You can also do some browsing on the Web for LDS-related products by going to http://www.ldsworld.com/marketplace/retailstores.asp. This site lists addresses, phone numbers, and names of LDS bookstores in every state.

You will likely not have to go as far as Salt Lake City

for your supply of Church-related material. Ask the members in your ward if there's a bookstore nearby that deals in LDS products. More than likely, somebody in your vicinity has opened a small bookstore, perhaps even in a basement or family room, that can supply most of your basic needs.

- ### Other Good Books
President Brigham Young counseled members of the Church to embrace truth wherever it may be found. Although our religion has more truth than any other church on the face of the earth, there are other people outside the Church who may have nuggets of truth we have not yet embraced. It is our responsibility to live so that we will recognize the truth whenever we find it, wherever we find it, and then to embrace the truth we ferret out. We should seek the truth by studying and improving our minds. Books should be our constant companions. (They're a lot easier to carry around than television sets, too!) We should ask questions to deepen our understanding of things we do not understand and keep our minds open to whatever truth finds its way there.

One caution is that some members of the Church depend too much on the wisdom of the world and set too much store in intellectual prowess. If you find yourself being seduced by intellectual topics rather than relying on simple faith, take care.

- ### Anti-Mormon Material
The fact that something has been published doesn't make it true. One wolf in sheep's clothing that you'll have to battle sooner or later concerns the anti-Mormon literature that springs up like weeds on a summer lawn.

Either through a misguided belief that they're helping you, or due to other more sinister motives, people will eventually give you pamphlets or books that may cause you to question your newly adopted religion. This "heresy literature" is skillfully worded and is produced by professionals with the purpose of causing you to doubt your faith. Many new members of the Church have been seduced by this literature and have abandoned the Church because of it. Through subtle and clever wording and extensive quoting (and misquoting) of long-dead Church leaders and others, these pamphlets distort our doctrine, giving our beliefs meanings that the prophets never intended. Don't get sucked into this quicksand. You don't need someone outside the Church to tell you what you believe. If you have any questions, look them up in the scriptures rather than using these pamphlets and books as your source code. And remember—if you don't hear something preached in general conference or written in the scriptures, it's almost certainly not a doctrine of the LDS Church.

Priesthood Blessings, Including Your Patriarchal Blessing

Imagine how it would be to get a personal letter from God—one that told you exactly what you needed to know to survive a crucial period of your life. This is what priesthood blessings are—they are personal messages of love and counsel from the Father.

Priesthood blessings can be given for several reasons. They can be used to heal the sick or to provide comfort during a difficult time of life. They can also give direction by offering insight as to what a person should do during a specific time frame, such as the setting apart that is done when a person receives a new calling.

When most people think of priesthood blessings, they're thinking about administering to the sick. This is normally done by two Melchizedek Priesthood holders, although one priesthood holder has authority to perform this ordinance alone if a second one is unavailable. Often fathers administer to members of their families, although home teachers or others may be asked to do so. Generally, priesthood holders wait until the person who is ill requests a priesthood blessing. This indicates that the person who is sick is willing to exercise his faith toward the fulfilling of the blessing that is given.

An administration to the sick is done in two parts. First, one of the priesthood holders will anoint the person being blessed by applying a small amount of consecrated oil to the person's head. A short prayer is said, giving the name of the person being anointed and saying that the anointing is being done by the authority of the priesthood. If consecrated oil is not available, or if this is the second blessing being given for the same illness, the anointing is not done. The prayer is closed in the name of Jesus Christ, as are all prayers.

After the anointing, both men will lay their hands upon the head of the patient, and one of the men will seal the anointing by giving the priesthood blessing. (This is also referred to as "acting as mouthpiece.") Again, the full name of the person being blessed is said, and the priesthood holder says that the anointing is being sealed by the authority of the Melchizedek Priesthood. Afterwards the speaker says the words that he is inspired by the Spirit to say, then closes in the name of Jesus Christ.

One should use some caution in making sure that priesthood blessings are not requested too often. They should not be used for every little sniffle or common cold that comes down the pike. But if a person has a serious illness, is about to undergo surgery, or is experiencing a great deal of pain, he should not hesitate to ask for a blessing.

Father's blessings and other blessings of counsel or comfort do not require anointing but are otherwise similar to administrations for the sick. If you need to know how to perform these blessings, the *Melchizedek Priesthood Leadership Handbook* gives detailed instructions. But for the purposes of this book, all you need to know is that such blessings are available to you if you need them.

Patriarchal blessings are similar to other priesthood blessings, but with a few major differences. First, most priesthood blessings cover a specific time frame. A blessing given to you when you are set apart for a Church calling, for example, will apply to you only during the period when you are serving in that particular calling. And you may receive more than one priesthood blessing during the course of a long illness or during crisis periods while battling a life-threatening illness. Fathers may choose to give priesthood blessings to a child on every birthday or at the beginning of every school year. But patriarchal blessings are different: except under unusual circumstances, a patriarchal blessing is a once-in-a-lifetime event.

Second, most priesthood blessings can be given by any Melchizedek Priesthood holder. Although it only makes sense that father's blessings can just be given by fathers, similar blessings of comfort can be given by other priesthood holders when a father is absent or does not hold the priesthood. Administrations to the sick can be given by any Melchizedek Priesthood holder, and the blessings that are conferred on you when you're set apart for a calling can be given by any one of a number of priesthood holders who have stewardship over you. But a patriarchal blessing can only be given by a patriarch who has been set apart to give patriarchal blessings to the members of his stake.

Third, most priesthood blessings shouldn't be recorded. It's acceptable to have someone take notes when you're being given a blessing, but recording devices are frowned on with the possible exception of during a father's blessing. During their lifetimes, Clark and Kathy have each had the experience of asking to tape record a particularly important priesthood blessing. In both cases, the person giving the blessing gave his permission for a recorder to be used. In both cases, the tape recorder malfunctioned. These were two new tape recorders, and they only malfunctioned during these particular instances. This tells us that even though the person giving the blessing may not object to the presence of tape recorders, the objection may come from a higher source.

In contrast patriarchal blessings are always recorded. They are then transcribed by someone who will send you a copy of the blessing. A copy of the blessing will be kept at Church headquarters forever, in case you lose your original copy and need a replacement. Your patriarchal blessing is a road map for your life. It may outline your strengths and occasionally your weaknesses, and it may also counsel you about some of the pitfalls that will beset you during your years on earth. If you ever lose your patriarchal blessing, it should be replaced so you can keep it and refer to it throughout your mortal experience.

When you decide you're ready to receive your patriarchal blessing, make an appointment with the bishop. You will be interviewed and issued a recommend for a patriarchal blessing, which you should take with you when you visit the patriarch to receive your blessing.

Unless an appointment is made for you to visit the patriarch, you should call the patriarch to schedule your own appointment. Don't be disappointed if your appointment is scheduled several months in the future. Giving patriarchal blessings is a grueling experience for patriarchs, involving fasting and pondering and prayer. Patriarchs can't do this preparation on the spur of the moment, and they can't just give ten blessings at a time to stay current if they receive a lot of requests at once. Make an appointment at the patriarch's convenience, not at your own.

Receiving your patriarchal blessing is a solemn occasion. Dress as you would dress for church. Your patriarch may allow your family to witness the blessing, but he may not. The more people who are in the room, the harder it may be for him to receive spiritual inspiration. Some patriarchs can give blessings in front of an audience, but others can't. Again, the patriarch's needs should take precedence over your own preferences or even your own family customs.

When you arrive for your patriarchal blessing, the patriarch will usually take you aside and visit with you for a few moments before giving you your blessing. Pay attention to what he says in this visit. It isn't uncommon for the patriarch to give advice before the blessing that is as important to the recipient as the blessing itself.

A patriarchal blessing is given by the patriarch, without other priesthood holders present to lay hands upon your head. He will not anoint your head with oil but will lay his hands upon your head and give the blessing he is inspired to give.

One bit of information you'll be told in your patriarchal blessing is your declaration of lineage. In this portion of the blessing, you'll be told which tribe of Israel you're descended from. In most cases, patriarchal blessings reveal that the person receiving the blessing comes from the tribe of Ephraim or Manasseh. In fact, a patriarch recently told us that in his experience, only one or two blessings per hundred reveal that the person comes from a different tribe.

This patriarch told us that people often put too much emphasis on their lineage. He said that lineage is important in that you have to have a declaration of lineage to have a valid patriarchal blessing, but as long as we live worthy lives, we'll *all* receive the blessings of Abraham, Isaac, and Jacob, no matter what our lineage happens to be. He counsels members of his stake to get past the declaration of lineage and concentrate instead on the rest of the blessing—the part that gives counsel and direction.

Don't expect to receive any new doctrine in your patriarchal blessing. Our patriarch friend said that if you were to lay out every verse of the scriptures on a floor and have God choose the ones that applied to you and put them together in one or two pages, a patriarchal blessing is what you'd get. At the end of your life, you'll be able to look back on the words of the blessing and see what they meant.

Patriarchal blessings give you general direction rather than answering specific questions. When you receive your patriarchal blessing, you won't be told when the world is going to end or the name of the person you're going to marry. A patriarch is not a fortuneteller. He uses inspiration, not a crystal ball. He receives enough information to guide you throughout your life but will not give you details that are specific enough to answer all your questions. Freedom of choice is such a big concept in the Church that no patriarchal blessing will ever tell you exactly what decisions you're supposed to make as you live your life. But patriarchal blessings can indicate where your talents and skills lie, helping you as you lay out the pattern for your future.

Although patriarchal blessings don't tell you everything you want to know, they can sometimes get pretty specific in small ways, letting you know in no uncertain terms that the patriarch is the conduit of the blessings rather than the source of them. Kathy learned this when she received her own patriarchal blessing. Her maiden name was Helms, and when she was in high school she ran a student council campaign with the slogan, "Put Kathy at the Helm." Years later, when she received her patriarchal blessing from a total stranger, the blessing counseled her to remember that "it is the Lord who is at the helm," and not Kathy herself.

When you get your patriarchal blessing, you may be so excited with it that you'll want to show it to all your friends. This is exactly the opposite of what you should do. Patriarchal blessings are sacred, and they are meant just for you. Although you may occasionally reveal select details of your blessing to others, and even let close family members read your blessing, you shouldn't pass around your blessing to everyone who wants to see it, and you shouldn't read it in public meetings. Put your blessing in a safe place, then take it out and read it occasionally. You'll be surprised how you will discover new things as you reread the blessing and how sections will become clearer as your life unfolds. But as with all blessings in the Church, the promises made in your blessing will only come to pass if you continue to do your best to follow the laws of the gospel.

The Law of the Fast

You already learned about fast and testimony meeting in chapter 2. Fast Sundays occur on twelve Sundays a year, usually the first Sunday of the month. At that time, Church members are counseled to give up food and drink for the space of two consecutive meals. But Church members are counseled to fast on other occasions, too.

There's a difference between fasting with a purpose and going without food. A lot of people who think they're fasting are just not eating. This isn't all bad. If your children see you fasting, you'll set an example for them. Also, the simple act of going without food is an act of obedience to the commandments, and that's a good thing too. Third, there are physical benefits that can be gained from fasting. Many doctors recommend an occasional fast just to cleanse the body, and many of us eat so much food that cutting back through fasting can't help but be beneficial.

But if all you do is go without food, you're missing the greatest benefit you would otherwise gain. When we subdue our bodies through fasting, our spirits grow stronger. Fasting brings us closer to the Lord than prayer alone. Fasting, in combination with prayer, is a powerful spiritual tool that can work miracles. Its importance shouldn't be underrated.

There are Church members who will tell you that a fast should be opened and closed with prayer. There are Church members that say in order to fast you should go without water as well as food, and other Church members who say that water is fine—you just shouldn't drink other liquids while fasting. There are Church members who fast for a full 24 hours, and Church members whose medical condition makes it impossible for them to fast for more than an hour at a time. As you can see, fasting is personal. The important thing is that no matter how you fast, you have the spirit of the fast with you.

Financial Support

Although no "plate" is passed and no money is collected during sacrament meetings, Saints are counseled to give generously to the Church. Contributions come in several forms, which will be outlined below. Payments are made by enclosing the contribution in an envelope that is set aside for the purpose. There is a contribution slip that should be filled out, giving the name of the contributor and how the contribution should be allocated to the various types of donation categories.

The LDS means of accounting is unusual in the Christian world. Most Christians, even those who tithe, are accustomed to giving their donations anonymously through the collection plate. Giving donations in such a forthright manner may be a culture shock for new members.

Kathy attended various wards for three years before she joined the Church. She had been a full-tithe payer all her life, ever since she'd read about tithing in Malachi when she was a child. But she had also read in Matthew that gifts should be given in secret, so she always just stuck a wad of cash in the envelope and turned it in without putting her name anywhere. She was unaware at the time how much trouble this caused in the financial clerk's office every week, but soon there were panicked announcements from the pulpit in sacrament meeting asking the person who forgot to put a contribution slip in the envelope to please come forward. Eventually someone must have made the connection that the anonymous donations were coming from the only Protestant in the congregation, because the bishop finally stopped pleading for the anonymous donor to come forth. Undoubtedly, the overworked financial clerk just filled out tithing slips in Kathy's name.

At the end of the year, the financial clerk will total up each member's financial contributions. Then each family in the ward should schedule an appointment with the bishop to have a tithing settlement. When you arrive for your appointment, the financial clerk will give you a printed summary of your contributions during the year, which you can accept or correct.

(These forms can be used to calculate tax deductions for charitable contributions, so they're important documents.) After you've looked over your records, the bishop will meet with the members of your family as a group and ask each member if he is a full-tithe payer, if he is a part-tithe payer, or if he pays no tithing at all. The bishop will also use the opportunity to visit briefly with your family as a group, so it's important to take the entire family to the annual tithing settlement. This is a good opportunity for your family to thank the bishop for everything he's done for you during the past year.

- **Tithing**

  Now that you know about tithing settlement, a word should be said about tithing itself. Before you joined the Church, the missionaries should have told you about the law of tithing. This is a law that isn't unique to the LDS Church. Indeed, tithing has been practiced since biblical times, and many Christians pay tithing today. Unfortunately, there isn't a guideline that tells us exactly what tithing consists of. We're told to pay ten percent of our "increase," so it's up to each of us to determine what our increase is.

  Clark once served as financial clerk in a ward where a Church member brought in ten radishes from her garden as a tithe on her "increase." This was an unusual situation, but it wasn't unique. Donations of produce, shares of stock, vehicles, or other tangible items are called tithing in kind. They are accepted as legal tender for tithing, although they are given rarely enough that such a donation always causes a stir in the financial clerk's office as the clerk researches how tithing in kind is accounted for. (The financial clerk will be able to get home to dinner much faster if you determine how much your radishes are worth and just pay that amount of money in tithing rather than producing the radishes themselves. In fact, Church members are encouraged to avoid paying tithing in kind, except under unusual circumstances.)

  Even your bishop usually won't counsel you whether to pay tithing on your net income or your gross income. When calculating your tithing, let your conscience be your guide. Determine your "increase" through study and prayer, and pay ten percent of that. When tithing settlement comes around every year, the bishop will only be interested in hearing whether you pay a full tithe. He doesn't care—and won't ask—how you made your calculations.

The paying of tithing often becomes a real test of faith for the new convert. Perhaps more than any principle you have learned, you might have problems obeying this law. In theory you may believe in the law of tithing, but you just don't know how you can afford to obey it. You might find yourself saying, "I want to pay my tithing, but I'm already living from paycheck to paycheck. Where will I ever find that extra 10 percent to give to the Lord?"

It may comfort you to know that most Church members report that the more consistently you pay your tithing, the easier it is to pay. Once people get in the habit of paying tithing, they usually wonder how they ever survived without paying it. If you have the faith to pay tithing, you will not miss the loss of income, and you will consider it a privilege and a blessing to be able to pay it regularly.

Many who have been in your place will tell you that making that first tithing payment was a gigantic leap of faith for them. Yet most of them will also tell you that they were able to get by as if by magic. Part of this is because you really do receive blessings by obeying this commandment. Many members can tell you that they received unexpected blessings, often financial blessings, after paying their tithing. But we think another part of this tithing miracle has a more simple explanation. Consider that as you embrace the gospel, your life will change in many ways. As you follow the Word of Wisdom, you will stop buying things that inflated your grocery bills. As you become involved in your ward, you will have less time for expensive leisure activities. As you receive priesthood and Relief Society lessons on budgeting and home management, you will learn to stretch your income farther. As you start to see the gospel work in your life, you will gain a more eternal perspective and be less interested in "keeping up with the Joneses." In short, living the Mormon lifestyle will often save you more than the 10 percent you will be paying in tithing. But the blessings you receive from paying tithing will more than compensate for a lifestyle that might be a bit more humble. When it comes to paying tithing, put your faith to work, and in the words of President Spencer W. Kimball, "Do It."

If you have tried paying tithing and still cannot get by, visit with your bishop. He can put you in touch with others in the ward who can help you with such skills as budgeting. Perhaps the solution is for you to upgrade your employment, and he can help you there too. Many people in the ward will want you to succeed and will want you to start receiving the blessings associated with paying your full 10 percent. We all are looking forward to the day when you can honestly say, "I can't afford *not* to pay my tithing."

- **Fast Offerings**

Going without food is only part of the monthly Church-wide fast. The other sacrifice we make on Fast Sunday is financial as Church members are asked to donate to the fast offering fund of the ward at least the cost of the two meals that were skipped. The money that is donated to the fast offering fund stays within the ward and is used at the bishop's discretion to help ward members who are facing a crisis of one sort or another. (See chapter 10 for a full explanation of how bishops help ward members in need.)

Church members are asked to give generously to the fast offering fund. Giving the cost of two meals is a minimum donation, but there are usually enough crisis situations in a ward at any given time that more money is often needed. Think of fast offering as an insurance policy. The more money that ward members give, the more money will be in the ward's checking account if ever you have a crisis of your own.

- **Ward Budget**

You may occasionally hear ward members referring to the ward budget. You'll be glad to know that you are not required to contribute to this one. Up until the early 1990s, families were asked to contribute every year to help with the expenses of running the ward. The size of each family's assessment was set by the bishop, who took into account the size of the family involved and the family income, as determined by the amount of tithing paid. Ward budget donations were used to finance the daily operations of the ward—including such things as utility bills, building repairs, office supplies, sacrament cups, choir music, ward parties, and the checkbooks that kept the various auxiliaries running. A family's ward budget assessment during the course of a year could be a considerable family expense.

Now, however, each ward is given an operating budget by Church headquarters. These annual stipends come from tithing dollars, and the amount that is given to a ward is based on the average number of people who attend sacrament meeting in that ward. The bishop will make a budget for his ward that is based on the amount of money he receives from the Church, dividing the funds among the auxiliaries and other people who need reimbursement for one ward expense or another. So while each ward still has a ward budget, the money comes from Church headquarters rather than from the members.

The financial donation slips still have a category for ward budget because sometimes you will need to put money back in the budget. Say, for example, that someone buys ten turkeys for a ward Thanksgiving party and gets reimbursed for them, but then only eight turkeys are used at the party. If you decide you want to buy the other two turkeys for your own use, you could write a check for their cost and submit it as a contribution to the ward budget.

- **Missionary Fund**

    Missionaries who go out into the field are expected to pay for their own support. For many years, the cost of that support could vary widely, depending on the place where the missionary was sent. You can imagine that the cost of living is somewhat higher in, say, Tokyo, than it is in Idaho. And the cost to clothe a missionary is considerably higher when the missionary goes to Russia than it is when he's sent to balmy Palm Springs.

    A few years ago, the Church took steps to equalize the burden on missionary families by setting an average fixed amount that families are expected to contribute for the upkeep of a missionary. Now, whether the missionary serves in Tennessee or Taiwan, his parents are asked to contribute the same amount each month toward his support. They do this by making monthly contributions to the ward missionary fund. Once a month, the Church Missionary Department will take the monthly payment from the ward missionary fund for each missionary serving from the ward. This pool of money will then be used to support all the missionaries in the world, no matter how high or low their actual expenses.

But you don't have to have a son or daughter serving a mission in order to contribute to the ward missionary fund. Any Church member can give a contribution to the missionary fund at any time. You can help a specific missionary in the field if his parents have financial hardships that may keep them from giving the full amount toward their missionary's support, or you can earmark your gift to go to the General Missionary Fund, where it will be used to help missionaries in other areas. Another option is a Book of Mormon fund that is set up by many wards. The money donated to this fund would be set aside to buy copies of the Book of Mormon to be distributed within your home stake.

When you give a gift to the missionary fund, be sure to let the bishop know the name of the missionary you want to help or designate that the amount you're contributing will go toward the Book of Mormon Fund. Otherwise, money that is received will be sent to the General Missionary Fund to be used as needed. We've heard rumors that writing the name on the donation form may jeopardize the tax-deductible status of the donation, but we haven't seen any evidence of that. Even so, be warned.

• **Other Contributions**

From time to time, ward members or Church members as a whole may be asked to contribute money toward an unusual circumstance. Perhaps a famine in Somalia or a flood in Florida may prompt the First Presidency to ask that Church members contribute money toward that cause. Perhaps a local Scouting program solicits money for camping equipment or some other Scout-related expense. These contributions can be given directly to the ward and

noted in the "other contributions" space on the donation
slip. That way the funds will be properly routed, and the
donor can receive credit for the donation against his income
tax. When you contribute funds in this area, be sure to designate where you want your money to go.

Advancing in the Priesthood

Faithful men who are members of the Church are given the
opportunity to receive two different priesthoods—the Aaronic
Priesthood and the Melchizedek Priesthood—and to advance
through the various offices of each. When you received your
instruction from the missionaries, they should have explained
the concept of priesthood to you, but we thought it might be
helpful to include a review here for your reference.

The textbook definition of the priesthood is "the authority
to act in the name of God." It can't get any simpler than that.
The Church of Jesus Christ cannot possibly be governed unless
His followers have the authority to act on His behalf. The
priesthood confers that authority on the people who hold it.

As much as you may want your child to learn to walk
without getting hurt, falling down is part of the process. We
learn to walk, as we learn everything else, through trial and
error. Eventually, through practice, we develop the faith to
stand on our own two feet and take steps to learn how to walk
without falling down, just as we learn to perfect the other skills
we need. Then, unless we forget to pay attention, we don't fall
down anymore.

So it is with the Church. If Jesus Christ came down to
earth and governed His Church directly, everything would run
perfectly, but the people on earth wouldn't grow and progress.
Just as a parent would let a child learn to walk, the Savior
stands back and lets His people learn through trial and error.
We often make mistakes in the way we perform our callings,
but we learn, grow, and progress because of those same mistakes.

There are limits, though. The Lord is also a God of order
and not confusion. If He let us run the Church without supervision, there would be all manner of confusion as each of us

tried to lead the Church in the direction we thought best. In order to maintain order while preserving free agency, the Savior governs His kingdom through the priesthood.

Priesthood is conferred by lineage. If you're a man, you'll have the priesthood conferred upon you by another priesthood holder, who had the priesthood conferred upon him by another priesthood holder, and so on up the line to Joseph Smith, who received it from Peter, James, and John, who received it from Jesus Christ. There is a similar lineage for your bishop, who received his authority to act as bishop through the stake president, who can trace his own authority back to the President of the Church, who was given his authority by Jesus Christ.

By the power of the priesthood, exercised through men, God can use His sons to govern, sustain, create, redeem, and exalt the whole human family. You might say that the priesthood is the "power of attorney" to act in Christ's name. Those brethren who use their priesthood in a righteous manner will build, govern, strengthen, and bless the Church and the lives of individual saints, just as Christ would if He dwelt among us.

There is a difference between knowing what the priesthood is and understanding how it will affect your life on a day-to-day basis. As to the practical application of the priesthood, there are a number of ways that you will be using it throughout your life.

- Holding the priesthood gives you the authority to perform the ordinances of the Church, and it is through those ordinances that you and those you love will progress through life and eventually return to God. You will use your priesthood to perform ordinances that bless the members of your ward or even strangers in the temple. Baptisms and confirmations and even weddings do not have to be performed by a paid clergyman but can be performed by priesthood holders who have been given the authority to perform these sacred ordinances.

- As already stated, the priesthood is the governing arm of the kingdom. Church leaders lead through the power of the priesthood. The prime example of this is your bishop. His priesthood not only gives him the power to preside over your ward, but also allows him to call other leaders and delegate some of that authority to them. Although your early callings in the Church may not involve much leadership, you may eventually receive callings where you are expected to lead your fellow Saints through the use of your priesthood authority. And although women do not directly hold the priesthood, they serve in their Church callings by authorization of this same priesthood authority, which has been delegated by their priesthood leaders.

- You will use the power of the priesthood to govern your own family righteously. As a husband and father, the Lord has given you the responsibility of caring and providing for the members of your family. The priesthood is a valuable help in exercising this important duty. You will exercise priesthood ordinances to help your family progress in the Church, such as the baptism of your children and the ordination of your own sons to the priesthood. Other ordinances will bless family members individually, such as blessings of the sick during times of illness and blessings of comfort during times of discouragement and confusion. You may also be assigned to home teach a person or family with no priesthood in the home, such as a widow, a divorced mother, or a family where the father is not a Church member. In these cases, you may also be asked to provide priesthood service, such as blessings or the baptism of family members.

- Receiving the priesthood also makes you a member of a quorum—a group of brethren holding the same priesthood office. When you attend priesthood meeting each Sunday, you meet with the members of your own quorum. Meeting together in a quorum provides strength and unity as you form a brotherhood of friendship, learning, and service.

- Just as Christ spent his life blessing the lives of others, the priesthood of Christ is based on service. We have all seen sad examples of corporate and political leaders who use their authority to dominate others or serve their own selfish interests. In contrast, priesthood leadership and authority should always be based on the principles of love, patience, charity, and service. Jesus preached often that the greatest among us must be the servant of all, and priesthood authority exemplifies that when it is properly used. Whether you'll be asked to visit the sick or to lend a strong back as part of the "Elders Quorum Moving Service," you will be given many opportunities for service as you exercise your priesthood in righteousness.

The Aaronic Priesthood

The Lord gave the priesthood to Adam, and it was passed down through him from father to son. At the time of Moses, the children of Israel had become so unrighteous that the priesthood was taken from them, only to be replaced by a lower priesthood with less authority and power. This is referred to as the Aaronic Priesthood (named after Moses's brother Aaron), the lesser priesthood, or the Levitical Priesthood.

During the time of Aaron, many of the duties of the Aaronic Priesthood related to the offering of animal sacrifices. As the Atonement of Christ abolished animal sacrifice, it also removed these duties from the Aaronic Priesthood. As exercised in The Church of Jesus Christ of Latter-day Saints today, the primary function of the Aaronic Priesthood is to prepare young men for the responsibilities of the greater priesthood. In fact, another common name for the Aaronic Priesthood in the Church today is the "preparatory" priesthood. Young men rise through the Aaronic Priesthood, moving from deacon to teacher to priest as they progress toward the ultimate goal of holding the Melchizedek Priesthood. As young men advance through the Aaronic Priesthood, each office in that priesthood provides them with more authority along with more responsibility.

- **Deacon**
  Worthy young men are typically given the Aaronic Priesthood and ordained to the office of deacon when they are twelve years old. Officers within a deacons quorum include a president, first counselor, second counselor, and secretary. These officers are called by the bishop from among the quorum members, providing the opportunity to develop leadership skills at an early age. If there are more

than twelve deacons in the quorum, the bishop has the option of creating multiple quorums, each presided over by the same officers. Generally, the second counselor in the bishopric oversees the daily operation of the quorum; other adult quorum advisers are called to provide Sunday instruction and assist the quorum in other ways.

According to the scriptures, the deacon "should be appointed to watch over the church, to be standing ministers unto the Church" (D&C 84:111). He does this by performing certain duties under the direction of his priesthood leaders.

A deacon's most visible assignment is to pass the sacrament. Deacons have one other conspicuous function in the ward, though, and that is to collect fast offerings. This is an assignment that is more commonly done in wards where the boundaries are close together. In wards where Church members live many miles apart, members more commonly give fast offerings as they do their other financial contributions—by sealing them in an envelope and giving them to a member of the bishopric.

Deacons have other assignments, too. They are instructed to follow the counsel of the bishopric and their quorum leaders, to speak in Church meetings when asked to do so, to notify quorum members of meetings, to participate in quorum instruction related to Church doctrine and priesthood duties, and to help the bishop administer after the temporal needs of the ward by looking after the poor and needy and caring for the meetinghouse and grounds. A deacon may serve as messenger for the bishop during Church meetings, and assist the bishopric in other ways when asked to do so. Finally, deacons look after the spiritual and temporal welfare of other quorum members, through love, fellowship, service, and example. They must be willing to serve on quorum committees and encourage other quorum members to live righteous lives.

- **Teacher**

Worthy young men are typically ordained to the office of teacher when they become fourteen years of age. Officers within a teachers quorum include a president, first counselor, second counselor, and secretary. These officers are called by the bishop and are selected from among the quorum members. If there are more than twenty-four teachers in the quorum, the bishop has the option of creating multiple quorums, each presided over by the same officers. Generally, the first counselor in the bishopric oversees the daily operation of the quorum; other adult quorum advisers are called to provide Sunday instruction and assist the quorum in other ways.

According to the scriptures, the teacher "is to watch over the church always, and be with and strengthen them" (D&C 20:53). Under the direction of his priesthood leaders, the teacher can perform all the duties assigned to a deacon, plus several additional responsibilities. Teachers prepare the sacrament table before sacrament meeting. Teachers can also serve as home teachers and as ushers for ward and stake meetings. Finally, they have the responsibility of serving as "a peacemaker, a calming influence, and an example of righteousness."

- **Priest**

Worthy young men are typically ordained to the office of priest when they reach their sixteenth birthday. Although deacons preside over the deacons quorum and teachers preside over the teachers quorum, the bishop presides over the priests. He calls two assistants and a secretary from among the quorum members to serve with him. If there are more than forty-eight priests in the quorum, the bishop has the option of creating multiple quorums, each presided over by the bishop, but with separate assistants and secretaries. As with the other Aaronic Priesthood quorums, other adult quorum advisers may be called to assist in the operation of the quorum.

Under the direction of his priesthood leaders, the priest can perform all the duties of a teacher and a deacon, and he also has additional responsibilities. The most conspicuous of these is that he can officiate at the sacrament table and say the sacrament prayers. (This is known as administering the sacrament.) But priests can perform two other ordinances. First, they can baptize new members into the Church and are often given the honor of baptizing a younger brother or sister. Second, they can confer the

Aaronic Priesthood on other worthy Church members and ordain them to offices within that priesthood, as directed by the bishop. One final responsibility is that priests can assist in missionary work.

Young men who participate in their Aaronic Priesthood quorums really do prepare to receive the higher, or Melchizedek, priesthood and be future leaders of the Church. If you go back and read through those duties again, you will see how much responsibility is placed upon young men in the Church at a very early age.

- **Bishop**

The office of bishop is really an office in the Aaronic Priesthood, and the bishop serves as president of the Aaronic Priesthood in the ward. When a man is set apart to be bishop, he is ordained to the office of bishop in the Aaronic Priesthood and is also set apart as the presiding high priest in the ward. Thus, he really wears two hats in the ward, one as the president of the Aaronic Priesthood and one as the leader of the Melchizedek Priesthood.

Receiving the Aaronic Priesthood

As a convert, you will not necessarily move through the offices of the Aaronic Priesthood as outlined above. Young men who join the Church during their teenage years are usually given the Aaronic Priesthood and ordained to the office appropriate to their age. For example, a convert boy aged fifteen would probably be ordained a teacher without having been a deacon first.

Similarly, male converts who are nineteen or older when baptized are usually ordained to the office of a priest within a month of their baptism. These men do not attend the priests quorum on Sunday but would instead attend a Melchizedek Priesthood quorum with brethren their own age. Ordaining adult converts to the office of priest gives them the opportunity to start using the priesthood in a few ways. They will be assigned as home teachers, allowed to administer the sacrament, and perhaps even be allowed to baptize their own children or ordain their own sons to the Aaronic Priesthood.

If you have been ordained to the office of priest, one of your first opportunities will be to administer (or bless) the sacrament. You will not have to memorize the sacrament prayers because the priests read the prayers from small cards that are held at the sacrament table. Before you bless the sacrament for the first time, you may want to read over the prayers several times first and practice saying them out loud. These prayers must be repeated exactly as written, and if even one word is missed, the prayer will have to be repeated until it has been said correctly. The world won't end if you have to say the prayer twice or even a half dozen times. Indeed, most men who have blessed the sacrament have needed to repeat a prayer at least once at some time or another. But practicing ahead of time may give you the self-confidence you need to get the ordinance right the first time you try it.

Because the keys to the Aaronic Priesthood reside with the bishop, he is the one who will contact you about being interviewed to receive the priesthood. He will interview you to determine if you are worthy, asking you questions that should be similar to the questions you were asked at baptism. Answer the questions honestly, even if you are not keeping all the commandments. The bishop will work with you to resolve those problems so that you may qualify to receive the priesthood at a later date.

If you are worthy to receive the Aaronic Priesthood, you will be sustained in a sacrament meeting. (Remember to sustain yourself!) After you are sustained, you will probably be ordained as part of priesthood meeting, either in the opening exercises or as part of the quorum in which you meet. This is done by a laying on of hands, similar to the laying on of hands you experienced when you were confirmed a member of the Church. Decide who you would like to have ordain you, and then let the bishop know. You can ask any worthy Melchizedek Priesthood holder, or someone who holds the office of priest in the Aaronic Priesthood. If you don't yet have any friends in the ward, you can ask the bishop or give the honor to one of the missionaries who converted you. You may also wish to select other worthy priests or Melchizedek Priesthood holders to stand in the circle when you are ordained. These could be friends, home teachers, quorum leaders, bishopric members, or other men in the ward whom you respect.

It is a tradition for men who have just been ordained or set apart to shake the hand of each man who stood in the circle. After you have been ordained or set apart, go around the circle of brethren and shake each hand, starting with the person who acted as "voice" during the blessing. Each of them will congratulate you and offer you encouragement in your new office or calling.

Within about two months, you should receive a certificate that records the important information about your ordination. Keep this certificate with your family history or other important records. If you do not receive this certificate, talk to your ward clerk.

Convert males who remain worthy and magnify their Aaronic Priesthood callings are usually given the Melchizedek Priesthood within a year of their baptism.

The Melchizedek Priesthood

Jesus Christ held the Melchizedek Priesthood and conferred the same priesthood upon His Apostles. After the Savior was crucified, the Church went into a period of gradual decline, and the Melchizedek Priesthood was taken from the earth. It was restored again when it was given to Joseph Smith by Peter, James, and John, sometime in late 1829 or early 1830.

As an investigator, you may have been puzzled by the unusual name given to this priesthood. The name of Melchizedek is mentioned twice in the Bible, once in Genesis and once in Psalms. The prophet Alma gives us a little more information when he mentioned that Melchizedek was a great high priest to whom Abraham paid his tithes. Section 107 of the Doctrine and Covenants explains that prior to Melchizedek, the name of the priesthood was called the Holy Priesthood after the Order of the Son of God. But to avoid too frequent repetition of the name of deity, the priesthood was renamed after Melchizedek. Section 107 is a good section to read if you're looking for a doctrinal explanation of this higher priesthood.

There are six different priesthood offices commonly associated with the Melchizedek Priesthood, as described below. Any office in the Melchizedek Priesthood gives the holder all the rights and privileges contained within the Aaronic Priesthood.

As you saw when we described the Aaronic Priesthood, there is a definite increase in authority that comes with each advancement to a new office. This is partially true with Melchizedek Priesthood offices, but to a much lesser degree. Some might give you the impression that a high priest is a "better" or "higher" calling than an elder. In fact, it is just a different office that contains keys specific to certain callings within the Church. Any man who holds the Melchizedek Priesthood worthily has ample authority to perform his duties, regardless of the priesthood office. Although the keys to the Aaronic Priesthood reside with the bishop, the keys to the Melchizedek Priesthood reside with the stake president.

The section on the Aaronic Priesthood described some of the ordinances that can be performed by that priesthood, such as baptism and the ordinances of the sacrament. You'll remember that any office within the Melchizedek Priesthood also encompasses all the rights of the Aaronic Priesthood. So, for example, an elder could administer or pass the sacrament. You may have already seen this if you have a ward that has a shortage of Aaronic Priesthood brethren.

There are also some ordinances that can only be performed by holders of the Melchizedek Priesthood. These include the naming and blessing of children, confirmation of a new member after baptism, the consecration of oil for use in blessing the sick, the ability to administer to the sick, the dedication of graves, and the ability to give father's blessings or other blessings of comfort and counsel. Other responsibilities that are unique to the Melchizedek Priesthood include ordaining brethren to offices in the Aaronic or Melchizedek priesthoods, setting apart members for new Church callings, and administering all of the ordinances performed in the temple (see chapter 9).

- **Elder**

This is the most common office of the Melchizedek priesthood and is the first step on the ladder of offices in that priesthood. Worthy young men may be ordained elders sometime after they turn 18. Young men preparing to serve missions are always ordained elders before being set apart as missionaries. Elders meet together in an elders quorum, one of which should exist in each ward in the stake. Being an elder entitles a man to enter the temple (if he holds a current recommend), preach the gospel, and perform all of the priesthood duties necessary to govern his family and fulfill his Church and priesthood assignments.

- **High Priest**

Certain high priests have special keys related to administration in the Church. Those who are called to serve in a bishopric, a stake presidency, or a high council must be ordained as high priests before they may serve in their callings. Typically, a man will hold the office of elder and then will be ordained a high priest when he is called to a leadership position that requires it.

In almost every ward, there are far more worthy men than there are positions in the bishopric or the stake presidency or on the high council. It only makes sense that not every worthy priesthood holder can be called to a position that requires the office of a high priest. Thus, many men are ordained high priests when they reach a certain age and would be more comfortable meeting with the high priests than with the elders. The bishop is the one who will usually make that recommendation to the stake president, as he holds the keys to the Melchizedek Priesthood in the stake. Whether a man is moved to the high priests quorum at a certain age depends on the size of the ward, the disposition of the bishop, and other factors. There is no shame in remaining an elder until late in life. But in wards where there are large numbers of men in each age group, it makes sense to divide them roughly according to their age and life experiences.

High priests also meet together as a quorum, and the stake president presides over that quorum. However, the stake president does not usually attend the weekly group meetings. (Seeing that there are often as many as ten high priests groups in a stake, the stake president would have to spread himself awfully thin to attend all of them.) The administration of the ward group is left to high priests within the ward, in the form of a high priest group leader and two assistants. Meetings are similar to those that are held in elders quorums.

- **Patriarch**

Patriarchal blessings are given by men who hold a separate office in the Melchizedek Priesthood, that of patriarch. Most stakes only have one or two patriarchs, so patriarchs do not meet in a quorum. Instead they usually meet with the high priests on Sundays.

Men who give patriarchal blessings must be so spiritually attuned that patriarchs are unique among Church members. First, theirs is a lifetime calling. Once a man is called as a patriarch, he's always a patriarch—even though the time may come when he is set apart to do something else. Usually, men aren't called as patriarchs until they have reached their 55th birthday and have no children living at home. Older men with no children living at home are less likely to have distractions that would cause a spirit of contention that would hinder the patriarch in his duties. It is so important for a patriarch to be able to receive spiritual inspiration that patriarchs aren't given any other callings in the Church. They are purposely kept away from any church "politics," because administrative issues could distract them from their all-important spiritual function. Indeed, they are the only men in the Church who usually aren't even asked to serve as home teachers. When they do serve as home teachers, they are assigned to families that aren't expected to have any problems that could distract the patriarch in his calling.

- **Apostle**

An Apostle is one of a group of men who are called to be special witnesses of Jesus Christ throughout all the world. You can read about them in chapter 6. Apostles meet together as part of the Quorum of the Twelve Apostles.

- **Seventy**

The Seventy is a priesthood office that is primarily concerned with missionary work. Currently, Quorums of the Seventy only exist at the general Church level. You can read about these quorums in chapter 6.

- **Presidency of the High Priesthood**

Some sources list the First Presidency of the Church

(also called the Presidency of the High Priesthood) as a separate Melchizedek Priesthood office. These brethren have the right to officiate in all the offices of the priesthood. They meet together as a Quorum of the First Presidency, which is composed of the President of the Church and his two counselors.

Receiving the Melchizedek Priesthood

When your bishop determines that you are ready to receive the Melchizedek Priesthood, he will hold an interview with you to make sure you are worthy. The questions he will ask you will be very similar to those asked of someone who desires to attend the temple (see chapter 9). If you are worthy, the bishop will then submit your name to the stake president. You must be approved by the stake presidency and the high council, and then you must have an interview with the stake presidency. This interview may be with the stake president, or it may be with one of his counselors. During the interview, you will be asked the same set of questions that you were asked by the bishop. You should be honest in your answers to the interview questions.

If the member of the stake presidency believes you are worthy, you will then have to be sustained before the entire stake. This can be done during a stake conference or a stake general priesthood meeting. Occasionally, men who receive the Melchizedek Priesthood are first sustained in their own wards, and then sustained before the stake in a later meeting.

Once you have been sustained, you will need to be ordained. This will be under the direction of the stake president, who will delegate someone to oversee the ordination and make sure everything is done correctly. As you did when you were ordained to offices in the Aaronic Priesthood, you will need to choose the person who will ordain you and see that your choice is approved by the bishop. You may also wish to select other worthy Melchizedek Priesthood holders to stand in the circle when you are ordained.

As with an Aaronic Priesthood ordination, you should receive a certificate of ordination within about two months. This certificate will contain the stake president's signature, because he holds the keys over the Melchizedek priesthood in your stake. Keep this certificate with your family history or other important records. If you do not receive this certificate, talk to your ward clerk.

The person who ordains you to the Melchizedek Priesthood may present you with a document tracing his line of priesthood authority. This is a record of how that person received his priesthood, starting with the person who ordained him, and going back to Jesus Christ. The practice of keeping a line of authority seems to have started more out of custom than doctrine, but it is important to some people, and it is interesting to know. That being the case, you'll want to keep your line of authority with your important documents. Now you will be a part of that line, so that if you ever ordain anyone else to the priesthood, you'll be a permanent link in his priesthood lineage. You can give him a similar document for him to keep with his own family records.

Continued Growth in the Kingdom

Active membership in the Church is a lifetime undertaking. There is no golden age when Church members can expect to sit back and rest on their laurels, letting younger and stronger people do the work. There is so much need for service in the Church that even people with severe handicaps or infirmities can be put to work in some capacity or another. No matter how old or frail people get, there is always something they can do.

By the end of your first year of Church membership, you as an adult member should have a home teaching or visiting teaching route, as well as some other Church calling. If you're a worthy man, you should receive the Melchizedek Priesthood within the first year of your membership in the Church. You should be looking toward attending the temple for the first time too, especially if you're married or are preparing for missionary service.

As your newness in the Church wears off, you'll be given assignments of increasing responsibility. You may feel inadequate to accept these callings, but as you accept challenges you'll grow in spirituality and capability until you're able to fulfill them. The leaders of your ward and stake were once as new in the Church as you are today. They took one step at a time to get them where they are today, just as you'll do.

At about the time men and women outside the Church are thinking about retirement, Church members begin to contemplate a new dimension of service. Many choose to serve missions. Others who live near temples spend years or even decades doing temple work. Family history centers are always looking for volunteers, or men and women can simply concentrate on doing their own genealogy. Ward nurseries can always use grandfather- or grandmother-figures to take care of the little ones during Church meetings. Church flowerbeds are always available to be tended by experienced gardeners.

This is a time of life when men and women who have spent a lifetime in learning are able to share their talents and their time with others, raising up a new generation of Church and community leaders. In the LDS Church, nobody is ever put out to pasture. They may slow down if they choose to do so, but opportunities for service are there for anyone who wants to serve.

A Convert's Questions

I heard about an oath associated with the priesthood. What is it?

Men who receive the Melchizedek Priesthood take upon themselves an oath and covenant of the priesthood—a series of promises between God and the priesthood holder.

The man agrees to acquire both the Aaronic and the Melchizedek Priesthoods, magnify the callings in both priesthoods, teach the word of God, and labor to advance the kingdom of the Lord. He also agrees to learn the gospel, render service, and comfort, strengthen, and perfect the lives of other Saints.

For His part, the Lord promises that those who keep these oaths will have their bodies renewed, will be counted in the seed of Abraham, will become the elect of God, and will receive all that the Father has.

The full text of the oath and covenant is contained in Doctrine and Covenants 84:33-42. We would encourage all men to read this section before receiving the priesthood, as it will remind them of the wonderful blessings and the great responsibilities associated with it.

I don't understand the difference between priesthood keys and priesthood authority. Help!

Holding the priesthood gives you the authority to perform certain ordinances, but not necessarily the keys to those ordinances. For example, if you have the Melchizedek Priesthood (or hold the office of priest in the Aaronic Priesthood) you can baptize new members. Does that mean you can baptize your own daughter in the bathtub when she turns eight years old? No, because while you hold the authority to baptize, the keys for baptism are held by the bishop, at least for the baptisms of youth. After the bishop interviews your daughter and finds her worthy and willing to be baptized, he will schedule a baptismal service. At the service, the bishop can delegate the actual performance of the ordinance to you or another worthy priesthood holder.

As a second example, you may have the priesthood authority to administer the sacrament. Does that mean if you would rather stay home next Sunday, you can bless the sacrament and pass it to your own family? No. Once again you have the authority for an ordinance, but not the keys. Your bishop can authorize you to administer the sacrament in your own home on rare occasions, such as if you lived a great distance from the meetinghouse. He can also delegate members of the ward to visit your home and administer the sacrament if you are ill.

Both of these examples used your bishop as the leader holding the priesthood keys. Other keys are also held by stake presidents, sealers in the temple, and General Authorities. The only individuals to hold keys in the ward are the bishop, the elders quorum president, the teachers quorum president, and the deacons quorum president.

While I was visiting a fellow quorum member, his wife was teasing him about something called "unrighteous dominion." What exactly is that?

Throughout this section, we have tried to emphasize that the priesthood should be used to bless the lives of others and should never be used to suggest or imply any kind of superiority or domination. Sadly, some men view the priesthood as something that permits them to abuse their wives and families. Occasionally this takes the form of physical abuse, but it is more often associated with the attitude that every decision in the home will be made by the man because he holds the priesthood.

The Lord condemns such attitudes, and promises that the priesthood of such misguided brethren will contain no power. Doctrine and Covenants 121 explains how the priesthood should govern, using principles of persuasion, long-suffering, gentleness, meekness, love unfeigned, kindness, and pure knowledge. Wouldn't the world be a better place if all our leaders could govern using such principles?

The priesthood is a tool for serving others. It should never be used in a misguided way to dominate or force others to obey your will. If you find yourself guilty of abusing the rights and privileges of the priesthood, go to your bishop for counsel.

Why don't women receive the priesthood?

This is a question that is often asked by women who are outside the Church rather than within it. When asked about the priesthood, most women inside the Church will say, "I don't want it. I have too much to do already!"

When you go to the temple, you may be surprised to find that priesthood ordinances are performed there by women. However, women do not perform priesthood ordinances outside the temple. Women are not formally ordained to the priesthood, although many Church leaders have taught that women hold the priesthood jointly with their husbands. This means that the righteous influence of the priesthood can be felt and enjoyed by all family members in a home where the priesthood exists. All family members do not need their own refrigerator.

Just one refrigerator that is "owned" and cared for by the mother can be shared and enjoyed by all family members. Similarly, the blessings of the priesthood can be brought into the home by the husband and father and then shared equally by the wife and children.

Although there are many who would have us believe that any suggestion of difference between the sexes suggests inferiority, the Church teaches that men and women have different roles and responsibilities in life. Most Mormons rejoice in this "separate but equal" philosophy and understand that the priesthood is just a tool for men to use in fulfilling part of their life's responsibilities—the duty of governing, both in the Church and in the home. Would any man feel inferior or resentful of his wife because she has a sewing machine and he does not? The sewing machine is a tool that the husband just doesn't need. Similarly, no woman should think any less of herself because she does not own a tool that is not needed to do the things she is asked to do.

A former bishop once asked a nonmember neighbor what he thought of the organization of the Church—particularly the doctrine that only men receive the priesthood. The neighbor replied, "I think your church has a pretty good idea. If your women could hold the priesthood, it would be like everything else in life. The women would be down at the church running things, and the men would be at home watching TV." Anyone who has ever watched the operation of the Church for any period of time will have to agree that giving men leadership responsibility makes them more equal to the women in terms of the time they donate to the kingdom.

But all these answers are simplistic. Perhaps the best answer to this question is simply that the women have not been given the priesthood because the Lord hasn't given us that instruction. We just don't know whether women will eventually receive the priesthood. If it ever happens, though, it won't be because it's politically expedient; it will be because the Lord tells the prophet that the time has come.

Experience has shown that the Church can move very fast when new revelations are received. If the Lord ever revealed that the time had come for women to start being ordained, you can be sure the policies would be in place practically overnight so that the Church could begin ordaining women. Until then, both the men and the women in the Church will just have to exercise faith that the Lord Jesus Christ still stands at the head of His Church and that things are proceeding according to His plan.

You say that a home teacher is "called." Is this similar to other callings in the Church?

Yes and no. All men who hold the priesthood are expected to carry out the responsibilities associated with it—and that includes home teaching. There are a few rare instances in the Church where a man who has unusual circumstances may request that he not be called as a home teacher. Sometimes, for example, a patriarch will not serve as a home teacher because worrying about the problems of his families could detract from the spirituality he would need to perform his calling. But some youth, and just about all adult men, should expect to serve as home teachers. Serving as a home teacher is a lifelong responsibility.

Even though men are expected to serve as home teachers, most good priesthood leaders will still be courteous enough to go through the formality of issuing a call when you are being asked to be a home teacher for the first time (or after you have moved into a new ward). Once your leader has the bishop's approval, he may wish to meet with you either at home or after your Sunday meetings. He will call you to be a home teacher and usually give you the name of your companion and the families you will be assigned to visit. Unlike other callings, you do not have to be sustained, nor do you have to be set apart. That already happened when you were sustained and ordained to the priesthood. A calling to do home teaching is simply a request for you to exercise the priesthood that you already hold in a specific assignment.

On rare occasions, a busy or absent-minded priesthood leader may just hand you a list of families that you are to home teach, without issuing a formal calling. You can either remind the leader that you have never been formally called (in which case he will probably be embarrassed and call you on the spot), or you can just accept the assignment, thank him, smile, and walk away, and go meet your companion and visit your families.

Although women do not have the priesthood, calls for visiting teachers are issued in a way that is similar to the way home teaching callings are issued. Relief Society presidents go on the assumption that any woman in the ward is willing to be a visiting teacher. The president will usually ask a woman if she's willing to take a route before assigning a route to her, but even if she forgets this step, it's not the end of the world. If circumstances prohibit you from being a visiting teacher during a particular time of your life, it's better to tell the Relief Society president so she can make other arrangements than it is to accept a route and just not go visiting teaching.

By the way, the best way to think of home teaching or visiting teaching is not as a short-term calling but as a lifetime commitment. If you can breathe, you can be a home teacher or a visiting teacher—and you *should* be. Home teaching and visiting teaching are so central to the foundation of the Church that the entire Church program wouldn't function nearly as well without them. If Latter-day Saints are the bricks that uphold our church structure, home teachers and visiting teachers are the mortar.

9

GOING TO
THE TEMPLE

One characteristic that sets The Church of Jesus Christ of Latter-day Saints apart from most other religions is its use of temples. There are currently more than 50 of these magnificent structures scattered throughout the world, and it was recently announced that by the turn of the century there will be twice that amount. Ask the man on the street what he knows about the Mormons, and you'll commonly hear responses such as, "That's the church that builds the temples."

We live close to the Washington Temple, which is actually located in Kensington, Maryland, just off the Washington Beltway. Seeing that temple at night is an experience never to be forgotten. As you drive west on the beltway toward Virginia, you round a corner and suddenly see the temple rising up from the darkness right in front of you—six gleaming white spires with bronze-colored caps, with the tallest spire accentuated by stained glass and topped by a figure of a golden angel. Shortly after the temple was completed, some vandals painted the words "Surrender Dorothy" on an overpass close to the temple—an obvious reference to *The Wizard of Oz*. It is almost a daily occurrence to hear the radio traffic announcers talk about the traffic that is "backed up all the way to the Mormon Temple." Thus, if you ask any resident of the surrounding Washington-Maryland-Virginia area about the "Mormon Temple," he will probably describe its beauty and give you directions for driving there—although you will doubtless get a variety of opinions if you ask people what goes on inside the temple walls.

So, although much of the world associates the Church with its beautiful temples, most people have little understanding of why the Church builds temples and what occurs within temple walls. As an investigator or recent convert, you might have some of these same questions yourself. The goal of this chapter is to answer most of those questions and fill you with an enthusiasm for becoming involved with the important work that is done there.

Temples Throughout History

To give you a better understanding of the function of temples, some historical background will be helpful. Here's a brief overview of temple building throughout history—both in biblical times and in the latter days of the restored Church.

Temples in Biblical Times

The Bible contains a rich history of temple construction by the Lord's chosen people. Shortly after the exodus of Israel from Egypt, the Israelites were required to build a tabernacle. This tabernacle had to be built exactly according to the Lord Jehovah's blueprint because the Lord Himself would visit there. Because the Israelites were a wandering people, this tabernacle had to be compact and portable. Nevertheless, it was built with the finest materials available to the people and according to specifications revealed by the Lord Himself.

King David wanted to build a more elegant and permanent house unto the Lord, but he was not allowed to do so because of the sins he had committed. The Lord told David that he would be allowed to gather materials for the temple but that the privilege of building the temple would fall to his son Solomon.

Solomon's temple was certainly one of the wonders of the ancient world. Using the materials and wealth provided by King David, who employed more than 30,000 workmen, the temple took more than seven years to complete. But for all its

majesty, the temple lasted only 40 years until it was dese-
crated by the wickedness of the people. This was a pattern
that would repeat itself often throughout history: wickedness
on the part of the people and their leaders would be followed
by the desecration of the temple and the withdrawal of the
Holy Spirit.

This was especially true in the Temple of Herod. Although
the temple was an architectural structure of beauty and
grandeur, the wickedness of the priests had corrupted many of
the practices and turned it into more of a marketplace than a
temple. It was from this temple that Christ cast out the money-
changers, as recorded in Matthew 21:12–13.

The Book of Mormon records that temples were built by the
Nephites on the American continent but provides few details of
their construction and the worship that took place within
them. The Nephite nation was destroyed within four centuries
after Christ's death, and there would not again be an earthly
temple recognized by the Lord until the gospel was restored by
Joseph Smith in the 1830s.

Temples in the Latter Days

Three years after the LDS Church was organized, the Lord
commanded Joseph Smith to build a temple in Kirtland, Ohio.
Despite poverty and persecution, the Saints responded to the
call, and the Kirtland Temple was completed and dedicated
within three years of the Lord's command. The days surrounding the dedication were filled with heavenly manifestations, as documented by sections 109–10 in the Doctrine and
Covenants. During one of these manifestations, Joseph Smith
and Oliver Cowdery were visited by Jesus Christ, Moses, Elias,
and Elijah. At this time, the Lord accepted the temple and
warned the people not to pollute the temple they had built.

Moses and the other ancient prophets had a purpose in
appearing in the Kirtland Temple. They were there to turn
over to the prophet various keys that would be used to administer the kingdom of God on the earth. Thus, we see that
another purpose of temples is to conduct such "heavenly business" as is necessary to further the Lord's work in both heaven
and on earth—and to link those two spheres together. This link

continues to be one of the most important functions of today's temples.

Within two years of the temple's dedication, the Saints were forced to flee Ohio because of persecution. The temple fell into other hands and is no longer owned by the Church. It has been restored today to its original condition and is an interesting place to visit if you are in the Cleveland, Ohio area.

When the Saints built a community in Nauvoo, Illinois, one of their first concerns was to build a new temple. The cornerstones of the Nauvoo Temple were laid in April 1841, and the building was dedicated approximately five years later. By the time the temple was completed, persecution of the Saints had accelerated again, and it was obvious that they would again be forced to flee. Yet, as a credit to the Saints who built it, the workers struggled to complete and properly furnish the temple they had built to their God. Even though persecution was intense, the temple was opened for a short time, and many Saints received blessings there before being forced from the state. In November 1848, the temple was mostly destroyed by fire, and the blackened walls that remained were claimed by a tornado in 1850.

It is interesting to note the spiritual evolution that occurred between the Kirtland and Nauvoo eras. The Kirtland Temple was certainly accepted by the Lord as His house, but its structure and function were similar to those of what we would call a tabernacle today. This temple was basically a large public meeting area that could be divided into smaller rooms for study. In the design of the Nauvoo Temple, we see that certain parts of the temple were designed to accommodate specific activities and ceremonies. In that regard, the design for the Nauvoo Temple is quite similar to the temples in use today.

After leaving Nauvoo, the Saints migrated west. They arrived in what is now Salt Lake City, Utah, on July 24, 1847. Four days after arriving in the Salt Lake Valley, President Brigham Young walked to a place in the sagebrush, struck the ground with his cane, and announced that a temple would be built on the site. Construction of the Salt Lake Temple took forty years, and Brigham Young did not live to see its dedication on April 6, 1893.

The Salt Lake Temple is a monument to the faith and

dedication of the early Saints, who sacrificed so much to build a temple to their God. This temple has the distinction of being one of the first temples built in the latter-days that is still in use as a functioning temple. Only the St. George, Logan, and Manti Temples—all three in Utah—were dedicated before the Salt Lake Temple; interestingly, all three were begun after the Salt Lake Temple was started.

The Salt Lake Temple was followed by others now in many countries throughout the world. Attending the temple in some far-flung areas of the world can be a once-in-a-lifetime opportunity. Many Church members sacrifice all their money and worldly goods to make the journey, which often takes days, weeks, or even months. But they make the sacrifice gladly, trading their earthly possessions for the blessings they receive when they attend.

Why Temples Are Needed

As shown in the short history just given, you'll find there are several recurring themes that run throughout the history of temple worship. Those who follow the Lord will often build temples. The Lord will always command His chosen people to build temples and will sometimes even specify the design Himself. No matter whether the blueprint comes from the Lord or from an earthly architect, the temple is always constructed using the finest materials available to the builders.

The word *temple* means "the house of the Lord." When a temple is accepted by the Lord and remains undefiled, it becomes a place where the Spirit of the Lord is often manifest to His people and where there is a closeness between the heavens and the earth.

Unlike a chapel or a synagogue, temples are not used for normal Sunday worship services. They are reserved for special activities and ceremonies not associated with Sabbath worship. That being the case, a temple is not a public building but is reserved as a sacred place where the Lord can bless those who are righteous and are chosen by Him. Even a king as great as David was not allowed to build or use a temple, because of his previous sins.

Temples provide places where the authorized servants of God can carry out sacred activities and ceremonies designed to bless the lives of the people. These ceremonies, or ordinances, are so sacred that they are never performed outside the temple, where those who don't understand them could make light of holy things.

Temple Ordinances

You should already be familiar with some of the ordinances performed in the Church. Baptism was the first ordinance performed on your behalf. Someone who held the priesthood recited the baptismal prayer and lowered you under the water. Likewise, when you were confirmed a member of the Church, an ordinance was performed. You are also witnessing an ordinance whenever you watch the priests administer the sacrament bread each Sunday during sacrament meeting.

Conferring the priesthood is an ordinance too. Receiving the priesthood is an ordinance that has great significance because, with one exception that will be mentioned later in this chapter, only men who have the priesthood have the authority to perform ordinances.

Before you began studying the LDS Church, you may have been baptized in another church. You might have even been a little offended at having to be baptized again after already being "saved" in your previous religion. Hopefully, you will now see that a second baptism was necessary because it had to be done using the proper procedure, and by someone holding the proper authority, which is the priesthood of God as restored to Joseph Smith and passed down through worthy Church members since his time.

But it isn't enough to be baptized. Being baptized is only the first step, just as going to the airport is only the first step in a trip to Hawaii. Yes, your baptism into the Church is what we call a saving ordinance. But just as there is a big difference between flying directly to Hawaii and flying to Los Angeles and standing on the beach, wishing you were in Hawaii, there's a world of difference between being exalted and just being saved.

When Adam and Eve sinned, they and all their descendants were cast out from God's presence. Upon their deaths, Adam and Eve could not return to God's presence, because they had sinned, and no unclean thing can dwell with God. Members of the Church do not believe that we've inherited Adam and Eve's sins, but we're fully aware that we commit sins on our own. Our own sins are enough to disqualify us from going back to the Father.

The only way out of this dilemma was to have our sins atoned for by a person who lived a sinless life. Jesus Christ made that sacrifice for us, and through his sacrifice all of God's children—Church members and nonmembers alike—will live forever. In addition, the Atonement gives us the opportunity to be forgiven, to come forth in the resurrection of the just, and to be restored to a perfect state.

Your baptism and confirmation made you a candidate for salvation. Through the gift of Jesus Christ, you will someday be resurrected and can live in a more perfect state. If that is all you want, you can achieve your goal by being baptized and then being faithful to the end of your life. The ordinances of the temple are for those who desire an even greater reward—exaltation.

Many Christians believe that the afterlife will consist of a heaven and a hell, but Christ taught that there are "many kingdoms" (John 14:2). Expanding upon this, section 76 of the Doctrine and Covenants describes three kingdoms of heaven, the most glorious of which is the celestial kingdom. The Apostle Paul mentioned these three kingdoms in 1 Corinthians 15, but he gave no clue as to what Christians had to do to attain them. It was the Prophet Joseph Smith who gave us that direction, when he said that "celestial thrones" can be attained through temple ordinances (see *History of the Church*, 6:319).

The true purpose of the ordinances of the temple is to qualify God's children to return to His presence and dwell with him in the celestial kingdom, thus becoming His equal in power, might, and dominion. This is the great plan of exaltation. Baptism opens the gate for us to live again, but the temple opens the gate whereby we can be equal in glory to God Himself. This concept is so foreign to the traditional idea of heaven that it is often viewed as blasphemy by those outside the Church, but those who ponder it for a time will soon understand the beauty and wonder of it and will gain an even greater appreciation for the great gift Christ has given to the faithful.

Ordinances for the Living

Before describing the various ordinances that occur in the temple, you need to understand that the recipients of these ordinances fall into two categories—ordinances done for the living and those performed for the dead. The first time you attend the temple, you will be receiving the ordinances for yourself. Thus, they will be called "living ordinances" because they will be done for you, a living person.

Just as you only need to be baptized one time by the proper authority, you only need to have the ordinances of the temple performed for you once. But if you've attended Church meetings for any length of time, you know that the Church encourages frequent temple attendance. If you live near a temple, you're probably aware that some Church members attend the temple monthly or even weekly. These people are performing temple ordinances on behalf of others who are no longer living. They are serving as proxies for the dead. If this confuses you, don't worry, it will be explained in more detail in the next section. For now, just concentrate on your first trip to the temple and on the ordinances that you will experience that first time. These living ordinances will be explained in the remainder of this section.

The Endowment

You may have heard the word *endowment* as it relates to universities or other institutions. Typically, an individual or corporation will endow the university with a generous financial contribution. The university will then establish an endowment fund that is used to finance studies or research or to help ease the financial demands placed on students. Similarly, the temple endowment is a gift from God to His children. It is not a financial gift, but an even more valuable gift of potential eternal life. The nature of the material presented during the endowment is to prepare God's children to return to Him.

If you think that the endowment is a "get into heaven free" pass, you're wrong. If such a free pass exists, we haven't found it yet! The temple endowment opens the door to the celestial kingdom, but we still must reach that door and walk through it. We accomplish this by continuing to live the commandments each day and by doing our best to become more perfect in every way. Receiving your endowment is an important stepping-stone on your path towards eternal life, but it is not the end of the path. In fact, it might more accurately be considered almost the beginning!

One phrase you'll hear often when people talk about the temple is that what goes on inside the temple is "sacred—not secret." This is true. We can't tell you exactly what goes on in the temple, because sacred things should never be mentioned in a forum where they could be held open to ridicule. But we do want to reassure you that you're not going to hear anything that will shock you. Almost everything that occurs in the endowment ceremony is found somewhere in the scriptures, often word for word. If you're familiar with the book of Genesis and the Pearl of Great Price, the endowment ceremony will contain no surprises for you when you visit the temple for the first time.

Although we can't tell you exactly what happens in the endowment ceremony, we can give you a few ideas of what to expect. The contents of the endowment can be put into three broad and somewhat overlapping categories.

First, there's an instructional portion of the endowment that teaches us about the nature of God and the details of his great eternal plan for his children. This covers the history of the earth beginning with the Creation and continues through the great Apostasy and the restoration of the Gospel. This is the portion of the ceremony that can be found almost word for word in the scriptures.

Second, as part of the endowment, you'll make certain covenants. A covenant is a promise made to God that you will obey certain commandments, and that He, in return, will bestow certain blessings upon you. You have already made certain covenants, such as the covenant of baptism, and (for men) the oath and covenant of the priesthood. The covenants made in the temple can be thought of as an extension to the covenants you have already made.

Don't be worried before you attend the temple that you'll be expected to make outlandish promises. Even these covenants are found in the scriptures, and they consist of living a life that is in accordance with the life you've been living ever since you joined the Church.

Third, as you participate in the covenants of the endowment, you are also taught certain things that will enable you to enter the celestial kingdom. These pieces of information aren't in the scriptures, because they don't need to be. You wouldn't need directions to a restaurant in a city you never planned to visit, would you? By the same token, there's no need to put these "directions" in scriptures, when most people would have no use for them. What you'll hear in this part of the endowment isn't shocking or horrible; it just doesn't apply to most people, so it isn't for their ears.

Sealing

Many converts who join the Church are first attracted to it because of the emphasis placed on families and family life. Latter-day Saints believe that marriages and families have an eternal nature, extending beyond the grave. It is in the temple where this "sealing together" occurs so that husbands and wives are bound together, along with their children, into a unit that can last through the eternities.

We have all attended weddings and heard the phrase "until death do you part." It's sad to consider the implication of this sentence as it is passed on to the new bride and groom. No matter how happy their marriage may be, and how much their love for each other will continue to grow, the contract of their marriage will be immediately dissolved upon the death of either partner. No wonder so many people are afraid of death!

The words "until death do you part" have no place in a temple sealing ceremony, in which a husband and wife are married for "time and all eternity." This is known as celestial marriage and is understood to be the order of marriage that exists in the celestial worlds. Children born to parents who have been married under the celestial law are likewise considered to be part of the eternal family unit.

In most states and nations, the government recognizes the

Church as an institution that is licensed to perform marriages. Men and women who are being married for the first time can have a temple marriage, whereby the sealing ceremony doubles as a legal marriage ceremony. If your government does not recognize the authority of the Church to perform marriages, you will have to get a civil marriage first outside the temple to fulfill the legal requirements, and then attend the temple to be sealed. If this is the case, you should try to have these done on the same day.

The sealing ceremony is performed in a sealing room, where the bride and groom kneel across an altar and take each other by the hand for this sacred ordinance. The ceremony is so short that the sealing itself takes less than five minutes. There is no bridal processional and no music. Even the exchanging of wedding rings isn't part of the ceremony but may be done after the sealing is over. The sealer will usually speak first to the bride and groom, reminding them of the significance of this sacred ordinance. Close friends and family members who have been through the temple (received their own endowments) can witness the sealing, but friends or relatives who have not been through the temple are not allowed to attend. As you can imagine, this can cause a lot of heartache in families where the son or daughter is married while the parents wait outside the temple.

As a new member, you may have already been married before joining the Church. If so, it isn't too late for you to be sealed to your husband or wife. After you and your spouse have received your endowments, you will be joined together in a sealing ceremony. Your children may also attend and will be sealed together as part of your eternal family. If, for various reasons, some children cannot attend, they can be sealed later in a similar ceremony. Any children that are born after your sealing are considered to be "born in the covenant," and do not need to be sealed to you.

You may have the impression that men and women get their endowment on the same day they get married, but this isn't necessarily the case. People who are called to serve full-time missions must receive their endowments before doing missionary service. It is common for them to receive their endowments, serve their missions, return and start dating again, and then eventually marry in the temple and be sealed. Likewise, single persons may want to receive their endowments but may have no current plans for marriage. Or, as a convert, your spouse may not have yet joined the Church or may not be progressing at the same rate as you are. All of these situations will require that you receive the endowment separately from the sealing ceremonies.

Although you may be disappointed to have to defer your sealing until the circumstances are right, you can take comfort from the fact that when you are finally ready as a family, the sealing power will be there for you.

Ordinances for the Dead

One of the most cryptic scriptures in the Bible is found in Paul's words to the Corinthians: "Else what shall they do which are baptized for the dead, if the dead rise not at all? why are they then baptized for the dead?" (1 Corinthians 15:29). Most Christians ignore that scripture, because they frankly don't know what to do with it. But as you learned in the missionary lessons, one major difference between Latter-day Saints and the rest of the world is that we believe gospel ordinances are necessary to save righteous souls no matter what state they're in—even if they're dead.

It only makes sense. Only a small percentage of people who have ever lived on earth have been fortunate enough to learn about Jesus Christ. It is incomprehensible to believe that God would send everyone else to an everlasting hell, just because they were in the wrong place at the wrong time.

God loves His children so much that He has established a series of ordinances that, when combined with a righteous life and the Savior's atonement, will return them to live with Him. Would a God capable of such love then devise a system that would save only the small percentage of people that were fortunate enough to live at a time when such ordinances were in operation? Any honest person who considers this situation will have to conclude that a just and loving God would never devise such an arbitrary and unfair system.

When a person dies, his body returns to dust (in time!), but his spirit goes to paradise. Much of the Christian world considers paradise to be a synonym for heaven, but Latter-day Saints believe that paradise is a waiting area where spirits await the resurrection and the final judgment. Souls are not idle in paradise but are growing and learning. Righteous people who have died serve as missionaries for those in paradise who died without a knowledge of Jesus Christ. Once these souls are converted, they must exercise faith in Jesus Christ, they must repent, and they must be baptized.

There's the rub. It's hard to be baptized when you don't have a body to go under the water. The only way this requirement can be satisfied is for the baptism to be performed on a living person, who serves as proxy for the person who is dead. The majority of ordinances that are performed in the temple consist of this proxy work, where living Church members stand in the stead of dead men and women who are receiving their own temple ordinances.

As you come to understand this principle of proxy ordinances, you may also see why Mormons are so interested in doing genealogical research to discover their ancestors. In return for giving you life, what better gift could you give an ancestor than to perform the saving ordinances of the kingdom for them?

As you do family research and submit names of your ancestors for temple ordinances, you can choose to have the names kept in a file at the temple called a "family file." Each time you attend the temple, you can go to the family file and get the names of the relatives for which you will serve as proxy during that visit. Once you have exhausted your list of family names, you can keep attending the temple. The only difference is that now you will do this work on behalf of strangers.

With all the billions of people who have lived when temples were not on the earth, it is a pretty safe bet that the temple will never run out of people who need ordinances. Some speculate that during the Millennium, that thousand-year reign of Christ on the earth, a good portion of our time will be occupied doing temple work.

The remainder of this section will describe the proxy ordinances that are performed in the temple. These will only be covered briefly, as you should be familiar with all of them, having been through most of them yourself.

Baptism and Confirmation

Baptism and confirmation provide access to Christ's atonement and to the kingdom of heaven and are required for everyone who wants to be saved. Even the Savior had to be baptized. Only those who die before the age of accountability (under the age of eight) are exempt. The scriptures make no distinction between the living and the dead in terms of the need for baptism.

The only baptisms that are performed in temples are baptisms for the dead. (Baptisms for the living are performed in chapels or other locations.) They are performed in magnificent temple baptismal fonts that rest upon the backs of twelve stone or bronze oxen, following the pattern given by the Lord and used in Solomon's temple. The twelve oxen represent the twelve tribes of Israel.

The ordinance of proxy baptism is followed by that of confirmation and the bestowal of the Holy Ghost. A living person will serve as proxy for the person receiving the ordinance of confirmation as well as the baptism, although the person who serves as proxy for the baptism isn't necessarily the same person who serves as proxy for the confirmation. The confirmation and conferring of the gift of the Holy Ghost constitutes the higher baptism of the Spirit that is required for both the living and the dead.

Although most temple ordinances are performed using adult proxies, temple baptisms can be performed by older children and young adults twelve years of age and older. Wards often conduct "youth baptism" trips, where young men and young women are taken to the temple to act as proxies for baptisms and confirmations.

Even though you cannot receive your endowment until you have been a Church member for at least a year, you can attend the temple before that to participate in proxy baptisms. Doing baptisms for the dead allows you to feel of the peaceful spirit within the temple and gives you an idea of the importance of the work that is done there. Perhaps you can participate in a youth baptism trip, if one is scheduled in the near future. Talk to your bishop if you have an interest in doing this.

Priesthood Ordination

Just as all living males must receive the Melchizedek Priesthood before receiving their endowments, all deceased males must also receive the priesthood. Males acting as proxy receive the Melchizedek Priesthood during the initiatory ordinances, which are a prelude to the presentation of the endowment.

Those who are concerned that women don't receive the priesthood will be comforted when they visit the temple and see that women perform ordinance work there. Not only do women serve as proxies for women who have died, but female temple workers always perform the initiatory ordinances when women are being endowed or serving as proxies.

Endowment

The ordinance of the endowment is almost identical for the living or the dead. Serving as proxy, you will be given a slip of paper containing the name of the person you represent. Several times during the endowment, you will be asked to repeat that person's name, or think about it. Saints believe that the dead experience the ordinance of the endowment through the person who serves as proxy, so it is important that you stay alert and pay attention to what is presented.

Many Church members spend their entire adult lives experiencing the endowment service again and again. It isn't uncommon for a man or a woman to go through thousands of endowment sessions during a lifetime. Some people, especially older ones who attend several sessions in the course of a day, may doze off during the presentation of the endowment, but those who attend the temple in the proper spirit are usually surprised how often they learn something new. The material presented in the endowment is both literal and symbolic and has meaning on several different levels. Those who keep their mind in tune with the Spirit will often emerge with new insights or new directions for their lives.

The conclusion of the endowment occurs in a room called the celestial room. This room represents our ultimate destiny, the celestial kingdom of God. This room is an ideal place to ponder the material presented in the endowment and to receive personal revelation from God related to your own path in life. Remember that the temple is the house of the Lord, and He manifests His Spirit there to His worthy children. It is a place where you can easily feel that Spirit and be guided by it.

Sealing Ordinances

As with the endowment, proxy sealing ordinances are almost identical to those for living temple patrons. A temple sealer will read the names of the deceased patrons, and you will kneel at the altar in proxy for them.

As with live ordinances, two types of sealings are performed. Husbands and wives are sealed together for eternity, and children are sealed to their parents.

There is no greater feeling than finding an ancestor's name through genealogical research, then taking that name to the temple and performing the ordinances on his behalf. Many times, people who attend the temple report they feel the presence of the person who is being served. The veil between the living and the dead is thin in the temple, and the person whose work is being done often manages to convey a sense of gratitude to the person who is serving as proxy. The work done in the temples is of great importance to those who have gone before us, and many Church members will tell you of great spiritual experiences they have had while performing genealogy and temple work.

Preparing to Attend the Temple

Going to the temple for the first time isn't something that you can do on the spur of the moment. A lot of thought and preparation should go into that first temple trip. You'll also have to meet with your bishop and your stake president to determine your worthiness to enter the house of the Lord. This section will give you some tips that should help you as you prepare to go to the temple. We will also describe the approval process you must go through to receive permission to attend and will make other suggestions so that your first experience is a good one.

Study and Preparation

No matter how much you prepare to attend the temple, we can guarantee that it will be different from what you expect. This is partly because the temple ordinances contain more ritual, ceremony, and symbolism than is found in a typical Sunday LDS worship service. As we surveyed friends about their first temple experience, we generally found that those who had done the most preparation were the ones who had the best experience. We will try to suggest some readings and activities that will make your first experience a positive one.

- **Scriptures**

  The scriptures contain much information that will give you a background for the information presented in the temple. We would suggest the following:

Genesis, chapters 1–3	Creation of the Earth; Adam and Eve
Moses, chapters 1–5	Creation of the Earth; Adam and Eve
Abraham, chapters 3–5	Creation of the Earth, God's Eternal Plan
D & C, section 76	The Kingdoms of Heaven
D & C, section 88	The Kingdoms of Heaven
D & C, section 95	Saints Reminded to Build the Kirtland Temple
D & C, section 109	Dedication of the Kirtland Temple
D & C, section 110	Heavenly Beings Appear in the Kirtland Temple
D & C, section 124	Functions and Ordinances of the Temple
D & C, section 132	The Ordinance of Celestial Marriage
D & C, section 138	Christ Preaches to Those in Paradise

- **Books**

  Several books and pamphlets have been published about the temple. If you live in an area where there are LDS bookstores, you'll be able to find a lot of information. It is best if you can browse through the books in person, as then you can eliminate those that are too general or too detailed. In general, the ones written by current or previous Church leaders would be the safest choices. Again, perhaps someone in your ward could give some recommendations.

  There are three that we would recommend:
  The House of the Lord, by James E. Talmage
  The Holy Temple, by Boyd K. Packer
  "Endowed from On High" (Church publication)

- **Temple Preparation Class**

The Church provides a series of classes designed for those who are preparing to attend the temple for the first time. This is called the temple preparation class, and it usually meets once a week for about two months. Some of the material presented in the lessons is quite general, but the student manuals provided with it are considerably more detailed. One of the most valuable parts of the class is the chance you'll have to meet with those who are already experienced in attending the temple. They can answer your general questions and clarify anything that is unclear from the course manuals.

Your bishop can tell you when you're ready to take a temple preparation class, and how to enroll for one.

Receiving the Melchizedek Priesthood

Men must receive the Melchizedek Priesthood before they can enter the temple. Church policy used to be that men had to wait a year before receiving this priesthood, but this policy has been changed. Bishops are now usually recommending that worthy men be ordained to the office of an elder after three to twelve months of Church membership.

If your bishop has not mentioned your advancement in the priesthood, you may wish to ask him about it. If he has talked to you about this, but you are still working out some issues relating to your worthiness, you need to resolve these issues. Don't deprive yourself and your family of temple blessings because you cannot change a few habits or forsake a few sins. Receiving your temple blessings is something that will have eternal implications for your family, and it should not be postponed.

Getting Your Recommend

Not all members of the Church can enter the temple. Although all Church members and even nonmembers are invited to attend Sunday services, admittance to the temple is reserved for those who keep all the basic commandments and teachings of the gospel. No one is perfect, and we all commit our share of sins each day, but there are minimum standards that must be met to allow access to the temple.

The first time you visit the temple, you will be given a worthiness interview to determine whether you are worthy to enter. This is done in two parts. In the first half of the interview, your bishop will ask you a fixed set of questions, which you must answer honestly. If your bishop believes you are worthy, based on the conversation you have with him, he will issue you a small slip of paper called a temple recommend. It is about the size of a credit card and will fit easily in your wallet or purse.

After you have a temple recommend that has been signed by your bishop, you must then meet with the stake president, who will ask you the same set of questions. If he decides you're worthy, based on your answers to the questions, he will also sign the recommend. Your temple recommend is not valid unless it has been signed by both your bishop and your stake president.

Whenever you enter the temple, the first place you will go is to a desk at the entrance. This is called a recommend desk. The temple worker who sits behind the desk will ask to see your recommend. He will verify that it is filled out correctly and that both signatures are present. The first time you visit the temple, he will stamp your recommend with an expiration date, which is approximately one year from the date it was issued. As long as you remain worthy, the recommend will be your key to enter the temple for the next year. As you approach the time when the recommend expires, you will need to schedule new interviews with a member of your bishopric and a member of your stake presidency in order to renew your recommend. Recommends must be renewed every year.

Questions you will be asked during a temple recommend interview cover such issues as your obedience to the law of chastity, the Word of Wisdom, and the teachings of latter-day prophets. You will be asked to confirm your belief in God, the Eternal Father, His Son Jesus Christ, and the Holy Ghost. You will also have a chance to discuss with the bishopric or stake presidency member any sins or issues in your life that have not been resolved with your Church leaders.

It is beyond the scope of this book to analyze interview

questions in detail. Feel free, however, to ask questions during the interview if you do not understand what is being asked.

It is important that you respond to each question fully and honestly. It's true that you won't be allowed into the temple if you are not worthy to do so but the covenants you'll be making in the temple are quite similar to the temple recommend questions. If you aren't obeying the commandments that give you access into the temple, then you'd probably break the covenants you made there as well. If you break the temple covenants, you'll be worse off than you would have been if you'd never gone to the temple at all.

If you can't honestly supply all the correct answers to the questions during your first visit, your bishop will give you the help and encouragement you need to develop a plan to get you to the temple. With that goal in mind, you'll be able to resolve your worthiness issues and eventually receive your endowment.

There are actually three different types of temple recommends that your bishop can issue. The first, which is called a Recommend for Living Ordinances, is the kind of recommend you'll get when you go to the temple for your own endowment. You'll also receive this kind of recommend when you are going to be married or sealed to your husband or wife. The only time you will use this recommend is on one of the few occasions in your life when you are attending the temple for living ordinances.

The most commonly issued recommend is one that allows members who have received their endowment to participate in all temple ordinances for the dead. This is the one you will use when you come back to the temple to perform proxy ordinances. Note that this type of recommend is also required when attending for living ordinances. So, when attending for your own endowment or sealing, you will need *both* types of recommends, properly completed and signed.

The third kind of recommend is issued to unendowed Church members. It allows them to be baptized for the dead, to be sealed to their parents, or (on rare occasions) to witness a sealing of their living brothers and sisters to their parents. The youth from your ward get this Limited-Use Recommend when they do youth baptisms. This is also the recommend your younger children will need if you plan to have them sealed to you.

The standards of worthiness are the same for all three types of recommends, so you will be asked questions similar to those previously listed for any of the three types.

Making an Appointment

Temple workers make every effort to accommodate the needs of the patrons, no matter what those needs may be. This means that if you walk in off the street with your temple recommend to receive your own endowment, they'll break their necks in a valiant effort to help you out. But common sense tells you that if the temple is prepared for your arrival, you'll have a smoother temple experience. That being the case, you might want to abandon the element of surprise and schedule an appointment for your first temple visit.

It's important to schedule that first temple visit for a couple of reasons. First, most temples are only set up to perform living ordinances during certain times of the day. Living ordinances usually take longer than proxy ordinances, and they involve temple workers who may not be at the temple if you just walk in off the street. Because of this, temple workers like to gather together the people who are receiving their own endowments into certain time slots, most of which are during times when the temple will be less crowded.

Another factor is that calling in advance will avoid delays due to scheduling. If twenty couples walk in off the street to be sealed in a temple that only has five sealing rooms, fifteen couples are going to be cooling their jets for a long time while they wait their turn for a sealing room. If you make an appointment, you'll save yourself the aggravation.

Making an appointment is especially important if you speak a language other than the language that is spoken at the temple, or if you have some sort of physical disability that may require different arrangements. Wheelchairs or even gurneys can be used in the temple. Interpreters are available for the deaf, and headsets are available in virtually any major language. But some of these arrangements need to be made ahead of time. If you walk in off the street, there may not be an opportunity to give you the accommodations you need.

Selecting Escorts and Witnesses

When you attend the temple to receive your own endowment, you should select one friend to go with you as your escort. You'll probably have many friends who will gladly volunteer for this assignment, and it's fine to have all your friends attend the temple with you that first time, but you can only choose one person to serve as your escort. The job of the escort is to help you through the experience, reassure you, help you find your way around the temple, and, in general, just provide moral support. The temple will provide an escort if you don't bring one, but it will probably be a better experience for you if you ask someone you know.

Your escort should be of the same sex as you are, because he or she will be navigating you through the dressing room. You should pick someone who is not only a friend, but who also attends the temple often, and who is familiar with the temple that you will be attending. It doesn't do much good to be led by someone who doesn't know what to do in the temple, or who will get lost somewhere between the front door and the dressing room, but you'd be surprised how often it happens!

Don't let someone railroad you into being your escort if you are uncomfortable around that person. Going to the temple for the first time is traumatic enough without having to spend those hours gritting your teeth and smiling at an escort who drives you crazy. If someone volunteers to be your escort—or even if someone insists on being your escort—only accept the offer if you want to do so. If you're uncomfortable with that person, *for any reason,* find some kind and gentle way of thanking him for volunteering, without letting him carry out his intent.

Once you've received your own endowment, you can be sealed to your spouse on the same day or on a subsequent temple trip. When you go to the temple to be sealed, you'll need to have your sealing observed by two male witnesses. A witness's responsibilities aren't as detailed as an escort's, so you won't need to be as picky about choosing your witnesses as you were when you chose your escort. Just pick two men who have current temple recommends, and whose names you'd like to appear on your sealing certificate. But if you'd rather not choose anyone, don't worry. The temple will assign witnesses to you if you come without them.

Surviving the Big Day

What to Take with You

Once you have your temple recommend signed by both your bishop and your stake president, keep it in a place where it won't get lost. You won't get inside the temple without it, even if it's your wedding day and the caterer has the food all fixed for your wedding brunch.

But that's not all you'll be taking with you when you go to the temple. You'll wear your normal "Sunday best" when you enter the temple, but immediately after you get there, you'll change into other clothing. If you're going to a full-sized temple, you may choose to rent these clothes. If you do, take a five-dollar bill with you to cover the clothing rental. This will be more than enough to pay for the rental of your temple clothing, including the ceremonial robes you'll need during the endowment ceremony. Otherwise, you should assemble the clothing yourself. Here is a summary of what you'll need.

Men will need a long-sleeved white shirt, white trousers, a white tie, white shoes, and white socks. If your trousers need a belt, that belt should also be white. By "white," we don't mean white with blue stripes, or white with a black manufacturer's logo, or something that used to be white before it faded to a dingy yellow. Everything you wear should be white, with the possible exception of the label that's hidden inside your shirt.

Women's needs are considerably more complicated. Women will need a floor-length white dress—one without a low-cut neck or back. The sleeves should go to the wrist, and there shouldn't be any transparent fabrics. By "white," we don't mean ivory, or ecru, or any one of those other popular off-whites. In this case "white" means "white." Period. Women also need white shoes, white pantyhose or knee-length nylons, a white bra, and a white full-length slip. Everything on this list—for either a man or a woman—can be rented at the temple, with the possible exception of the white bra, for well under five dollars.

For some reason, there are a lot of women who think these rules can be thrown out the window on their wedding day. They'll look through the bridal catalogues and find dresses with sheer sleeves or no sleeves at all, or dresses that are front-less or backless (or both!), or dresses that meet all the other requirements except that they're in a stunning tint of bone. You're welcome to look all you want at dresses like these, but you're going to be embarrassed to wear them at the temple. Temple workers will do what they can to add fabric panels to make your wedding dress acceptable as temple wear, but it will never look the same as it did on the model once you've got a white polyester dickey covering your cleavage.

Another point to ponder for brides is that no matter how pretty your veil is, you're not going to be wearing it when you get married. You can buy a veil to wear outside the temple and at the reception, and all your pictures can be taken with you wearing the veil. But when you're actually kneeling across the altar, the veil won't even be in the same room with you. Don't get too attached to it.

Ditto for flowers. You won't be carrying a bouquet into the sealing room, and your groom-to-be won't be wearing a bouton-niere. Save your flowers for the pictures afterward.

Another thing you'll want to take on your first trip to the temple is your checkbook. After you have been endowed, you'll wear "garments" instead of traditional underwear. (Learn more about garments in the question section at the end of this chapter.) Garments are not expensive, but you'll want to pur-chase enough sets of them while you're at the temple that you can wear them every day. Don't leave home without your checkbook or a decent amount of cash to cover this expense.

Now that you know what to take with you to the temple, here are things you might as well leave at home. Cameras are not allowed inside the temple, although you are welcome to take pictures outside. Tape recorders are not allowed inside the temple. Cellular phones and beepers are not allowed inside the temple. If you carry any of these things with you, you'll have to check them at the recommend desk.

To Eat, or Not to Eat

How much you should eat before you go to the temple—or whether you should eat anything—is a private matter. You'll probably have several well-meaning people tell you that you should fast before your first visit to the temple. The proper answer to this is, "Thanks for the suggestion. I'll consider it."

Everyone's digestive system is different. For some people, fasting is entirely appropriate. If you're one of those people, fasting may heighten the spiritual experience for you. But you need to keep in mind that you'll be spending several hours in the temple, and once you get started there's no time for a lunch break. If you think you may experience some dizziness if you go without food, by all means eat before you go. Kathy fainted at the altar once, and the embarrassment she suffered far outweighed any spiritual benefits she might have received from fasting.

But be sure you don't eat too much. You don't want to be worried about emergency trips to the bathroom when you're supposed to be concentrating on the endowment session. Nor do you want the huge meal you ate beforehand to put you to sleep. You won't be the first person who's ever fallen asleep inside a temple, by any means, but this is one time you'll want to be awake and alert.

The best advice about food is this: Do whatever it takes so that food isn't a factor for the three to four hours you will be spending in the temple. Make sure you aren't distracted by worrying about the food you've already consumed or by fantasizing about the food you're going to consume on this landmark day in your life.

When to Get There

When you make an appointment to go to the temple, you'll be told what time you need to arrive there. The time that was given to you was not pulled out of a hat just to entertain the temple worker. If the temple worker says you're supposed to be at the temple at noon, that's when you should walk through the front door. Plan your travel time with enough leeway that you won't be delayed by traffic or by anything else that could come up at the last moment. And if you're going through the temple on a Saturday, add extra time to circle the parking lot. Saturdays are the busiest days in the temple.

Your first trip to the temple is a big day in your life. In some ways, you'll be the center of attention. At least, the people in your ward will think you're the star of the day. But once you get to the temple, you may find that you're only one star in a whole constellation of people who are attending the temple for the first time. And every one of those stars, together with the cast of thousands of people who may be accompanying them, will have to wait for you if you decide to wander in a half hour late.

Plan your trip to the temple so that you're early rather than late. You can always go to the visitors' center or take pictures outside the temple to take up your extra time. If something horrible happens to make you late for your appointment, make every effort to call the temple and tell them how late you'll be. That way, the temple workers can decide whether to hold up the process or to send the rest of the constellation ahead without you. Even if you're late, you'll still be able to go to the temple that day—it will just be a lot more complicated for everyone involved.

Behavior Inside the Temple

Going to the temple is not the same as going to an ice cream parlor. Even though you may have a dozen or more friends attending the temple with you when you go for the first time, you should leave the party atmosphere at home. People pay lip service to reverence in sacrament meeting and then jabber a mile a minute, but the temple is a different situation entirely. Here are a few guidelines that will keep you from being embarrassed at the temple.

- **Keep Your Voice Down**

   There's not much to say about this one. Loud voices are out of place in the temple, even if you've just seen your old high school sweetheart for the first time in twenty years and are trying to flag him down. It's fine to visit in the dressing rooms or to a limited extent even in the halls, as long as you do it quietly, but be careful not to distract others by speaking in the endowment room. If you have something you absolutely have to ask your escort, do it in a whisper. Otherwise, sit quietly and meditate before the session begins. The people around you will be glad you did.

- **No Peacocks, Please**

Although you'll want to look your best when you're inside the temple, looking your best inside the temple is entirely different from looking your best at a fancy-dress ball. If you're a woman, keep your hair and makeup simple. Leave the flashy jewelry and dangling earrings at home. The object is to keep from calling attention to yourself. It's fine to be a peacock in your normal life, as long as you shed your plumage inside the temple.

Because so many people are sensitive to the environment these days, it's good advice to leave your perfume and hairspray at home as well. Any temple worker can tell you horror stories about people who have had asthma attacks after walking into a dressing room where another patron sprayed hairspray ten minutes before. Sometimes people have to leave endowment sessions because a patron's perfume has made them sick. If you want to bring your perfume and hairspray and stinky hand lotion with you to put on after you leave the temple, that's fine. But for the sake of those with asthma or other health problems, wait until then.

- **Leave the Chewing Gum at Home**

If there are places where it's appropriate to chew gum, the temple isn't one of them. If you have an oral fixation that must be satisfied, carry breath mints or cough drops instead. Cough drops often come in handy in the temple, where the dry atmosphere lends itself to coughing attacks. (If your cough drops or breath mints are wrapped in cellophane, you may want to put them in a small plastic bag so they won't make so much noise when you unwrap them.) Rental temple dresses have conveniently placed pockets where you can hide these treasures until they're needed.

- **Be Prepared for Temperature Extremes**

Nobody likes the temperature in the temple. This is a fact of life.

A small percentage of people find the temple too cold. There are shawls (white shawls, of course!) to accommodate these people. When you put on your ceremonial robes in the endowment room, the shawl goes under the robe, right next to your dress. It looks funny, but it's warm.

Most people, however, find that temperatures in the temple are sweltering. Things only get worse when you're dressed in layers of polyester rental clothes. There's nothing you can do to make yourself feel cooler. But if you feel as though you're going to faint from the heat, put a pathetic look on your face. If you're lucky, a temple worker may notice and bring you a glass of water.

- **Be Careful About Noise in the Celestial Room**

  Although it's important to be quiet everywhere in the temple, that goes double in the celestial room. No matter what temple you visit, the acoustics in the celestial room can be downright amazing. Words that are uttered in the smallest whisper can reverberate around the room in stereophonic tones. When Kathy has been on duty in the celestial room, she has overheard people talking about their children's soccer teams, choosing restaurants, discussing business, and going into embarrassing detail about their medical problems—all from people who were whispering at least thirty feet away from her. Don't say a word in the celestial room unless you absolutely have to. Even then, keep your conversations to a bare minimum. Remember, there are people who have come to the celestial room to pray over desperate situations. Don't drive them away with your casual laughter and chitchat.

  And while you're in the celestial room, there are other things to consider. Reading material of any kind is not allowed in the celestial room. (In fact, the celestial room is one of the only places on earth where it isn't even appropriate to read the scriptures!) And although praying is definitely encouraged, all prayers should be silent. Patrons are asked not to pray aloud or to kneel in this public place.

- **Expect to Be Overwhelmed**

  No matter how well prepared you are to enter the temple, your first experience will very likely be different

from what you expected. You're going to be barraged with so
much new information that there's no way you'll be able to
remember it all. Absorbing all the information that is presented in the endowment and sealing ceremonies in one
trip is like trying to fill a drinking glass from a fire hose. It's
not going to happen.

Never fear. If you start to get nervous at any time
during the day's proceedings, remind yourself that there's
nothing to be afraid of. You won't be tested afterwards to
see how much you remember. And you won't be embarrassed or humiliated in any way.

Just in case your escort forgets to give you a pep talk,
here's one that you can read before you ever attend the
temple. As you go through your own endowment ceremony,
there is not a single thing that should frighten you. When
you're around other people, you will always be wearing
some sort of clothing. You will never—not one time—have
to memorize anything. You will never—not for a moment—
have to stand up by yourself and do something alone, with
the whole congregation watching you. You will never, never,
never be left on your own, being expected to do something
but not knowing what it is. At every moment when you
could possibly need assistance, there will be a temple
worker available to help you. The rest of the time, there will
be temple workers nearby, ready to spring to your aid. Even
if you just need a Kleenex, or if you're feeling faint and need
a cracker, or if you're coughing and need some water, or if
your bladder can't make it through the temple session, all
you have to do is raise your hand, and a temple worker will
be with you to help you before you know it. Temple workers
love to do things like that. It makes them feel useful.

- **Keep the Temple Sacred**

This chapter probably hasn't been as specific as you
hoped it would be. There's a reason for that. Those who
don't have the background of Church membership would
not understand the temple ordinances and might ridicule
them or make light of them.

You will be told in the endowment ceremony that you
have a sacred obligation to not discuss what you have seen

there. This means you shouldn't discuss the temple ceremony with nonmembers *or* with Church members. Although it is usually permissible to talk about the temple in a general way (as we have tried to do in this chapter), your conversation should never go into specifics.

Some Church members make a habit of repeating some of the words of temple ceremonies in their regular conversation. Nonmembers or unendowed members have no idea what they are hearing, so this becomes somewhat of an inside joke between the speaker and other endowed members. This practice should be avoided, because it also makes light of sacred things.

If you have any questions about the endowment ceremony, ask your escort in the celestial room after your session. Any questions that can't be answered by the members of your party should be taken directly to a member of the temple presidency. At no time should the specifics of the endowment ceremony be discussed outside the temple. Remember—these things are "sacred, not secret."

After Your Endowment

Going to the temple isn't a one-time experience. Unless you live so far from a temple that you'll have to cross a continent to get there, you should return often. Once you've been to the temple that first time, you can see that you'll have to go back to the temple again and again before you'll begin to absorb everything you were taught on your first visit. Many people spend a lifetime attending the temple regularly, and they continue to learn new things from the endowment ceremony throughout their lives. The endowment ceremony is like an onion, with layer after layer that can be peeled away to expose yet another layer underneath.

A few people attend the temple once and then never go back. Some of them do this because they think of the temple as a spiritual "vaccination" that only needs to be injected once in a lifetime. Others were so unprepared for the experience that they were shocked by the foreignness of it, and now they have no desire to go back again. If you're one of those people, try to

overcome your reservations. The temple gives you great blessings the first time you attend, but also blesses you each time
you return. Here are some suggestions that may help as you
plan to continue your spiritual growth associated with the
temple.

• Why Go Back?

Regular temple attendance results in a triple blessing.
First, you are blessed because of the charity you show when
you serve as a proxy for others. Second, each time you attend,
new insights and understandings can be opened to you,
resulting in personal spiritual growth and maturity. Third, the
temple is a haven of peace that can calm you in times of
trouble. If you go to the temple for no other reason than to take
yourself away from the cares of the world, your trip to the
temple will be well worth the time you spend there.

• A Place to Receive Personal Revelation

As Latter-day Saints, we believe in personal revelation.
Each of us has the right to petition God for comfort and understanding. Each of us has the right to ask for spiritual help in
making decisions or solving problems. If we follow the commandments and keep ourselves close to the Spirit of the Lord,
this personal revelation will come when we need it.

Because the temple is the house of the Lord, it is a good
place to feel His Spirit and feel close to Him. After participating
in temple ordinances, patrons often take advantage of the
celestial room to sit quietly and pray. It isn't appropriate to
kneel or to pray aloud or to read in the celestial room, but
patrons may spend as much time as they want in quiet meditation. These are the times when the Lord really does speak to
His children, comfort them, and answer their prayers. If you
need comfort during times of trial, or if you have important
decisions to make, consider taking your problems to the
temple.

• Family History and Genealogy

You may go back to the temple because your ancestors
want to see you there. A good friend of ours was told in her
patriarchal blessing that there was a great work for her to do
in finding the names of her ancestors and in doing the work for

them in the temple. She firmly believes that her ancestors might have been doing a little "pushing" from the spirit world to get her into the Church so that they could continue their progress on the other side. Perhaps your ancestors had a similar influence on your own conversion.

If you are the first convert in your family, there is a pretty good chance that some of the research for your ancestors has not been done. Many of those ancestors might be anxiously awaiting your help. Think about visiting your local family history center and getting started on this important work. Those who immerse themselves in genealogy are always glad they did.

 • **Temple Missions**

In chapter 8, you learned about missionary work. In that chapter, we told you that one option for retired couples is to serve temple missions. These callings usually last from 6 to 24 months. The couples are assigned to a particular temple. They live near the temple and work there 4 to 6 days each week.

It is a real joy to work with these temple missionary couples. Many of them are in their 70s or their 80s, yet they work a schedule that would put many younger people to shame. It is not uncommon to see them leaving the temple at 10:30 P.M., only to see them back at 6:00 A.M. the next morning. Elderly temple workers have their share of illness and other age-related problems, but they seem to have a zest for life that is unmatched in other people their age. Working in the temple seems to magnify their strength, bring increased satisfaction into their lives, and bring them closer together as couples.

If you are approaching retirement age and are in reasonable health, consider serving a temple mission. If you're nervous about going, you can agree to serve for just six months, and then you can extend your mission when you find out how much you enjoy it. If retirement is still down the road, start planning now so that you and your spouse can have this great experience. One of Clark's coworkers in the Washington Temple said, "I feel guilty calling this a mission. We've had so much fun and made so many friends that I prefer to think of it as a vacation."

A Convert's Questions

Why are you baptizing all my relatives and making them Mormons?

The idea of proxy ordinances raises the hackles of many outside the Church who believe that the Church is trying to steal all their dead relatives and turn them into Latter-day Saints. The truth is that nobody can be "turned into" anything against his will. The ordinances performed in the temple open certain doors for a soul, but the person in question still has to choose to enter those doors. It doesn't matter how much temple work you do for your Great-Aunt Eliza—if she doesn't want to join the Church, the temple ordinances you do in her behalf won't make any difference.

You can get a million letters in the mail, offering you to visit the Such-and-Such Resort for a fun-filled free vacation. Sometimes it seems that you get the whole million of them in one day! But unless you take advantage of the offer, it's as though you never received the invitation. It's the same thing with temple ordinances—unless you accept them, it's as though they were never done for you. Your Great-Aunt Eliza has everything to gain and nothing to lose by having the ordinance work done for her. That's why Church members are so enthusiastic about doing it.

Latter-day Saints are under no delusions that everyone who has ordinances performed in his behalf is going to accept the work. On the contrary, we're taught that people enter the spirit world with the same personalities they had when they died. The people who would have been receptive to the gospel when they were alive are the ones who are likely to receive the gospel on the other side. We have had many feelings while working in the temple that led us to believe the work we were doing was accepted by the person for whom we were acting as proxy. Other times, we have had no such feelings. Because Church members can't know who would accept the gospel and who wouldn't, we make every effort to at least give everyone the opportunity to accept the gospel if he wants it. When people on the other side reject the ordinances that are done in their behalf, at least the Saints who attended the temple for them will benefit from performing that act of charity.

When non-Mormons complain about the temple work that is being done in behalf of their ancestors, Church members have trouble understanding what all the fuss is about. If the doctrines and authority of the Church aren't legitimate, any work that is done in the temple isn't going to do any good. The ordinances will be null and void, and the dead relatives will be entirely unaffected by the work that has been done for them.

On the other hand, if the ordinances are true and valid, why wouldn't the complainers want us to bless their relatives? They should be lined up at the temple doors, asking that the work be done for them and for their ancestors—just in case.

You can't have it both ways. Either the ordinances are legitimate, or they aren't. Either they have the power to bless the lives of those who receive them, or they don't. It's a no-lose situation for men and women who have the work done in their behalf. Either they'll be greatly blessed by the ordinances, or they'll be in exactly the same situation they were in before the ordinances were performed.

LDS temples vary greatly in terms of their external appearance. Are they the same inside, and are there some temples that are better than others?

Despite their external appearance, all of the latter-day temples are identical in terms of their function. Smaller temples are just as legitimate as large temples—they just have fewer rooms. For example, a large temple may have six rooms where endowments are presented, while a smaller temple will only have one or two. In 1997, the Church announced a program of building "small" temples that can be added to existing structures such as stake centers or that can be built on smaller pieces of property. The goal of this program is to bring temples closer to the members so that members in remote areas can attend the temple without traveling excessive distances. You can rest assured that these small temples will allow the performance of all necessary temple ordinances.

There is some variation in temples, based on when they were built. In at least two temples in the Church, Salt Lake and Manti (Utah), the patrons move through a number of rooms as they participate in the endowment, with each room decorated to represent a step in our eternal journey. Newer temples tend to have smaller rooms, but the patrons stay in one room for most of the endowment ceremony.

In general, modern temples are designed so that the most sacred ordinances are performed on the higher floors of the temple. As we perform progressive ordinances we move upward, symbolizing the way we get closer to the Lord as we progress in the kingdom. The baptistry is always located at the lowest point of the temple. This represents the symbolic act of burial during baptism, and also reminds us that Christ descended below all things to redeem us.

The higher floors of the temple contain the endowment rooms, the celestial room (representing the highest kingdom of heaven), and the sealing rooms. Larger temples may also contain an assembly room (also called the priesthood room), that is used occasionally for special meetings.

Additional rooms include the offices of the temple presidency, waiting areas, the family file office, and dressing rooms. Larger temples usually have cafeterias, so that patrons spending long hours in the temple can purchase meals without leaving the temple.

Although some members may have sentimental attachments to certain temples, all temples provide for performing the same ordinances and are all equally valid and important in the eyes of the Lord.

What do I keep hearing about some kind of temple underwear?

When people work in the temple, they dress in clothing that is worn only in the temple. This clothing is mostly white, which is a symbol of purity. The uniform clothing represents equality, too. Because everyone dresses alike inside the temple, everyone in the temple is equal. Once you enter temple doors, it doesn't matter how rich you are, or how famous, or how poor and nondescript. The only factor that is important in temple worship is that those who enter the temple are spiritually worthy to be there.

When you receive your own endowment, you will wear ceremonial clothing, including sacred white underclothing known as garments. Before you leave the temple that first time, you'll take off the ceremonial outer clothing, but you'll wear the garments out of the temple under your regular clothes. Your garments are designed to replace the underwear that you wore into the temple. You will promise to wear these garments for the rest of your life, day and night, as a constant reminder of the sacred covenants you made in the temple.

When new Church members first learn about garments, their eyes often get as wide as saucers. But once you see garments for the first time, you'll see that the concept isn't as terrible as it sounds. You can choose from numerous styles and fabrics, some of which are pretty close to underwear that you may be wearing now. You don't have to keep them on when you bathe, or when you have marital relations, or when you do certain other activities. You don't have to wear them to the doctor's office. You don't have to burn them if they touch the floor. The instruction you receive as part of your endowment will explain proper care of your garments, and when you should and should not wear them. Once you get used to them, garments are actually quite comfortable and should interfere very little with any of your regular activities. It will only be a short time until garments feel natural to you, and you will not want to go back to the "pre-temple" underwear that you used previously.

You may be forced to make some changes to your wardrobe after you start wearing garments. This is because garments cover certain portions of your body that extreme fashions often expose. Thus, wearing garments properly will also have an added benefit (you might not consider it that!) of forcing you to dress more modestly. Look around at the temple-going members of your ward. Do you notice a certain modesty in their dress? Do you see many sleeveless dresses, short skirts, low necklines, tank-tops, skimpy shorts, or bare midriffs? Some members who are overly concerned with fashion or comfort will modify their garments so they may wear some types of clothing. Similarly, some members look for any excuse to remove their garments, such as when they're washing the car or mowing the lawn. This is wrong. We encourage you therefore not to participate in either of these practices, because they show a disregard for the covenants you made in the temple.

Garments are made by a subsidiary of the Church known as Beehive Clothing Mills. There are usually Beehive Clothing outlets within or close to the larger temples, where you can go to buy garments or other ceremonial clothing that is used in the temple. You can also order them by phone and have the garments mailed to you. Although you do not need to have your own set of temple clothing if you attend a full-sized temple (you can rent it in the temple for a modest fee), it is nice to have a set if you are planning to attend the temple often.

As already mentioned, garments serve as a reminder to you of the covenants you made in the temple—those things you promised to do, and the rewards the Lord promised you in return if you are faithful. Garments also serve as a form of spiritual protection from the evils of the world. If you are faithful to your covenants, they will serve to protect you from temptation and other evils.

There is some debate as to whether garments provide a physical protection as well. We will not take sides in this issue, but will leave this discussion with a statement by President Spencer W. Kimball: "Temple garments afford protection. . . . Though generally I think our protection is a mental, spiritual, moral one, yet I am convinced that there could be and undoubtedly have been many cases where there has been, through faith, an actual physical protection, so we must not minimize that possibility" (*The Teachings of Spencer W. Kimball,* p. 539).

If my spouse is not a member, should I still go to the temple?

There's no easy answer to this question. Every situation is different. Whether you should go to the temple without your spouse depends entirely on who your spouse is—and who you are.

If you joined the Church without your spouse, there is already somewhat of a gulf between you and your spouse because of the Church. The Church takes a huge chunk of your time and your commitment. This is a justifiable cause for jealousy from a spouse who didn't count on your divided loyalties when the two of you got married.

Receiving your endowment could widen that gulf between you and your spouse. The temple covenants you make will underscore the differences between you and may make it harder for you to live in a situation where you're "unequally yoked." Similarly, your spouse may find it harder to live with you. After all, when you go to the temple, you're going to change all the way down to your underwear.

A litmus test for this situation would be to ask yourself how well your spouse supports your current activity level in the Church. If he or she is very supportive and has respected your newly found beliefs, it's entirely possible that he would support your decision to attend the temple. If your spouse resents the time you are involved with Church activities or ridicules your beliefs, perhaps you might be better off to wait before taking such a step.

Other factors might be your age, the length of time you have been married, and the possibility that your spouse might eventually join the Church. If you're still young, have been married quite recently, or if there's a possibility your spouse will be baptized within a year or two, you might be better off just to be patient and see what happens before you take such a big step alone.

The whole idea of attending the temple is to build eternal families. If your decision to attend the temple destroys your current family, you may be taking a step in the wrong direction. The Lord knows your heart and will bless you, even if you have to postpone the blessings of the temple for a short season. Before making any decision, you will need to have an honest discussion with your spouse and your bishop. Once you have made a decision, have the Lord confirm that decision through fasting and prayer.

Should I attend the temple if I'm not married yet?

The answer to this question depends upon who you are.

Because young men are more likely to go on missions than young women, men generally tend to receive their endowments before they reach age 20. This isn't usually the case with women, however. Young women aren't prohibited from getting their endowments at this age, and some choose to do so. But traditionally young women who do not serve full-time missions are likely to wait to go to the temple until they marry. If they reach a mature age without getting married, they may then choose to go to the temple alone, rather than not to go at all.

In general, we suggest that any unmarried person should attend the temple when he believes he is in a position to appreciate the experience and when he is convinced he is mature enough to understand the seriousness of the covenants he will make. Some of these covenants are hard for single people to keep. The covenant regarding chastity strengthens the commitment to chastity and high moral standards with the opposite sex. Thus, the consequences of moral sins will be greater if you have made temple covenants.

As with any important decision, make your first trip to the temple a matter of fasting and prayer. Also make sure to counsel with your bishop and other ward leaders whose opinions you respect.

As a convert, why do I have to wait a year before I can attend the temple?

We have all seen converts who come into the Church going 90 miles per hour and act as though they have been members their entire lives. These members are usually anxious to get to the temple and often count the days until their year's "probation" is over so they can finally receive their temple blessings.

The one-year waiting period is designed to make sure converts really understand the gospel and to make sure their testimonies are solid enough that they will remain active in the Church. Many people embrace the gospel and are excited about it for a while, but they have no real roots and no real understanding of certain gospel principles. When friends ridicule them, or when they get distracted by other things, or when they learn of doctrines they cannot accept or commandments they cannot obey, they fall into inactivity. It would not benefit these converts to experience the temple shortly after their baptism. Not only would they not understand much of the proceedings, but their fate would be worse if they went to the temple and then fell away from the Church than it would if they had never made their temple covenants.

Progressing in the kingdom of God is like climbing a ladder. Each time we take a step, our vision of the world expands and we understand more. But for each step, we rise that much higher off the earth and increase the potential of eternal injury if we fall off the ladder. We want new converts to expand their vision of eternity by attending the temple. But we also want to make sure their footing on the gospel ladder is solid enough that they will not fall off and suffer eternal injuries.

I've heard that I cannot attend the temple if I have a tattoo. Is this true?

We're not sure which is more outrageous—the crazy stories nonmembers tell about the temple or the even crazier stories that our own members sometimes spread. This is just one of many silly myths about the temple we have heard from our own members. (Another weird piece of folklore is the idea that Church members have to always be touching their garments, even when they're sitting in the bathtub.)

It is true that the typical Mormon lifestyle probably does not involve spending a lot of time at the local tattoo parlor, but there are certainly converts who get tattoos prior to joining the Church. There are also lifelong Church members who got tattoos during the "wild" years of their youth, before settling down to Church activity. Their tattoos do not stop them from going to the temple as patrons, or even from becoming temple workers later in life.

The standards for entering the temple were outlined in the previous section on preparing to attend. The same questions apply for the newest convert or for a lifetime member. Before you believe any of the wild rumors that circulate about the temple, have a discussion with a trusted ward friend. Life is too short to entertain all the silly falsehoods you will hear about the temple.

What if I get sealed to my spouse, and then we get divorced?

If you're worried enough about your relationship to even ask that question, maybe you ought to postpone any temple visits until things are more solid.

The good news, though, is that once you go to the temple, the odds are in your favor. People who have been sealed in the temple are statistically much less likely to be divorced. Usually these couples understand they have the potential to be together through eternity, and they make an extra effort to develop an eternal relationship.

You might say that temple marriages may have a higher chance of success because the participants have their eyes on a higher goal from the start. Rather than run for the nearest attorney at the first sign of trouble, they try to work out their problems and be worthy of their sealing.

Despite the statistics, there are times when even temple marriages end in divorce. This usually happens when one spouse has been unfaithful, but it can happen for other reasons as well. In this situation, the couple will first execute the legal procedures to obtain a civil divorce. But even after the civil divorce is final, the temple sealing remains in effect.

If the couple wants to nullify the sealing as well, there is a procedure that can be followed to permit a temple sealing to be canceled. This is not a common procedure, and it must be approved by the President of the Church. The name for this procedure is a "cancellation of temple sealing," but is often incorrectly referred to as a "temple divorce." Cancellations of sealings are usually not granted until immediately before one of the parties plans to go back to the temple to be sealed to someone else. Even if you are the innocent party in a divorce situation, it may take some time to get your cancellation approved. Cancellations are not simply an exercise in paperwork but are obviously treated as a serious matter.

Meet with your bishop if you are having marital problems. He will either counsel you himself, or will recommend a qualified counselor—or perhaps he will do both. If, despite all your efforts, a divorce is the final result, your bishop can explain the procedures and options available to you in terms of your temple sealing blessings.

Grandpa Jones was a horse thief. Do I have to be sealed to him?

One of the reasons many people are attracted to the Church is because of its doctrine of eternal families. In a family where there is true love between husband and wife and children, the idea of an eternal family unit holds great appeal.

Sadly, not all of us come from perfect family situations. If your parents were divorced, or you grew up in an abusive family situation, the idea of being sealed to your family may seem like a punishment rather than a reward. There have been many people who have joined the Church despite the doctrine of eternal families rather than because of it.

Perhaps your situation isn't as extreme as that. Perhaps, for the most part, you love your family. Except there's one relative who doesn't like you, or has cheated you, or has done some other terrible injustice to you during the course of your life. As much as you've tried to forgive and forget, you can't see spending an hour with that person, much less all of eternity.

Odds are, you won't.

Many Church leaders have reminded us of our responsibility to perform temple ordinances for all the people who will ever live on the earth. Part of these ordinances includes the sealing together of the entire family of man, all the way back to Adam and Eve. It's not our job to judge whether our ancestors deserve these blessings. Our job is simply to see that the opportunities are given.

You may do Grandpa Jones's temple work for him, but that doesn't mean he's going to be tied to you forever. On the contrary, if Grandpa Jones did not repent of his evil ways, you're not going to spend eternity with him no matter what temple work was done on his behalf. If he *does* repent, however, he'll be a different person from the Grandpa Jones you know and loathe.

We know that the Lord will judge all men fairly. God loves Grandpa Jones despite his wickedness, but God also loves you. You will not be forced to endure an eternity of unhappiness, just to keep your family intact. If your family situation is a bad one, God certainly has the power to graft you into another family tree. This already happens when a child is adopted by

Mormon parents and then sealed to the new family. It can also happen for you.

Those of us with less than perfect family situations will have to develop some extra faith to help us believe that somehow God will work things out. If this issue troubles you, talk with your bishop or take your concerns to God in fasting and in prayer.

10

WHERE DO I TURN
FOR HELP?

Being members of The Church of Jesus Christ of Latter-day Saints doesn't exempt us from the problems of life. As a new convert, you'll find that you're just as susceptible to illness and death as you always were. You're just as likely to suffer the pangs of misfortune. You're just as likely to be the victim of crime, accident, or unfairness. You're just as likely to lose a job or to become physically incapacitated so you can no longer do your work. And although your chances of marital problems will drastically decrease if you're sealed in the temple, being a member of the Church is no silver bullet. If you and your spouse aren't equally committed to making your marriage work, you will not be immune from marital problems or even divorce.

One of the teachings of the gospel is that at times problems in the life of a good person may be placed there for the good of the person—because it is through adversity that we grow. While most of us are not spiritually mature enough that we are actually grateful when problems come our way, we can at least take consolation from the fact that our dark cloud will eventually have a silver lining.

Our membership in the Church gives us the spiritual tools to cope with adversity, but it also provides a support system made up of real flesh-and-blood people and the programs they run. You have not been left alone to deal with the vicissitudes of life—you now have a ready-made group of people to love you and support you in times of trouble. This chapter covers where you should go for help—and when.

Those Who Help

Spiritual Resources

Sometimes problems come to us for no apparent reason. Other times they're given to us for a purpose. Without trials and tribulations in our lives, we would never grow spiritually because we would have no need to depend on God for help.

When trials come, the first thing we should do is turn to God in prayer. Answers to prayer can reveal to us why a particular difficulty has come to us at a particular time, and can also show us how to resolve that difficulty. Through answered prayers, God can show us the shortcomings that may have caused our problems, or comfort us with the knowledge that our problems came to us through no wrongdoing of our own. God can solve problems for us, he can show us how to solve our own problems, or he can make the difficulties of life easier to bear. Do not underestimate the power of spiritual resources during difficult times.

There are several avenues open to us as far as spiritual resources are concerned, but prayer is foremost among them. We can pray in secret for ourselves, and we can have others pray on our behalf. The prayer rolls in the temples have been established to give Church members the opportunity to pray for themselves or others in need. In times of trial, you may want to call a temple and have your name or the name of a loved one put on the temple prayer roll.

If you have a temple recommend, you can go to the temple and pray for guidance. If you don't have a temple recommend, that doesn't mean you can't have the same results. Kathy once went to the temple with a problem, only to realize when she saw the empty temple parking lot that it was a Monday, and the temple was closed. She prayed in the parking lot and received the answer she was looking for. Remember—the location of your prayer is less important than the content of it.

Fasting is another vital spiritual resource. Through the discipline of fasting, we make ourselves spiritually open to receive answers we might not otherwise receive. If health problems prohibit you from fasting for any length of time, a fast lasting even just an hour or two can be equally effective if it is done in the right spirit.

Scripture study is another tool that is available to help us in times of need. The answers to any problem can be found in the scriptures, if only you look for them. We once knew an inspired Relief Society teacher who began her lesson on scripture study by having every class member write down the problem that plagued her most in her life. She told class members to be specific and to write down exactly what was troubling them. She then passed a hat and had each member randomly draw a piece of paper from the hat. A miracle occurred in that classroom when the women who had randomly drawn those pieces of paper saw that their specific questions were answered by the scriptures they had drawn. Most of us don't have the faith of that Relief Society teacher, but we can learn from her lesson that the scriptures have an answer to every problem that may afflict us.

Priesthood blessings can also offer spiritual strength, as long as they're used correctly. Inspired guidance can be given through the power of these priesthood blessings. It is wise to remember, however, that priesthood blessings are not one-a-day vitamins. They are given on unusual occasions when divine intervention is needed to restore health or solve a specific problem. Your home teacher will be happy to give you a priesthood blessing if you believe you need one, but priesthood blessings were never intended to be used instead of aspirin at the first sign of a cough or a sniffle, and they weren't designed to take the place of a visit to the family doctor. Nor should they be looked upon as spiritual pick-me-ups to be dispensed during monthly home teaching visits. Priesthood blessings are powerful tools, and they should be respected as such.

Home and Visiting Teachers

When home teachers and visiting teachers function the way the program was designed to do, they're a wonderful resource in helping you to solve your problems. These are

Church members whose stewardship is to love you and care for you. They represent the Lord as His hands to do work on your behalf—whether that work be in the form of lessons your family needs, companionship in times of loneliness, helping hands when you need a strong back, counselors when you are trying to see your way through a dilemma, or a pot of soup when you have the flu. Home teachers and visiting teachers should be vitally interested in you and should be ready to help you when you have difficulties in your life.

Your quorum leader or Relief Society president tried to choose home teachers and visiting teachers that were best suited to your needs. This doesn't mean the teachers who have been assigned to you will always be perfect. We must constantly remind ourselves that the Church is a volunteer organization, and people have the agency to fail as well as to succeed.

If your home teachers or visiting teachers fall down on the job, they may just need a little encouragement. Call your home teacher and invite him to teach your family a specific lesson this month. Call your visiting teacher and tell her you need a visit. Show your appreciation to home teachers and visiting teachers when they do come and make it easy for them to do so.

If you've done all you can do and still don't receive your home teaching or visiting teaching visits, talk to your quorum leader or Relief Society president. It's a sad fact of life that there aren't enough reliable home teachers and visiting teachers to go around, but if your family is experiencing problems and needs the extra attention a good home teacher or visiting teacher can give, your auxiliary leader can try different home teachers or visiting teachers until you find a companionship that more fully meets your needs.

Quorum or Auxiliary Leaders

There may be times when you'd feel more comfortable going to your quorum leader or Relief Society president with a problem than you would taking the problem to your home or visiting teachers. Perhaps you don't have a rapport with your home or visiting teachers. Perhaps your home or visiting teachers are part of the problem. Perhaps the problem is so sensitive that you want as few people to know about it as possible. If for some reason you don't feel comfortable going to your home or visiting teachers with your problems, your auxiliary leaders should be next on the list.

Ward or Stake Specialists

Sometimes, members of your ward or stake may be called as specialists over an area where you need help. Ward librarians can help you find research materials for gospel-related subjects. Ward or stake family history specialists can teach you how to begin tracing your family's genealogy. Ward or stake employment specialists can help you find employment. Ward welfare specialists may teach you how to plan and maintain your food storage, how to grind wheat and bake bread, or how to manage your finances. Ward or stake cultural arts specialists may help you put on that play you've been writing or get you involved in local theater productions. Relief Society compassionate service leaders can tell you who in the ward needs a helping hand if you're looking for an outlet for service you can perform. Choir directors can help you learn to lead music, and organists can give you tips on how to play the organ.

In every ward, there's somebody who's an expert on just about anything you need to learn. Although you wouldn't want to ask for somebody to give you a professional service for free, you can probably ask for advice and help on Church-related issues. If you're unsure whether it would be appropriate to ask a ward member to give you advice, ask your quorum leader or Relief Society president—or counsel with your trusty home and visiting teachers.

Bishop

On rare occasions it's appropriate to go to the bishop when you have a problem. If you have committed a sin that needs confessing, if you're having marital conflicts or financial difficulties, or if you're having a disagreement with a ward member that the two of you can't reconcile on your own, the bishop is the person you'll want to consult. He is the "common judge in Israel," and the buck stops with him. However, please remember that your bishop has several hundred other sheep in his fold. If everyone went to see him whenever a problem arose, he wouldn't have time to go to work or spend time with his family or perform any of his other duties.

Every ward has a handful of "squeaky wheels" who take almost all the bishop's counseling time. Don't be too quick to become one of those squeaky wheels. If you really need to counsel with the bishop, make an appointment through his executive secretary. Unless it's a dire emergency, don't call him directly, and especially not late at night. On the other hand, no bishop worth his salt would deny that losing a little sleep is well worth a life saved or a divorce prevented. The point is, God has appointed bishops to be used but not abused.

We once had a bishop who was fond of saying that the Holy Ghost goes to bed at 10:00 P.M. That was a discreet way of saying he didn't want to get phone calls after that hour. It's amazing how many people will call a bishop at 1:30 A.M., or even later, with a problem that could just as easily wait until tomorrow—or next week. Don't demand any more of your bishop than you'd want to give if you were the bishop of your ward. Remember, he isn't on a salary. He performs his duties out of love for the Lord and for the ward members. Don't take advantage of his generosity.

When you do go to a bishop to ask for counsel, it is wise to remember that your bishop has been given stewardship over you. He is entitled to receive personal revelation and inspiration regarding you and your situation. Do not take his counsel lightly. If necessary, he may consult with the stake president on your behalf.

Stake President

Most Church members go a lifetime without ever seeking the advice of the stake president due to personal difficulties. But on extremely rare occasions it is appropriate to take problems to a stake president that would normally be taken to the bishop. This could happen when a bishop has not been responsive to a ward member's needs, if the member has a sin to confess but feels uneasy going to the bishop, when a bishop suggests that the member seek the advice of the stake president, or if the bishop is part of the problem.

Just remember—your bishop is responsible for hundreds of Church members, but your stake president is responsible for thousands. He doesn't have the time or the energy to make a hobby out of your personal challenges. If you absolutely must see the stake president, the rules are the same as for making an appointment with the bishop. Do it by calling the stake president's executive secretary to set up an appointment. And unless it's a life-or-death situation, don't even think about calling in the middle of the night.

When you make an appointment with the stake president—or with the bishop, for that matter—keep it. Sometimes a stake president may drive for more than an hour to get to the place that was determined for you to meet him. But even if the appointment is in his own home, he has set aside other needs or even canceled other commitments to meet with you. The least you can do to is to do your best to meet at his convenience rather than yours, to keep the appointments you've made with him (and to arrive promptly for those appointments!), and to show appreciation for the effort he's made on your behalf.

Types of Help Provided

In addition to acts of compassionate service by ward members and visits by your home and visiting teachers, there are several means of counseling and aid that are available to members of the Church. Among them are financial aid, personal and family counseling, and help for those who have committed serious transgressions.

Financial Advice and Support

Members of The Church of Jesus Christ of Latter-day Saints are participants in what may be the only welfare system in the world that works. Church members contribute fast offerings monthly according to their ability to pay. When Church members need financial assistance, they can have short-term help given to them through the bishop or his appointed representative.

If you find yourself in severe financial circumstances, you

should try to dig yourself out of the situation. If you find that you're stuck, go to your family members. If they are at all able to help you, they should be the resource of first resort. If they can't help you, you should make an appointment with the bishop and discuss your situation with him.

Instead of telling the bishop what you want, tell the bishop your situation and let him determine what the ward can do for you. The bishop may determine that what you need is financial counseling, which he can provide to you in a meeting or series of meetings over an extended period. The Church strongly counsels that its members stay out of debt. Your bishop may focus on a way for you to reduce your indebtedness and reform your financial excesses.

The bishop may determine that your greatest need during a time of crisis is food. If groceries are your need, he will probably go through the Relief Society president to get supplies from a bishop's storehouse to feed your family.

If your family is being fed through the bishop's storehouse, it is appropriate to tell the bishop or the Relief Society president what allergies or food sensitivities your family members may have, so grocery lists can be planned that fill your needs. But if you have expensive tastes, it is not appropriate to expect the ward to indulge them. We once had a friend who said the biggest challenge she faced as a Relief Society president was when she had to go to the bishop's storehouse to buy steaks that had been demanded by a family in the ward, and then go home to feed hot dogs to her own husband and children.

On some occasions, fast offering funds are used to pay the bills of families who are experiencing an emergency situation. The bishop will not give you cash but will instead direct his financial clerk to write checks to your creditors. Perhaps he'll authorize a check to buy a new appliance, if a good used one isn't available from a member of the ward. On rare occasions, a mortgage payment may be made for a month or even two. However, it's unrealistic to expect that the ward will foot a large monthly mortgage payment while the breadwinner of your family is unemployed for six months or a year. If unemployment seems to be a long-term prospect, it would not be unreasonable for the bishop to recommend you sell your home and find less expensive living quarters. The fast-offering funds are not an open checkbook that is available to be used at your discretion.

Financial assistance that is given to you in emergency situations is not a loan. It doesn't have to be paid back when you are financially solvent. However, it is hoped that beneficiaries of financial aid will remember what was given to them when the time comes for them to pay their monthly fast offering. The Church asks that its members give generously when Fast Sunday comes around.

Personal, Marriage, and Family Counseling

For general information about marriage and family-related problems, there are resources available through the Church. Ask your home teachers or visiting teachers for a lesson concerning a facet of home relationships that seems to be an issue for you, or see if your local Church bookstore has books that can be of help.

However, if there is a crucial problem in your marriage or family life, or if you are having serious personal problems and need help, it is appropriate to seek counsel from the bishop. Be mindful when you do this that the bishop is not a family therapist. Unless he is a psychologist by profession he is not trained in psychology, and he probably hasn't had a single class that would help him deal with your situation. But despite his lack of formal training, he is entitled to receive spiritual inspiration on your behalf. His counsel may help show you ways to strengthen your own emotional situation or bolster your marriage, or he may help you find ways to get along with your children.

It is important to remember that the bishop's priority is to keep your family together. It is not likely that he will counsel you to seek a divorce, no matter how hopeless the situation may be. Nor should you expect him to take sides in a family squabble—no matter how right you may believe you are— unless you or your spouse have been convicted of physical or sexual abuse. The bishop has been called to be the spiritual leader of every member of your family, and he can't do that if he has thrown himself in one warring camp or the other.

If your personal or family problems are complex and of long

duration, the bishop may recommend that you seek out a family counselor through LDS Social Services. These counselors are trained to give therapy and counsel that will conform to Church teachings, but they are not infallible. Unlike your bishop, they do not have a spiritual stewardship over you that would allow them to receive inspiration on your behalf. Nevertheless, they are available to Church members who need help on an individual or family basis.

Help for Those Who Commit Spiritual Transgressions

Where you go for help with spiritual transgressions depends on the spiritual transgression. If you've committed a sin against another person—if you've stolen something from the grocery store or gossiped about a ward member or done something along those lines—the best thing to do is to pray and ask forgiveness, and then go immediately to the person you've wronged, ask for forgiveness and offer restitution for what was taken or damaged. If the person you've wronged accepts your apology, and if you don't commit the sin again, that sin can be put behind you.

If the sin was a major transgression, however, the ward member should seek the bishop's counsel. Sexual sins and any form of abuse are examples of grievous sins that need reconciliation from Church leaders as well as from the victims. If you are guilty of any grave sin, make an appointment to see the bishop as soon as possible. And if you aren't sure whether a sin is serious enough to merit a visit with the bishop, it's better to err on the side of caution.

A Convert's Questions

I'm embarrassed to take help that is offered, even when I desperately need it. What should I do?

This is a common situation in the Church. People often feel more comfortable stepping in and offering service than being on the receiving end. We once had a saintly Relief Society president who fell from a horse and broke her back in three places. It was nearly a month before she accepted any form of compassionate service from ward members—and only then because ward members finally stopped taking no for an answer. Even then she was so accustomed to being the giver rather than the receiver that she sneaked half the meals that were taken to her family over to other families because she thought they needed the food more than her family did.

What we need to remember that it is often a service to allow people to perform acts of kindness for us. Sister Merriwether down the street may need to provide soup to soothe your strep throat even more than you need to eat the soup. It's a form of pride to deny that we need help when we're in desperate need of it. If you suffer from that kind of pride, pray for the humility to be able to receive as well as to give. Then practice the art of saying, "Thank you. You're a lifesaver. It's so kind of you to help." That's what mirrors are for.

And while you're standing in front of the mirror, practice telling people what you need. If somebody volunteers to bring you a pan of lasagna, but seven other women have already put pans of lasagna in your refrigerator, it isn't considered rude to say, "We have tons of food, but I sure could use somebody to throw a couple of loads of laundry in the washing machine for me," or, "I could use the company far more than I need the meal. Would you mind visiting me for a few minutes instead?" Just remember to suggest an alternative that would cost no more time or money or effort than the person was already planning to spend. If somebody offers you a plate of brownies, don't suggest a three-course dinner.

How do I ask for help?

Ideally, members in the ward who have stewardship over you should see your need and step in without your ever having to ask. But Church members are human, and sometimes they fail to see needs that should be glaringly obvious.

When you experience problems and need help from the ward, what you should do depends on what the problem is. In most circumstances the first place you should turn should be your home teachers or visiting teachers. They are the ones who are specifically assigned to care for you both spiritually and temporally.

If you do not have a rapport with your home teachers or visiting teachers, the place to go would be to a friend in the ward who could be conduit between you and the Relief Society president or your quorum leader. If you don't receive satisfaction that way, you can go directly to the Relief Society president or your quorum leader. Go to the bishop as a last resort. He has plenty of other people making demands on his time, and the best way for him and the ward to deal with members' problems is through the chain of command the prophets have set up for us. Even then, the bishop can help with immediate, short-term needs, but help over the long haul is the responsibility of quorum and Relief Society leaders.

The circumstances of your problem will be relayed to the people who can help you, strictly on a need-to-know basis. If you've broken your leg, your situation will naturally be broadcast to more ward members than if you've had to declare bankruptcy. Don't assume that everyone in the ward is familiar with your circumstances. If close friends fail to help you in a time of need, they may not have been told you had a problem and needed their help.

How much help can I expect?

Earlier in this book, we compared a ward to a bathtub full of water. During the normal course of life, there are times that every Church member drains water from that tub by accepting service from others. But nobody has exclusive rights to the water in the tub. Nobody can expect to have his needs met constantly, without ever adding water back into the water supply.

Ideally, every member of the Church should be ready to drop things at a moment's notice to provide service whenever it's needed, but life doesn't always work that way. Realistically speaking, there are only a finite number of hours of service a ward can be expected to provide during the course of a month—and those hours have to be divided among all the members of the ward. There may be a time in your life where some catastrophe overtakes you and when your needs will consume quite a bit of the ward members' time. This crisis may take weeks or even months to resolve. But the ward can't be expected to provide daily care to a chronic invalid forever, or make monthly house payments for a family whose bread-winner can't find a job to suit him. Eventually, service that is given to you will be given at the cost of service that would otherwise be given to others. This could cause resentment and bitterness.

There's a saying in the Church that may be of help here. When trouble comes, first try to solve the problem on your own. Then turn to members of your family for help. Only when all else fails should members turn to the Church. This is especially true when your problems are of long-term duration. Ward members may be delighted to watch your children every day for a week when you first get home from the hospital, but it's unreasonable to expect them to watch your children every day after school so you can work a later shift.

Look upon service that is done to you as a privilege rather than a right. And be ever mindful that the ward needs you to add water to the communal bathtub, and not just to drain it. Even invalids can find ways to perform service, and Church members are expected to give as well as to take. Don't ever take service that you wouldn't give to somebody else.

You may want to consider one more thing. Before you ask for service, ask yourself if you really need help or if you just want it because you think you deserve it. We once knew a visiting teacher who was diagnosed as having a life-threatening illness (wrongly, as it turned out). As she lay moaning in bed, one of the women whom she served as a visiting teacher called and asked that a meal be brought in that night because she was recovering from surgery. The visiting teacher was surprised by the request because the woman had a house full of teenagers, any one of whom should have been able to cook. Nevertheless, she got up from her sickbed and prepared the meal for the family in need. When the meal was taken over, it was accepted by a teenage daughter because the woman who was recovering from surgery was out playing tennis. Needless to say, the visiting teacher felt less than charitable about the act of service she had been called upon to perform.

My bishop asked me to work to pay for the help I was given from the Church. Why did he do this?

Church leaders have found that taking welfare without giving something in exchange can be devastating for the person who is on the receiving end. The loss of self-esteem that is experienced by the recipient can sometimes be worse than the original lack of food or clothing or shelter. Thus, when the recipient is physically able to work, the bishop will usually ask that time be served at Church welfare facilities such as bishops' storehouses or canneries, or in performing some other labor that will benefit other members of the Church. This is not a punishment; in fact, most Church members who are given the opportunity to receive "workfare" consider it a blessing. People who are asked to work will not be pushed beyond their physical capabilities. In fact, they may be given a list of possible work assignments and allowed to choose an activity that makes use of an interest or a skill.

If you end up accepting an assignment to work in your local meetinghouse, don't worry that people who happen to see you working will know you're on Church welfare. On the contrary, most people will naturally assume that you've volunteered to plant the garden or clean the ward kitchen or do whatever task you've been assigned to do out of the goodness of your heart. You don't need to worry that the bishop is going to tell anyone you're getting help from the Church. In fact, if anyone talks behind your back, they'll be telling their friends that they saw Brother So-and-So digging out that dangerous old tree stump on his day off, and isn't he a terrific person for doing it!

Sometimes I see people who have problems but aren't getting any help. I'm not a ward leader. What should I do?

In every ward, there are people who fall through the cracks. Sometimes there are so many "squeaky wheels" in a ward that ward members who aren't as vocal or whose needs aren't as obvious are left to fend for themselves.

We once lived in a ward where our new bishop had a heart attack. People flocked to visit him throughout the entire period of recuperation, but nobody seemed to notice that the bishop's wife was feeling frightened and angry and neglected. Finally she said to us, "People think it was my husband's heart attack, but they were wrong. It was *our* heart attack. Why isn't anyone taking care of *me*?"

As things turned out, the bishop recovered in a couple of months, but the bishop's wife took more than a year to recover. Perhaps she would have made a quicker recovery if people had seen her suffering and had helped her rather than giving all the attention to her husband.

If you're the first person to spot a need, you may want to bring it to the attention of the Relief Society president or your priesthood quorum leader. But even the most diligent Relief Society presidents have been known to drop the ball—or they have good intentions, only to be distracted by those squeaky wheels. If someone needs a service you can perform, do it. Visit the lonely. Comfort the grieving. Give your used goods away rather than selling them. Write a letter of appreciation or make a phone call. Service is the foundation of the gospel, and the person who performs the service eventually benefits from the service more than the beneficiary.

Remember that we are the Lord's representatives on earth. Our eyes are His eyes, if we look for people in need. Our hearts are His heart, if we recognize the suffering of others and feel compassion for them. Our hands are His hands, when we perform service to others. And our voices are His voice, when we offer kind words to those who are in desperate need.

EPILOGUE—
ENDURING TO THE END

There are more than a dozen places in the scriptures where we are admonished to "endure to the end." Thus, not only does God expect us to do everything we can to follow His commandments but He also expects us to continue doing all those things throughout the rest of our lives.

In one sense, you have "endured to the end" of this book, although we hope it has not been a painful process. If we've fulfilled our purpose, you have learned something and been entertained along the way. But as a new (or soon to be new) convert, you have taken the first step on a journey that will continue even beyond the end of your life on this earth. We have tried to give you a road map and point out some of the potholes along the way, but you are ultimately responsible for arriving at that destination.

Sometimes we look at an errant child and wonder, "How will this child ever grow up to be a responsible adult?" Similarly, you may wonder how you will ever be able to be anything more than a new convert with a few limited responsibilities. Yet, just as that child, with proper nourishment and training and care, will eventually mature into a responsible adult, you will also mature. You and your fellow converts will be the future bishops, Relief Society presidents, and temple workers of the Church.

But regular spiritual nourishment is the key. Even strong members of the Church require a daily vaccination of faith, prayer, repentance, and scripture study. These, along with regular doses of Church meetings, temple attendance, and family home evening will inoculate us against the spiritual viruses of the world.

Have you ever noticed how painful memories seem to fade over time? Unfortunately, this seems to apply to spiritual memories as well. Most of us have had profound spiritual moments in our lives, only to have the memory and the intensity of those moments fade with the passing of time. As the memories fade, we may forget them. Worse, we may eventually convince ourselves they never happened. Despite the outpouring of love we received in a moment of spiritual enlightenment, the passing of time may convince us that our answers to prayer were no more than a case of indigestion or some other delusion. This is a common human failing.

No matter what spiritual gifts you may have been given, your spiritual reservoir is really a leaky bucket, and you must constantly add more water or the bucket will run dry. When you were investigating the Church, you probably had one or more of these spiritual downpours that filled your bucket. But no matter how strong those feelings are now, they will eventually evaporate until your bucket is dry unless you are adding more spiritual water each day.

In the parable of the sower, Christ likens converts to His kingdom to seeds scattered by a sower. Some seeds fell in stony places, sprouted, but then were scorched by the sun because they had no deep roots. Some fell among thorns, and the thorns choked them. As a convert, you need to work daily to avoid these two fates. You can deepen your spiritual roots by using the tools already mentioned. You can avoid the thorns by limiting your association with those who ridicule your membership in the Church. This may not be as easy as it sounds, especially if the thorns are within your own family. But many converts can testify of the way in which the Lord has softened the hearts of unbelieving associates over time. Once they see how your membership has enriched your life, many of these cynics will become more tolerant, if not outright accepting of your decision to join the Church. It is our hope that *all* converts can become like the last group of seeds mentioned in Matthew 13:8: "But other[s] fell into good ground, and brought forth fruit, some an hundredfold, some sixtyfold, some thirtyfold."

A radio advertisement for a national accounting firm claims that "There has never been a better time to be a [company name] client." We could take some license with that, and claim that "There has never been a better time to be a member of The Church of Jesus Christ of Latter-day Saints." Much like the stone cut out without hands in Nebuchadnezzar's dream, the kingdom of God continues to fill the whole earth, gaining in speed, size, and power with each passing year. In the same letter to the newspaper editor where Joseph Smith defined the Articles of Faith, he made the following bold statement:

> The Standard of Truth has been erected; no unhallowed hand can stop the work from progressing; persecutions may rage, mobs may combine, armies may assemble, calumny may defame, but the truth of God will go forth boldly, nobly, and independent, till it has penetrated every continent, visited every clime, swept every country, and sounded in every ear, till the purposes of God shall be accomplished, and the Great Jehovah shall say the work is done. (In *History of the Church,* 4:540.)

We have seen much of this come to pass in our own lifetimes and continue to see this prophecy fulfilled with each passing day. We have seen the Church grow from less than two million members to more than ten million. We have seen a Utah-based religion grow into a worldwide Church, with more than 55,000 missionaries currently serving in almost every country of the world. We have seen the Berlin wall tumble, and the gospel being preached in the former Soviet Union—a suggestion that would have been laughable two decades ago. We have seen the number of temples almost quadruple, until they dot the land and are found in just about every corner of the world. We have seen the Church grow out of obscurity into a well-respected organization featured in prime-time television programs and on the covers of national magazines.

None of this could happen if it were the work of men. It is not the work of men, but the work of Jesus Christ, who stands at the head of His kingdom. A few critics say that Latter-day Saints are "sheep" who follow blindly without question or reason. Our experience refutes this simplistic argument. We have found our Mormon friends to be intelligent, thoughtful, sincere, and interesting. They are successful in business, in the arts, in the community, and at whatever they decide to do. They are role models for their friends, neighbors, and associates. Their testimonies of the gospel are as varied as they are, but all are based on individual study followed by spiritual confirmation.

As one of the newest members of this army of God, we welcome you. President Spencer W. Kimball had a sign on his desk that said, simply, "Do it." Perhaps that should be the motto for every new member. Just start each day with the determination that you will learn a little more, do a little more, and grow a little stronger. A daily cup of such spiritual water will fill your bucket, fill your home, fill your life, and fill your soul. Then when the day comes that you meet your Savior, He will say as He said in Matthew 25:21, "Well done, [thou] good and faithful servant: thou hast been faithful over a few things, I will make thee ruler over many things: enter thou into the joy of thy lord."

GLOSSARY

It's only a matter of time before those attending LDS meetings or associating with LDS members hear words new to them, or familiar words used in an unfamiliar manner. As with any group, members of the Church seem to have a lingo unique to them. This glossary will attempt to identify and clarify some of these terms. All of these words or phrases are used elsewhere in the book (see the index), but they are defined here in one place as a handy reference. Just as those vacationing in a foreign land will keep a translation dictionary nearby, keep this glossary handy when you come in contact with Church members or Church activities.

Although some callings are found here, we have tried not to clutter the glossary with all the different callings you will find in the Church. Refer to the index and chapters 4–6. You will find some callings here, but they are usually generic. For example, you will not find Sunday School secretary, but you will find secretary.

– A –

Aaronic Priesthood—one of two priesthoods within the Church. The Aaronic Priesthood is given to worthy young men age 12 and older and also to worthy convert adult males shortly after baptism. Also called the lesser, Levitical, or preparatory priesthood. *See also* Melchizedek Priesthood.

Aaronic Priesthood Committee—a stake committee charged with the task of strengthening the Aaronic Priesthood members within the stake. It is composed of members of the stake presidency, stake high council, and stake Young Men organizations.

accountability, law of—the doctrine that individuals are accountable for their own actions, not the actions of others. This doctrine does not excuse parents from accountability for their children's actions, if they are the ones who have trained their children to err. *See also* agency.

active—Church members who attend their meetings, fulfill their assignments, and otherwise live the gospel to the best of their ability. *See also* inactive, less active.

activities committee—the committee responsible for organizing most of the cultural and athletic activities in a ward. The committee usually consists of a chairman, a cultural arts director, a physical activities director, and other specialists.

activities music director—a member of the activities committee in charge of secular musical presentations, such as talent nights and musical productions. He may also be asked to provide musical training to others.

activity day—a quarterly Primary activity during which the children meet together for some type of educational or social activity. This is usually held on a weekday or a Saturday.

activity night—when multiple wards meet in a meetinghouse, the night that a particular ward is assigned to use the meetinghouse for Mutual and Relief Society meetings.

administer—to perform an ordinance. The two most common usages refer to administering the sacrament and administering to those who are ill.

administering the sacrament—blessing the sacrament. This is done as part of every sacrament meeting by either a priest in the Aaronic Priesthood or a holder of the Melchizedek Priesthood.

administering to the sick—the ordinance of blessing an individual who is ill. This is usually done by two Melchizedek Priesthood holders using olive oil that has been consecrated for the blessing of the sick. One man usually anoints the head of the person with oil, and then the second man usually joins in to seal the anointing. If two men are not available, one priesthood holder can perform both functions.

advance—a general term used to indicate age-driven growth in the Church. Young women will advance through the classes of the Young Women program, and young men advance through the offices of the Aaronic Priesthood. Primary children who have their 12th birthday advance to Mutual.

age of accountability—the age when individuals in general are considered to be old enough to know right from wrong. In the Church, this is age eight.

agency—the concept that individuals should be free to make decisions that affect their own lives, even if those decisions are wrong. This is often referred to as *free agency*, but the *free* is misleading because although we are free to make our own choices, we are not free from the consequences of them.

agent bishop—the bishop in a Church meetinghouse who is responsible for the upkeep and use of the meetinghouse for all wards that meet within the meetinghouse. Usually, this assignment rotates from bishop to bishop in some established way.

agent ward—the ward that is responsible for the upkeep and use of the meetinghouse. *See also* agent bishop.

anoint—the first portion of a blessing given to a sick person. A Melchizedek Priesthood holder will anoint the top of the person's head with a small drop of consecrated olive oil, place his hands on the person's head, call the person by name, and state that he is anointing the person's head by the authority of the Melchizedek Priesthood and in the name of Jesus Christ.

anti-Mormon literature—books, pamphlets, or videos prepared to discourage those with an interest in the Church. Some specimens are ludicrous, but others are skillfully prepared to subtly distort Church doctrine.

Apostle—an office in the Melchizedek Priesthood, held by those twelve General Authorities who belong to the Quorum of the Twelve Apostles.

Area Authority Seventy—a Church authority called to assist an Area Presidency in administering the affairs of the Church in a certain area. Although similar to General Authorities, they are different in that they can preside only in one area, and they are expected to keep their regular employment while serving.

Area Presidency—usually a group of three General Authorities (although an Area Authority Seventy can serve as a counselor) who are responsible for administering the affairs of the Church in a particular geographical area. The presidency consists of a president and his two counselors. The presidency has regular contact with all of the stake presidents in their area.

assistant—used in some callings to denote those assigned to assist the leader. Although most church organizations are led by presidents and assisted by counselors, some priesthood groups—such as priests and high priests—use the term assistant instead.

assistant clerk—a man called to assist the ward (or stake) clerk in performing his duties. An assistant clerk will often be assigned specific responsibilities, such as financial matters or membership records.

assistant executive secretary—A man called to assist the ward (or stake) executive secretary in performing his duties.

assistant meetinghouse librarian—a person called to assist the meetinghouse librarian or the associate meetinghouse librarian in performing duties related to the library.

associate meetinghouse librarian—a meetinghouse librarian for a ward that is not the agent ward. When multiple wards share a building, the librarian from the agent ward is called the meetinghouse librarian, and the librarians from other wards are called associate librarians.

auxiliary—one of the nonpriesthood organizations within the Church, such as Primary, Relief Society, Sunday School, Young Men, and Young Women. Priesthood quorums are not considered to be auxiliaries.

auxiliary leaders—a generic term usually used to refer to the presidencies of any of the auxiliary organizations. For example, the Young Men and Young Women presidencies are referred to as auxiliary leaders.

auxiliary music staff—members of the ward music committee who provide musical support for the ward auxiliaries. Examples would include the choristers and pianists who work with the Relief Society and the Primary.

auxiliary president—a generic term referring to the president of an auxiliary organization. For example, the Relief Society president and Sunday School president are both auxiliary presidents.

auxiliary training meetings—meetings sponsored by ward or stake leaders to help train those who work in the various ward auxiliary organizations.

– B –

baptism—the ordinance that marks your admission into the

Church. Previous baptisms in other faiths are not recognized because you must be baptized by one having the proper priesthood authority. Within the Church, baptisms may be performed by men holding the Melchizedek Priesthood or the office of priest in the Aaronic Priesthood. Baptisms are performed by immersion.

baptismal font—the sunken pool especially constructed in some church buildings for the performing of baptisms. Fonts are also found in temples but are only used when performing baptisms for those who are deceased.

Bear—one of the ranks associated with the Cub Scout program. Young boys in the Church may participate in the Cub program while they are in Primary.

bearing testimony—the act of publicly declaring your spiritual beliefs. Members usually bear their testimonies during the monthly fast and testimony meeting, but testimonies may be borne at other times. Missionaries often bear testimony to investigators of the principles and doctrines they have taught them.

Beehive—the youngest class of girls in the Young Women program. Girls who are Beehives are 12–13 years of age.

Bible—one of four volumes of scripture recognized by the Church. In general, the King James Version of the Bible is used by most Church members. *See also* standard works.

bishop—an office in the Aaronic Priesthood given to those who are called to preside over a ward. The bishop presides over the Aaronic Priesthood but is also the presiding high priest in the ward and the common judge over ward members. A bishop is roughly equivalent to a pastor, minister, or priest in other denominations.

bishop's storehouse—a facility containing an assortment of food, clothing, and other supplies. The storehouses are run as part of the welfare program of the Church. With the bishop's approval, needy ward members may visit the storehouse to obtain supplies.

bishopric—the three men that form the governing body of a ward, which consists of a bishop and his two counselors. *See also* branch president.

blessing of babies—an ordinance performed by the father of a new baby or by another Melchizedek Priesthood holder. The one giving the blessing declares the baby's name and gives the child a blessing. This is usually done during fast and testimony meeting.

blessing of comfort—a blessing given by a Melchizedek Priesthood holder to someone who is in need of comfort or guidance.
Fathers or home teachers are often asked to give these blessings to those who need guidance or reassurance in their lives.
Unlike blessings of the sick, no consecrated oil is used.

blessing of the sick—an ordinance usually performed by two
Melchizedek Priesthood holders at the request of someone who
is ill. The blessing consists of two parts, the anointing and the
sealing. *See also* anoint, seal the anointing.

Book of Mormon—one of four volumes of scripture recognized as
official canon by members of the Church. Translated by the
Prophet Joseph Smith from golden plates maintained by
ancient civilizations that lived on the American continent.

boundary—used to define the neighborhoods included in a particular ward or stake. Each ward has a defined boundary, and
all members living inside the boundary should attend that
ward. Boundaries usually follow physical or logical divisions,
such as rivers, roads, and county borders.

boundary realignment—the act of redefining the boundaries
between two or more wards. This is usually done when a
growth or decline in Church membership makes it necessary
to create new wards, dissolve old wards, or change the boundaries between wards.

Boy Scouts of America—*see* Scouting.

branch, branch president—a branch is similar to a ward but
contains a smaller number of Church members. Branches are
formed when there are not enough members for a ward in a
particular geographic area. Branches are designed to be
staffed with fewer people than a ward, and they are led by a
branch president rather than a bishop.

Brigham Young University—a large university in Provo, Utah,
owned and operated by the Church.

brother, brethren—terms used in the Church when referring to
men. These are used to imply a close kinship, as we literally
are brothers in the kingdom of God. Those who speak in public
meetings often refer to the congregation as "brothers and sisters." Individual members may also be addressed or referred
to as "Brother Jones" or "Brother Smith." Some also use the
term *Brethren* (note the capital B) to refer to the general
authorities of the Church. *See also* sister.

building coordinator—someone assigned to schedule all activities in the meetinghouse and to let people in the building if

they do not have keys. Building coordinators are especially important when multiple wards share a building. The building coordinators from each ward should meet together often.

BYU—*see* Brigham Young University.

– C –

calling—an opportunity to perform service within the Church, also known as a job or position. Examples of callings would include bishop, Sunday School teacher, and Young Women president.

camp director—a calling within the Young Women organization. The camp director is expected to organize and participate in the annual girls' camp.

cannery—Church facilities used to can food as part of the welfare program of the Church. Ward members may occasionally be asked to work at the cannery for several hours on a volunteer basis.

celestial kingdom—the most glorious of the three kingdoms of heaven, reserved for those who have been the most valiant in keeping the Lord's commandments.

celestial marriage—*see* temple marriage.

celestial room—a room in LDS temples used to symbolize the glory and beauty of the celestial kingdom.

CES—*see* Church Educational System.

chapel—the room where sacrament meeting and other worship services are held. Church members often use the word chapel mistakenly, when they really mean meetinghouse.

choir accompanist—the person assigned to play the piano or organ for the ward choir.

choir director—the person assigned to lead the ward choir.

choir librarian—the person assigned to maintain the music for the ward choir.

choir president—the person assigned to preside over the ward choir. The president usually calls rehearsals to order, introduces new members, makes announcements, and solicits new members from the body of the ward.

choir secretary—the person assigned to perform clerical duties for the ward choir.

choir section leader—the person assigned to supervise a section of the ward choir.

choose the right—*see* CTR.

chorister—one of several callings involved in leading the congregational singing. The ward chorister leads the singing in sacrament meeting, while auxiliary choristers do the same for their organizations.

Church, the—an abbreviated way of referring to The Church of Jesus Christ of Latter-day Saints, especially among its members. It is common to hear expressions such as "I joined the Church in 1988."

Church discipline—formal discipline imposed upon Church members who commit serious transgressions. Church discipline is determined by disciplinary councils that are held at the ward or stake level.

Church Educational System—a Church headquarters department responsible for administering the seminary and institute programs. More often referred to using the initials CES.

Church magazine—one of several magazines published by the Church to strengthen its members. In English these are the *Ensign, New Era, Friend,* and *Liahona.*

Church News, the—a weekly newspaper section published by the Church-owned *Deseret News* newspaper in Salt Lake City. Church members outside of Utah may subscribe to the *Church News* to keep informed of Church events.

civil marriage—generally, any marriage not performed in an LDS temple. Also, couples who have been widowed during their previous marriages can become married in a temple for "time only." This also could be referred to as a civil marriage.

clerical staff—those called to provide administrative support to Church leaders. For example, the bishopric is supported by a clerical staff of executive secretaries and ward clerks.

clerk—a male member assigned to do clerical functions, such as completing reports and certificates. The two most common clerks are ward clerks and stake clerks.

coach—a member of the ward or stake activities committee assigned to manage an athletic team. In wards where the Scouting program is implemented, the adult leader of the Varsity Team is also called a coach.

Committee for Single Members—a committee that may exist at either the ward or the stake level to consider the needs of single members and to organize activities and classes for them.

common judge—one of the five responsibilities of a bishop. He is the common judge of the people in his ward. The bishop is performing this duty when he holds worthiness interviews or disciplinary councils.

community relations specialist—a stake calling that involves building better relationships between the Church and the community. Those in this calling often involve wards in local community service projects.

companionship—two people called to serve together in a Church calling. Home and visiting teachers serve together in a companionship, as do full-time missionaries.

compassionate service leader—a member of the ward Relief Society board assigned to coordinate acts of compassionate service towards members, such as preparing a meal for a sister who is ill.

conduct—to take charge of a meeting, introducing the speakers and the hymns, and giving announcements. See preside.

conference—a special gathering of Saints for instruction outside of the normal Sunday meetings. Common examples include stake conference and general conference.

confirm—a Melchizedek Priesthood ordinance given to a newly baptized person that declares him to be a member of the Church and bestows upon him the gift of the Holy Ghost.

consecrated oil—pure olive oil that has been blessed and is used only for the healing of the sick by two Melchizedek Priesthood brethren. *See also* anoint, seal the anointing.

conversion—the process an investigator goes through to gain a testimony of the Church and a desire to be baptized and become a member.

convert—a person who was not born as a member of the Church but who joined later in life, usually because of the influence of friends, neighbors, or LDS missionaries. Also, the person to whom this book is written.

counselor—a person who is called to assist someone else in a Church calling. Most leadership callings within the Church consist of a president and two counselors.

Course 12–Course 17—names of Sunday School classes for young people age 12–17, where the course number corresponds with the age of the student.

covenant—a promise made between a person and God. The person promises to follow certain commandments, and God promises to bless and reward the person in certain ways. Examples of covenants you make include baptism, receiving the priesthood (for men), and the covenants that are made inside the temple.

CTR—Choose the Right (what Church members are admonished to do). This is the name for an age group of Primary children, and also a slogan that is popular on jewelry items.

Cub committee—a group that works under the direction of the ward Scout committee chairman, in wards that participate in Scouting. The Cub committee specifically addresses the needs of boys under 11 years of age who participate in the Cub program.

Cub Scout—a Scouting program designed for Primary boys age 8–11. When the boys reach the age of 12, they graduate from Primary and the Cub program and become regular Boy Scouts.

cultural arts director—a member of a ward or stake activities committee who helps plan cultural activities, such as talent shows, dramatic productions, or musical programs.

cultural arts specialist—similar to a cultural arts director, except he is usually called for a shorter period of time to work on a particular project or program or to practice a particular specialty.

cultural hall—a large room within an LDS meetinghouse used to hold cultural or athletic events. Usually easily recognized because of the presence of basketball hoops. Old-timers still call it the "gym."

– D–

dance director—a specialist that serves under the cultural activities director on the ward or stake activities committee. Responsible for organizing dances and giving dance instruction.

deacon—an office in the Aaronic Priesthood usually given to young men age 12–13. Duties of deacons include passing the sacrament and gathering fast offerings.

deacons quorum—a group of young men who all hold the office of deacon. They meet together as a group on Sunday and during Mutual activities.

deacons quorum presidency—the presiding body over the deacons quorum, and staffed by members of the quorum itself. The presidency consists of a president and two counselors.

declaration of lineage—a portion of each patriarchal blessing in which you are told through which tribe of Israel your lineage is derived.

dedication of graves—a Melchizedek Priesthood ordinance that involves the blessing and dedication of a grave site before the casket is placed into the ground. This is performed at the cemetery after the funeral.

delegate—the process by which certain responsibilities are given to others. For example, the bishop will not try to run the entire ward himself but will delegate some of his duties to his counselors.

den chief—a Scout-age boy assigned to assist the Cub dens. He attends their meetings, gives advice, and serves as an example for the Cubs.

den leader—an adult leader called to supervise one of the Cub dens. Works with the den chief to plan activities and serve as a good example.

deseret—an Book of Mormon term that means "honeybee" (see Ether 2:3) and is used to signify industriousness. Deseret is a common name for Church-related businesses, such as Deseret Industries and the *Deseret News*.

director of libraries—a stake calling concerned with the proper training of the librarians who serve in the meetinghouse libraries throughout the stake.

disciplinary council—a formal meeting held to consider the membership status of a member who has committed serious transgressions. Disciplinary councils may be held at both the stake and the ward level. The focus of such a council is usually to help the member repent.

disfellowship—one outcome of a disciplinary council. Disfellowshipped members are still members of the Church, but they cannot participate in certain activities, such as giving talks or public prayers.

distribution center—Church-operated centers that contain the supplies necessary for running the Church, such as manuals, videos, forms, and certificates. Supplies are available for free or for a nominal charge and may be ordered by Church units or individual members. A distribution center catalog is published each year.

district—an organization unit similar to a stake but smaller and usually composed of branches rather than wards. In locations where Church membership is small and scattered, you often find branches and districts rather than wards and stakes.

doctrine—beliefs of the Church, as found in the scriptures. The law of tithing and the Word of Wisdom are both doctrines of the Church because they are both contained in scripture. It is important for all Church members to understand the difference between doctrine, practice, and opinion.

Doctrine and Covenants—one of four volumes of scripture recognized by the Church. The Doctrine and Covenants contains revelations received between the founding of the Church in 1830 and the present day. *See also* standard works.

drama director—a specialist who serves under the cultural activities director on the ward or stake activities committee. He is responsible for organizing plays, roadshows, and other dramatic presentations.

– E –

education counselor—the first counselor in the Relief Society, who is responsible to coordinate the Sunday Relief Society lessons that are taught to the women of the ward.

elder—an office in the Melchizedek Priesthood, usually held by younger men in a ward. The term *elder* is also applied when referring to full-time male missionaries or General Authorities of the Church.

elders quorum—the group of men holding the office of elder in the Melchizedek Priesthood that meet together in a ward.

elders quorum presidency—the men called to preside over the elders quorum in a ward. The presidency consists of a president and his two counselors.

employment centers—facilities run by the Church to help members find or upgrade their employment.

employment specialist—a person called at the ward or stake level to help others find or upgrade their employment. In addition to matching job openings with applicants, this person usually provides training in such areas as job interviews and résumé writing.

endowment—an ordinance presented in temples that prepares those who live worthily to return to the presence of God. Endowments are performed for the living and for those who are deceased.

Ensign, the—*see* Church magazines.

exaltation—a higher reward for those who have been especially valiant in keeping the Lord's commandments. Salvation is given to all through the Atonement of Jesus Christ, but exaltation is a gift from God for those who have been willing to sacrifice and obey at all costs.

excommunicate—the most serious decision of a disciplinary council. An excommunicated member is no longer considered a member of the Church. He can attend meetings, but he cannot participate by taking the sacrament or by holding any Church position.

executive secretary—a calling involved with performing administrative duties for other Church leaders. Both bishops and stake presidents have executive secretaries and use them to schedule appointments, prepare agendas, and perform other duties.

– F –

family council—often held as part of family home evening, family councils allow family members to discuss family problems, give assignments, make decisions, or plan family events such as vacations.

family file—an office in a temple containing names of deceased persons for which temple ordinances need to be done. Names in the family file are submitted by the relatives of the deceased, who usually then participate in performing the ordinances.

family history—the activities associated with creating and maintaining a history of your immediate family and other relatives. Although family history often refers to genealogy, it also includes other activities such as maintaining journals or photo albums.

family history center—facilities maintained by the Church to assist members in performing genealogical research. They are also open to nonmembers of the Church.

family history center director—a stake calling involved with the operation of family history centers. The director is charged with the overall performance of the center.

family history center specialists—those called to assist the family history center director in the operation of the family history center. They usually assist patrons who come to use the center.

family history class—a class taught during Sunday School time designed to teach members the basics of doing family history and using the family history center.

family history consultant—a ward calling oriented toward getting ward members involved in family history work and answering their questions. The consultant often teaches the family history class in Sunday School and organizes trips to the family history center.

family home evening—a Church program designed to bring families together one night per week for spiritual instruction, family council, and other family activities. The official night for family home evening is Monday, but it may be held on any night that is convenient for the family.

family home evening group leader—a single male holding the Melchizedek Priesthood and assigned to supervise a family home evening group composed of single members.

family home evening manual—a book containing lesson materials and other ideas to be used as part of family home evening.

family night—*see* family home evening.

fast and testimony meeting—the name of the sacrament meeting held on fast Sunday, so named because the members are given an opportunity to bear testimonies after the sacrament is administered.

fast day, fast Sunday—one Sunday every month, typically the first Sunday of every month, when Church members go for two meals without food and then donate an equivalent amount of money to the Church for the benefit of the poor and needy.

fast offering—the amount of money that is donated for the benefit of the poor and needy on fast Sunday. This amount should be at least the cost of two meals, although Church members are counseled to give a generous fast offering.

fasting—the act of praying and going without food for spiritual reasons.

fellowship, fellowshipping—the act of making others feel welcome and wanted. Church members are expected to fellowship, or friendship, members who move into the ward, as well as converts.

finance clerk—an assistant clerk called to deal specifically with financial matters. He may serve at either the ward or the stake level.

fireside—a special Church meeting, usually with a spiritual theme and often involving a particular group. For example, most bishops sponsor regular youth firesides for the young men and young women of the ward.

First Presidency—the presiding quorum of the Church, which is composed of the President, or prophet, and his two counselors.

food production—an important element of the welfare program of the Church. Members learn to be self-sufficient by producing a portion of their food and then preserving it.

food storage—*see* home storage.

four-generation program—a family history program of the Church where each member is asked to trace his genealogy back through at least four generations.

foyer—a meeting area or hallway just outside of the chapel in most meetinghouses. A lot of meeting, greeting, and Church business occurs in the foyer.

free agency—*see* agency.

Friend, the—*see* Church magazines.

full-time missionary—someone called to devote his entire life to missionary service for a period of 18 to 24 months. Most missionaries are young men approximately 19 to 24 years of age, but women and older couples may also serve.

– G –

garments—the underclothing worn by Church members who have received their temple endowments.

genealogy—*see* family history.

General Authorities—those leaders called to preside over the entire body of the Church, rather than just a particular stake or ward. Examples of General Authorities include the First Presidency and the Quorum of the Twelve.

general auxiliary presidencies—those called to serve in leadership positions that will help set policy for auxiliaries throughout the Church. For example, the general Relief Society presidency must be concerned with the operation of the Relief Society in all the units worldwide.

general Church officers—a generic term used to include all those called as general officers of the Church. For example, the General Authorities and the general auxiliary presidencies would be included.

general conference—a conference of all members of the Church held twice per year, in April and October. Sessions are held at the tabernacle in Salt Lake City and broadcast throughout the world via television, radio, and satellite.

general priesthood meeting—a stake meeting to which all priesthood holders in the stake are invited, both Aaronic and Melchizedek.

general session—a session of general conference to which all members are invited. *See* priesthood session.

golden questions, the—an old missionary term. Church members were challenged to ask nonmembers, "What do you know about the Mormon Church?" "Would you like to know more?"

gospel—the pattern for successful living as taught by God and Jesus Christ. It is often said that Joseph Smith gave us the restored gospel, because through him God gave us back those important parts that had been lost over time, such as baptism for the dead.

Gospel Doctrine—the weekly Sunday School lesson for adult Church members, drawn from the scriptures.

Gospel Principles—a series of Sunday School lessons that are designed to teach prospective Church members and new Church members the basics of the gospel.

graveside service—the second portion of a funeral service, which is performed at the grave. The first portion, or funeral program, is usually held in a meetinghouse. Sometimes the funeral is omitted, and the graveside service serves as the only program.

– H –

heresy literature—*see* anti-Mormon literature.

high council—a group of twelve men who assist the stake president in administering the stake. Those called to serve as high councilors must hold the office of high priest in the Melchizedek Priesthood and usually have much experience in Church leadership.

high council Sunday—a Sunday when a stake high councilor attends your ward and serves as the primary sacrament meeting speaker.

high priest—an office in the Melchizedek Priesthood given to those who are called to Church leadership positions, such as bishops and stake presidents. *See also* elder.

high priests group—the group of high priests that meet together in a ward. They are not called a quorum, because all the high priests in the stake comprise one high priests quorum.

high priests group leader—the calling that provides leadership for a ward high priests group. The leader is not called a quorum president, because the president of the stake high priests quorum is the stake president.

home management teacher—a Relief Society board member assigned to give a short lesson on some home management topic during each homemaking meeting.

home name extraction workers—workers who search vital records, prepare the names on the records for computer input, and then submit the names to the Church Family History Department, where others may use them for their own family history research.

home storage—food, clothing, fuel, water, and other necessities of life that are accumulated by a family and used in rotation. The purpose of home storage is to sustain families during times of emergency.

home teaching—a program in which two priesthood holders visit each home in the ward at least once per month. As directed by the head of the house, the home teachers may pray, teach lessons, and check on the physical and spiritual condition of the family.

homemaking counselor—the second counselor of the Relief Society, whose assignment covers the monthly homemaking meeting and other home arts.

homemaking leader—the Relief Society member who is in charge of planning the monthly Relief Society homemaking meeting.

homemaking meeting—the monthly meeting of women in a ward, allegedly designed to teach home arts to the women, and more practically designed to give women an opportunity to spend time in each other's company.

homemaking night—another name for homemaking meeting. The night of the month on which the homemaking meeting is scheduled.

– I –

inactive—*see* active, less active.

institute—a program sponsored by the Church Educational System (CES) designed to provide religious instruction to college-age students. Others who are not students may also attend the classes.

investigators—individuals who are studying the Church but have not yet committed to be baptized.

– J –

job—*see* calling.

Joseph Smith—the founder and first President of The Church of Jesus Christ of Latter-day Saints.

– K –

keys—certain powers and authorities that are bestowed when Priesthood holders are set apart for certain callings within the Church. For example, a bishop is set apart with certain keys that allow him to minister to the members of his ward. Other callings that have keys include stake president and elders quorum president. Auxiliary presidents do not hold keys.

kingdom of God—a phrase used to describe the body of the Church that emphasizes its more spiritual aspects. Someone might say, "I hope to use this calling to help build the kingdom of God," or "Good home teachers help the kingdom grow stronger."

– L –

Latter-day Saints—a nickname for members of The Church of Jesus Christ of Latter-day Saints.

Laurel—a member of the senior class in the Young Women program, whose members are age 16–17.

law of common consent—a concept that members of the Church must approve all callings that are issued to members who will work with them or preside over them. Each member is given a regular opportunity to approve ward, stake, and general Church leaders. *See also* sustain.

law of consecration—a law that requires the dedication of all one's time, talents, and possessions to the building up of the Church and the kingdom of God. President John Taylor said that the celestial kingdom operates under this law, as did the people in Enoch's day.

lay ministry—spiritual leadership provided by those who receive no pay for their services. Except for a few General Authorities, no Church leaders receive payment for their services.

LDS Church—a nickname for The Church of Jesus Christ of Latter-day Saints.

LDS Social Services—*see* Social Services.

leadership meeting—meetings designed to instruct those with leadership callings on how to be better leaders. Usually presented by the stake to ward leaders.

leadership training missions—a type of full-time mission where the missionaries serve in weaker areas of the Church and teach the local leaders to be more effective. Older couples are often asked to serve this type of mission.

less active—in these politically correct times, the name for Church members who rarely darken the door of a church. Basically, you stay off the less-active list by showing up for a Church meeting once every three months. The name would perhaps have greater meaning if it applied to Church members who usually come to church but who can't be relied on to take callings or otherwise commit themselves—but it doesn't. *See also* active.

lesser priesthood—*see* Aaronic Priesthood.

Levitical priesthood—*see* Aaronic Priesthood.

Liahona—*see* Church magazines.

library—*see* meetinghouse library, family history library.

lifers—individuals who were born to parents who were members of the Church. *See also* convert.

line of authority—when a man is ordained to the Melchizedek Priesthood, the person ordaining him often gives him a document tracing his line of priesthood authority back to Jesus Christ through the earliest Church leaders of the restored church.

living ordinances—temple ordinances performed for the living person who is receiving them. *See also* proxy ordinances.

– M –

magazine representative—a ward calling that consists of helping ward members get subscriptions to any of the Church magazines.

magnify—a term often used in connection with callings. Church members are urged to magnify their callings, or to do more than the minimum required in the description of the calling.

manifest—a term that means raising your right hand to sustain an action or an individual. If someone says, "All who can sustain Brother Farley in this calling, please manifest it," the proper response is to raise your right hand to signify your agreement. *See also* sustain.

media relations specialist—a person who reports to the stake public communications director. This calling is to establish relationships between the stake and the media so that Church events are given positive attention in the local newspapers and other media outlets.

meetinghouse—the place where wards hold church services and other meetings. Sometimes erroneously called the chapel.

meetinghouse library—a room in most meetinghouses that contains Church-related books, videos, photographs, and recordings. It is supervised by a meetinghouse librarian, who makes materials available to teachers and individual members.

Melchizedek Priesthood—one of two priesthoods given to worthy men within the Church. The Aaronic Priesthood is a preparatory priesthood, but the Melchizedek Priesthood contains all the authority necessary to lead the Church and to return all worthy members back into God's presence.

Melchizedek Priesthood committee—a stake committee composed of high council members that attempts to strengthen the Melchizedek Priesthood quorums in the wards.

Melchizedek Priesthood holder—*see* priesthood holder.

Melchizedek Priesthood Leadership Handbook—a short manual that teaches Melchizedek Priesthood leaders their duties and also gives instruction on the performance of Melchizedek Priesthood ordinances.

member activation—stake programs designed to help wards increase the activity levels of its members, particularly the ones who never attend church.

membership clerk—an assistant ward or stake clerk called specifically to deal with membership records.

membership records—a record that is created when you are baptized and follows you throughout your life in the Church. It moves when you move and is updated to reflect important events such as ordinations and marriage.

MIA—*see* Mutual.

Mia Maid—a class in the Young Women for young women age 14–15.

military relations—a stake program that is designed to keep the Church in contact with those members of the stake who are away from home serving in the military.

mini-mission—an activity designed to prepare youth to serve full-time missions. They are called, set apart, and expected to preach the gospel and live mission rules for several days.

mission—geographic regions of the world into which full-time missionaries are sent. The missionaries in each mission are presided over by a mission presidency. The term *mission* is also used to refer to the calling to be a missionary, as in, "I'm going on a mission next year."

mission leader—a man called to help direct the missionary work in each ward. He works closely with the stake missionaries, the full-time missionaries, and the members of the ward. This is a stake calling, and the ward mission leader reports to the stake mission presidency.

mission of the Church—the goal that all Church programs are designed to accomplish: Invite all to come unto Christ and be perfected in him. This is done in three ways: perfect the Saints, proclaim the gospel, and redeem the dead.

mission presidency—the governing body assigned to supervise the full-time missionaries assigned to a specific mission. The mission presidency consists of the president and his two counselors. *See also* stake mission presidency, stake mission president.

mission rules—a fairly rigid set of rules that all full-time missionaries are expected to follow. These rules help 19-year-old boys to act like missionaries, rather than 19-year-old boys.

missionary—someone called to preach the gospel to others. Although all members are expected to be missionaries, stake missionaries and full-time missionaries have specific Church callings for missionary work.

Missionary Department—the department at Church headquarters that coordinates all activities with the missions and the full-time missionaries of the Church.

missionary fund—a fund maintained by each ward and used to support the full-time missionaries serving from the ward. Members may donate to the missionary fund to help provide financial support for the ward's missionaries.

missionary open houses—programs designed to allow members to introduce their nonmember friends and neighbors to the Church. These meetings are held at the meetinghouse and usually involve missionary talks, a video or satellite broadcast, and light refreshments.

missionary preparation classes—classes to help prepare those who desire to serve a full-time mission for the Church. These classes often emphasize important scriptures that missionaries use regularly.

missionary splits—the act of putting a pair of missionaries in two places at once by pairing each missionary with a ward member of the same sex for a brief amount of time.

Mormon Church—a nickname for The Church of Jesus Christ of Latter-day Saints.

Mormonism—a term for the doctrines, principles, and beliefs that comprise The Church of Jesus Christ of Latter-day Saints.

Mormons—a nickname for members of The Church of Jesus Christ of Latter-day Saints, derived from the ancient prophet who gave the Book of Mormon its name.

mouthpiece—*see* voice.

music adviser—a member of the bishopric assigned to work with the ward music committee.

music chairman—a person called to head the ward music committee. This person works with the music adviser and the other committee members to provide the worship music for the ward.

music committee—a ward committee organized to oversee all worship music presented in the ward.

Mutual—a weekly activity planned for the Young Men and the Young Women. They usually meet in their separate classes for some type of recreational activity or service project. On occasion, they may meet together for a joint activity. Mutual is usually held on a night during the week.

– N –

name and a blessing—*see* blessing of babies.

New Era, the—*see* Church magazines.

new member discussions—a series of lessons designed for new converts. These lessons should be given within the first two months after a convert joins the Church. They are usually presented by the home teachers or the stake or full-time missionaries and are designed to reinforce the principles already taught during the missionary discussions.

newsletter editor—someone called to edit, copy, and distribute a ward newsletter. These are usually produced monthly, bimonthly, or quarterly and contain articles and announcements about members and activities.

nonmembers—a term used by members of the Church to refer to those who are not members.

nursery—the place where children between the ages of 18 months and three years are taken while their parents are in Sunday School and Priesthood or Relief Society.

nursery leader—someone called to oversee the ward nursery.

– O –

oath and covenant of the priesthood—a promise made by men who receive the priesthood that they will honor the priesthood, magnify priesthood callings, and keep all of the commandments. God then covenants that men who obey that oath will receive all the blessings that He has.

opening exercises—short meetings where an organization meets together before separating for individual classes. For example, priesthood meetings usually start with all priesthood members meeting together for a song, a prayer, and general announcements. At the conclusion of these opening exercises, each quorum will then go its own way and hold its own meeting.

ordain, ordination—giving someone the authority to hold a specific priesthood office. When a young boy first receives the Aaronic Priesthood, he has the priesthood conferred upon him and then is ordained to the office of a deacon within that priesthood. As he advances through the Aaronic Priesthood, he will later be ordained a teacher and then a priest.

ordinance—a ceremony or rite performed by the power of the priesthood that is recognized not only by the Church but also by God. Examples of ordinances include the blessing of babies, baptism, confirmation, ordination to the priesthood, blessing of the sick, administration of the sacrament, and the ordinances performed in temples. One of the greatest blessings of having the priesthood is the ability to bless the lives of those around you through priesthood ordinances.

ordinance workers—those assigned to perform ordinances in the temple. Also known as temple workers.

organist—a member of the ward music committee assigned to provide organ and piano music as part of worship services, primarily sacrament meeting.

overflow area—an area behind the chapel that may be opened when more space is needed or may be left closed and used as a classroom. In many meetinghouses, the chapel, overflow area, and cultural hall are grouped together so that large meetings may be expanded into the overflow area and then the cultural hall.

– P –

PAF—*see* personal ancestral file.

patriarch—an office in the Melchizedek Priesthood, and also a stake calling within the Church. Patriarchs are called upon to give patriarchal blessings to members within the stake.

patriarchal blessing—a blessing given to a Church member by a stake patriarch. Blessings declare the lineage of the members, and give them a roadmap for their lives, including blessings they will receive if they live worthily.

Pearl of Great Price—one of four volumes of scripture held to be sacred by Church members. *See also* standard works.

PEC—*see* priesthood executive committee.

perfect the saints—*see* mission of the Church.

personal ancestral file (PAF)—a computer program sold by the Church that helps keep track of family lineage and other genealogical information. Don't even think about looking for it in a Windows format.

personal journals—used by members to record important events that occur in their lives. One of the aspects of family history is the keeping of personal journals.

personal priesthood interview—*see* priesthood interview.

personal progress program—a portion of the Young Women program that allows young women to set personal goals and then strive to accomplish them.

personal revelation—the right of every Church member to receive individual guidance from God in regard to his own life and the lives of those over whom he has stewardship.

phase—used when referring to the size of a meetinghouse and congregation. A phase one building is the smallest meetinghouse the Church builds and is designed for small congregations. As membership increases, buildings may be remodeled and upgraded, until the third phase, which is a full-sized meetinghouse. Programs and curriculum materials parallel the meetinghouse phases.

physical activities director—a member of the stake or ward activities committee who plans and coordinates athletic events.

physical activities specialist—similar to a physical activities director, except he is usually called to assist with one event or to serve in one particular area.

physical facilities representative—a member of the stake high council who is responsible for all of the buildings within the stake. He is the liaison when buildings are built or upgraded, when a building must be repaired, or when maintenance problems arise.

pianist—a calling on the ward music committee, which may or may not be tied to a particular organization. Pianists are often needed by many of the ward auxiliaries, such as the Primary and the Relief Society, but are also needed for general ward meetings.

podium—properly called the pulpit but almost always misnamed the podium, it is the speaker's rostrum at the front of LDS chapels, usually with a microphone attached.

position—*see* calling.

PPI—*see* priesthood interview.

preparatory priesthood—*see* Aaronic Priesthood.

preside—the person in a meeting who holds the most authority. For example, a stake president visiting a ward meeting always presides at that meeting, even though he probably won't conduct and may not even participate on the program.

president—the person called to provide leadership over a particular group. Examples include a stake president, an elders quorum president, and a Relief Society president.

President and prophet—a term often used to refer to the President of the Church, as it emphasizes his dual role as both a President and the prophet of God.

Presiding Bishopric—three General Authorities who are assigned the responsibility of maintaining the physical assets of the Church. The group is composed of the Presiding Bishop and his two counselors.

priest—one of the offices in the Aaronic Priesthood, usually given to young men age 16–17, but also to male converts shortly after baptism. Priests have authority to baptize and to administer the sacrament.

priests quorum, priests quorum president—a group of young men in the ward who meet together and all hold the office of priest in the Aaronic Priesthood. The president of the priests quorum is the bishop, who calls two priests as his assistants.

priesthood—power given to worthy men in the Church to officiate in the name of Jesus Christ. Men use the priesthood to lead the Church and to perform priesthood ordinances to bless the lives of others. *See also* Aaronic Priesthood, Melchizedek Priesthood.

priesthood advancements—the act of moving from one priesthood office to another, particularly within the Aaronic Priesthood. For example, a deacon will be advanced to the office of a teacher when he turns 14 if he is worthy.

priesthood blessing—a blessing of comfort or counsel given by a man holding the Melchizedek Priesthood. Men often give such blessings to their children at the start of each school year.

priesthood executive committee (PEC)—a group of priesthood leaders who meet together to discuss the needs of those they serve. Such meetings are known as "PEC meetings" and occur regularly both in wards and stakes.

priesthood holder—a generic term used to refer to any man who holds the priesthood.

priesthood interview—an interview between a priesthood holder and the person in authority over him. Home teachers use regular priesthood interviews with their leaders to discuss the status of the families they teach. Bishops also have regular interviews with the stake president. This interview used to be known as a personal priesthood interview, or PPI; though this term has been officially obsolete for a number of years, it lingers on in LDS culture.

priesthood leader—a generic term describing anyone in a position of priesthood leadership over others. Examples of priesthood leaders include quorum presidencies, bishops, and stake presidents.

priesthood leadership meeting—a stake meeting designed to teach leadership skills to those who have been given priesthood leadership callings. For example, the elders quorum presidencies from each ward may be invited to learn how to lead more effectively.

priesthood meeting—a portion of the three-hour meeting block in which priesthood holders meet together, first in opening exercises, and then later in individual quorum and group meetings. This may also be used as a generic term to refer to any meeting to which only priesthood holders are invited.

priesthood quorum—*see* quorum.

priesthood quorum leader—*see* priesthood leader.

priesthood session—a meeting of general conference to which only priesthood holders are invited. *See also* general session.

Primary—the auxiliary organization of the Church tasked with teaching children. Boys and girls participate in Primary from age 3 to age 12, at which time they move into the Young Men and Young Women programs.

Primary presidency—the leadership of the Primary organization, consisting of a president and her two counselors.

probation—one outcome of a disciplinary council. Those on probation are still members of the Church but are restricted from doing certain activities, as determined by the council.

proclaim the gospel—*see* mission of the Church.

prophets—those who are authorized by the Lord to receive revelation for large groups of people. The President of the Church is known as the prophet because he is the one who receives revelations from the Lord applicable to the entire church and the entire world. All General Authorities in the First Presidency and Quorum of the Twelve Apostles are also sustained as prophets, seers, and revelators because they are entitled to receive revelation related to their stewardships.

proselyting mission—a full-time mission whose primary focus is the finding of converts.

prospective elder—any male Church member who has passed his 19th birthday but has not yet been ordained an elder. Also, any married male who does not yet have the Melchizedek Priesthood.

proxy—someone serving as a substitute for someone else. Church members may serve as proxy for their deceased relatives when they attend the temple and perform ordinances for them.

proxy ordinances—those ordinances performed in the temple on behalf of persons who are deceased. *See also* living ordinances.

public communications—any number of callings that involve working with the media and the community to publicize Church functions and correct false beliefs about the Church.

public communications director—a stake calling involved with the supervising of all public communications activities occurring within the stake.

– Q –

quad—an abbreviation for quadruple combination. A book of scripture that contains all four of the standard works of the Church. *See also* standard works.

quiet book—a book with features that are designed to keep small children quiet during church meetings.

quorum—a group of brethren that meet together and all hold the same priesthood office.

quorum adviser—an adult called to assist in the operation of the Aaronic Priesthood quorums. He is often a member of the Young Men presidency.

quorum business—general activities that take place in a quorum meeting before the lesson is presented. Includes such things as announcements, sustainings, and the ordination of new quorum members.

quorum committees—three committees that should be organized in each quorum to help accomplish the mission of the Church. *See also* mission of the Church.

quorum instructor—the person called to teach the weekly lesson in quorum meeting.

quorum leaders—a generic term referring to the leadership of priesthood quorums. This would include all the presidencies of all the quorums, and usually includes the high priests group leaders, although they technically are not a quorum.

quorum meetings—the main portion of the weekly priesthood meeting, where members meet together with their individual quorums to receive spiritual and practical instruction.

Quorum of the Twelve, Quorum of the Twelve Apostles, Council of the Twelve—much like Christ's twelve Apostles, the Quorum of the Twelve Apostles is composed of twelve General Authorities who help lead the Church and serve as personal witnesses of Jesus Christ to all the world.

quorum presidency—*see* quorum leaders.

Quorums of the Seventy—additional groups of General and Area Authorities who assist the Quorum of the Twelve and the First Presidency in the operation of the Church throughout the world. The scriptures provide for up to seven Quorums of the Seventy, each with 70 members. As of this writing, five quorums are active.

– R –

recommend desk—an area just inside the temple where those desiring to enter must show their temple recommends, each signed by a member of their bishopric and stake presidency.

recommend for a patriarchal blessing—a form that must be completed by the bishop of any Church member who wants to schedule an appointment with a stake patriarch to receive a patriarchal blessing.

redeem the dead—*see* mission of the Church.

regional conference—a Church meeting scheduled on an occasional basis to which the stakes within a specific geographic region are invited.

release—the opposite of being called to a Church assignment. At the conclusion of your calling, you will be released. As with a sustaining, this will usually be done in a public meeting. Often, your replacement will be sustained at the same time.

released time—in areas with large LDS populations, schools will often legally release students during the school day to attend seminary. This is known as released time.

Relief Society—the main auxiliary designed to meet the needs of adult women in the Church, whether single or married.

Relief Society board—those women with callings in the Relief Society are considered part of the Relief Society board, which meets occasionally to be trained and to discuss the needs of the women in the ward.

Relief Society compassionate service leader—*see* compassionate service leader.

Relief Society presidency—those women chosen to preside over the Relief Society in the ward or the stake. The presidency is composed of a president and two counselors.

Relief Society single adult representative—a member of the Relief Society board who represents the needs of the single women in the ward. She should serve on the ward single adult committee.

roadshow—a short dramatic production involving ward

members who act, sing, and dance; often designed with minimal scenery so the production can be loaded onto a truck and hauled to other meetinghouses.

– S –

sacrament—an ordinance performed as part of each sacrament meeting. Members of the Aaronic Priesthood bless and distribute bread and water to the members of the congregation. Members partake of the bread and water to remember the Atonement of Jesus Christ and the covenants they made when they were baptized.

sacrament meeting—the Sunday worship service for members of the Church, so named because its primary purpose is to allow members to receive the sacrament.

sacrament service—the portion of the sacrament meeting when the sacrament is prepared, blessed, and presented to the members. Sometimes used incorrectly to refer to sacrament meeting.

Saints—members of The Church of Jesus Christ of Latter-day Saints.

saving ordinance—a priesthood ordinance that is required for those who would return to the presence of God. Baptism and confirmation are examples of such ordinances, while the blessing of babies is not.

Scout—for wards that are affiliated with the Boy Scouts of America, a Scouting program that usually includes young men age 12 and 13.

Scouting—a general term used to describe any of the three programs associated with the Boy Scouts of America (Scout, Varsity Scout, and Venturing). Many wards include the Scouting program as part of their program for Young Men.

Scout troop—a group of Scouts that meets together.

Scouting committee—one or more committees of adults that coordinate all Scouting programs within the ward. Members and nonmembers of the Church may serve on these committees.

Scoutmaster—the adult leader called to provide instruction and supervision for the Scout troop.

scriptures—sacred writings containing instructions from God to His children through His prophets. Church members recognize four different books of scripture. *See also* standard works.

seal the anointing—the second portion of a blessing given to a sick person by one or two Melchizedek Priesthood holders. The brethren place their hands on the head of the sick person and pronounce a blessing upon the person as directed by the Holy Ghost. *See also* anoint.

sealer—a temple ordinance worker who has the authority to perform sealings.

sealing—an ordinance performed in the temple where a husband and wife, along with any children they might have, are joined together as a family for all eternity. This may be done as a living or proxy ordinance. *See also* temple marriage.

sealing room—a room in the temple where sealing ordinances are performed.

seminary—a program of daily gospel instruction designed for youth of approximately high school age. Classes may be taught early in the morning or during the school day and may meet in a seminary building, a meetinghouse, or a member's home.

senior companion—the man considered to have the most experience in a priesthood companionship. For full-time missionaries, this will be the missionary who has served the longest. When an Aaronic and Melchizedek Priesthood holder home teach together, the Melchizedek Priesthood holder is the senior companion.

senior patrol leader—a young man selected from a Scout troop to provide leadership to the other boys in the troop. He works with adult leaders to help lead the troop.

service projects—Church activities designed to provide service to the community or to others. Examples would include gathering trash from the roadway or cleaning the house of someone who is ill.

session—used to designate different portions of the same activity. During general conference there is a morning session, an afternoon session, and a priesthood session.

set apart—a priesthood ordinance that gives a person the authority to perform a certain calling within the Church. For some callings, the person being set apart is also given spiritual keys that will assist him in performing the calling. (Note: only four individuals hold keys in a ward, those being the bishop, the elders quorum president, and the presidents of the teachers and deacons.)

Seventy—Melchizedek Priesthood office that is primarily concerned with missionary work and the spreading of the gospel throughout the world. *See also* Quorums of the Seventy.

sharing time—a portion of Primary where classes meet together to practice songs and do other activities of a group nature.

single adult—an unmarried member of the Church age 31 or over. This includes members who are single because of death or divorce (but only after the divorce is final).

single adult committee—a group organized in a ward to consider the needs of the single adults in the ward. The committee usually includes a bishopric member, the single adult representative and other priesthood and auxiliary leaders.

single adult council—a group organized at the stake level to consider the needs of the single adults. The committee usually includes high council members, ward single adult representatives, and other stake priesthood and auxiliary leaders.

single adult representative—a single adult called by the bishop to represent all the single adults in the ward. He should expect to attend ward meetings, such as ward council, and certain stake meetings.

single member, singles—generic terms used to represent adult members of the Church who are unmarried. Single members are classified as either young single adults or single adults.

single member representative—a generic term used to refer to either a young single adult representative, or a single adult representative.

singles ward, single adult ward—wards where the members are all single, except for the members of the bishopric, who are usually married. These wards may be designed for either young single adults or single adults and usually span an entire stake or even a multistake area.

sister—a generic term to denote any adult female within the Church; a form of address used instead of Miss, Ms, or Mrs. The term reminds us of our relationship to God and to each other.

sister ward—a ward that shares a meetinghouse with another ward; a ward that shares a name with another ward (i.e., the Warrenton First Ward and the Warrenton Second Ward).

Social Services—a group within the Church that provides social services to Church members, such as marital counseling and adoption assistance. Bishops can refer members in need to these specialists.

speech director—a person who works under the cultural arts director as part of the ward or stake activities committee. Involved with the organizing of speech festivals and similar events.

spirit of the fast—a general feeling of sacrifice and humility that accompanies fasting. Those who have physical limitations that prevent them from fasting may still partake of the spirit of the fast through meditation, study, and prayer.

split—a slang term used to describe a change in ward boundaries, particularly when a large ward is divided into two smaller ones. People will say that the ward is about "to divide" or "to be split." *See also* missionary splits.

sports director—someone called to serve under the physical activities director as part of the ward or stake activities committee. This person is usually given such tasks as the organization of athletic teams.

square, the—those performing the ordinance of baptism are instructed to raise their right arm "to the square" while saying the baptismal prayer. This simply means raising your hand so that the elbow is bent at a 90° angle.

stake—a group of approximately eight wards or branches that are grouped together and governed by common leadership.

stake center, stake house—one of the ward buildings in your stake that is designated as a stake center. It will be a little larger than the other buildings and will have an extra set of offices for stake leaders such as the stake presidency and the high council. Stake meetings will often be held at the stake center. The term *stake house* means the same thing, but is not used much any more.

stake conference—a group of Saturday and Sunday meetings that include all the wards in the stake. Stake conference is usually held twice per year, and the meetings are usually held at the stake center. On Sundays when stake conference is held, there are no ward meetings.

stake dances—dances sponsored by the stake to which all of the youth in the stake are invited.

stake mission—an organization within the stake that is responsible for coordinating all the missionary work within the stake. The stake mission works with the full-time missionaries, the ward mission leaders, and the stake missionaries.

stake mission presidency—the brethren called to lead the stake mission. The stake mission presidency consists of a president and his two counselors.

stake missionary—a Church member called to do missionary work on a part-time basis. This is a stake calling and is governed from the stake, but most of the work occurs in the ward.

stake presidency—the men called to lead a stake. The stake presidency consists of the stake president and his two counselors.

standard works—the four books of scripture that are accepted as scriptural canon by the LDS Church. These include the Bible, the Book of Mormon, the Doctrine and Covenants, and the Pearl of Great Price.

stewardship—a term referring to the people, programs, and property over which a leader has responsibility. For example, a bishop has stewardship over everyone in the ward. A home teacher has stewardship over the families he home teaches.

study guide—a guide or curriculum manual from which the Sunday lessons are taken for the Relief Society and the Melchizedek Priesthood quorums. Each member of those groups should have a study guide so he or she can read the lesson material in advance.

Sunbeams—the youngest Primary class, consisting of children 2–3 years of age.

Sunday program editor—the person called to edit, copy, and in some cases distribute the program that announces the schedule of speakers in sacrament meeting.

Sunday School—an auxiliary of the Church designed to teach members about the gospel and the scriptures. A portion of the Sunday meeting block is devoted to Sunday School classes.

Sunday School class president—a member chosen to preside over each Sunday School class. The president usually introduces new members and visitors, arranges for the prayers, and turns the time over to the instructor.

Sunday School presidency—the men called to lead the Sunday School organization. The presidency consists of a president and his two counselors.

sustain—the process of allowing all ward members to approve those who will lead them. During ward and stake conferences, members are asked to raise their hands to approve all officers at the ward, stake, and general Church levels. But sustaining means more than just raising your hand for the person. It also means you will support and assist him through your actions. *See also* law of common consent.

sustaining list—the list of people that are to be sustained in their callings. Formal sustaining lists are used when there are a large number of people to be sustained, such as at ward and stake conference.

– T –

talent and interest survey—a survey that can indicate to ward leaders where their members' talents and interests lie, if only the members will consent to filling out such a survey. These surveys are compiled by the ward activities committee.

talk—an oral presentation on a gospel subject. Unlike some churches where the ministers do all the preaching, the LDS Church relies on its members for most of the teaching. Thus, members will be found giving talks in many Church meetings, including sacrament meetings and Primary.

teacher—a person called to teach the gospel and the scriptures. Teachers will be found in just about every ward organization and auxiliary. A teacher also refers to an office in the Aaronic Priesthood, usually held by young men age 14–15.

teacher development basic course—a course designed for those training to become teachers. It is often taught during the Sunday School class time, usually by the ward teacher development coordinator.

teacher development coordinator—a ward calling tasked with the responsibility of training teachers. The coordinator will conduct the teacher development basic course and will also prepare regular training meetings for the teachers in the ward.

teachers quorum—a group of young men who meet together on Sundays and hold the office of teacher in the Aaronic Priesthood.

teachers quorum presidency—the young men called from the teachers quorum to provide leadership for that group. The presidency is composed of a president and two counselors.

"Teaching—No Greater Call"—a manual available at the distribution center that contains advice for becoming an effective teacher. Recommended reading for anyone called to be a teacher.

temple—a building constructed by the Church for the performing of sacred ordinances designed to save and link together the entire family of man. Also a place to receive comfort and personal revelation.

temple clothes—sacred white ceremonial clothing worn by those who attend the temple. White is used because it symbolizes purity before the Lord. An additional benefit is that when all people are dressed alike, there are no distinctions between them and a sense of equality prevails.

temple dedications—ceremonies held to consecrate new temples so that ordinance work may begin. After dedication, public tours are no longer given and only worthy Church members may enter.

temple marriage—a marriage performed in the temple that includes a sealing ceremony to seal the couple together for eternity, if they remain worthy. Any children born to the couple after their marriage are automatically sealed to them. *See also* sealing.

temple matrons—the wives of the temple presidency. They are called to serve in the temple along with their husbands.

temple mission—a type of mission whereby the missionaries are called to work in a temple full time rather than go out and preach in public. Older couples and single women are often called on temple missions.

temple preparation class—a class taught at the ward level designed for those who plan to attend the temple for the first time. Converts preparing for the temple should make sure to ask about this class.

temple presidency—a group of three men called to direct the operation of a temple. The presidency is composed of a president and his two counselors.

temple recommend, temple recommend interview—those desiring to attend the temple must participate in a temple recommend interview, where they are asked about their worthiness by members of both the bishopric and the stake presidency. If they are worthy, they are issued a recommend that admits them to the temples of the Church for the next year. A Church member must show a valid recommend each time he attends the temple.

temple work—a generic term used to refer to attending the temple and performing ordinances there.

temple worthy—a term used to describe those that are worthy to enter the temple. The youth of the Church are often urged to keep themselves temple worthy, even though they may not be ready to attend for several years. New converts should also strive to always be temple worthy.

testimony—a personal conviction that a person develops regarding the truthfulness of the Church and its teachings, doctrines, and leaders. Testimony meeting is the time for sharing those feelings with the other members of your ward. All members must work to strengthen their testimonies each day.

three-hour block—the current meeting schedule followed by most Church wards each Sunday. Each ward will meet for a three-hour time period that includes sacrament meeting, Sunday School, Relief Society, priesthood, Primary, and youth programs.

tithing—a financial donation to the Church that represents one-tenth of a person's income. The payment of a full tithing is expected of worthy Church members and is necessary to progress in the kingdom of God. It is the first step in living the law of consecration.

tithing in kind—payment of tithing using goods rather than money. This was more common in the early days of the Church when a farmer would donate ten percent of his crops. Some people still pay tithing in kind but usually donate financial instruments such as stock certificates.

tithing settlement—a yearly meeting with the bishop to balance the Church's donation records with yours. The bishop will also ask you to state whether you pay a full tithing or only partial tithing.

tracting—an activity performed by full-time missionaries where they walk through a neighborhood, knocking on all the doors looking for investigators. This activity may involve passing out Church-related tracts.

triple combination—a book in which are bound all of the standard works except the Bible.

– U –

unit—a generic term that is used interchangeably to mean either a ward or a branch of the Church, such as, "Our stake has really grown, and now we have twelve units."

– V –

Valiant—classes of children in the Primary program who are age 8–11.

Varsity Scout—a Scouting program designed for young men age 14–15.

Varsity Scout coach—an adult leader assigned to encourage and supervise the Varsity Scout team.

Varsity Scout team—the group of Varsity Scouts that meets together in a ward.

Varsity team captain—a young man called from the Varsity Scouts to provide leadership to the team. The team captain meets with the coach to plan activities.

Venturing Crew—a group of young men who participate in the Venturing Scouting program. In wards that participate in the Scouting program, Venturers are young men age 16–17 who are usually also priests in the Aaronic Priesthood.

Venturing Crew leader—an adult leader called to supervise the Venturing Crew in a ward.

Venturing Crew president—a young man called from the ranks of the Venturing Crew to preside over it.

visiting teacher, visiting teaching—the visiting teaching program of the Relief Society is similar to the priesthood home teaching program. Each pair of visiting teachers is assigned to visit one or more Relief Society sisters each month, providing a lesson and support to the member and reporting any serious problems back to the Relief Society president or the visiting teaching board member.

visiting teaching board member—a member of the Relief Society board who calls each visiting teacher monthly, compiles statistics about which sisters were and were not visited, and reports any problems found during the visits to the Relief Society president.

visiting teaching supervisor—in wards with a large number of visiting teaching companionships, these supervisors are called to assist the visiting teaching board member in performing her job.

visitors' center—an information center designed to teach non-members and investigators about the Church. These centers are usually located near temples or Church historical sites and have many different programs and videos designed to help investigators understand the doctrines, history, and beliefs of the Church.

voice—when multiple priesthood holders are involved in an ordinance, one man serves as the voice, or mouthpiece, for the entire group. Thus, he speaks for the group and also for the Lord in performing the ordinance.

– W –

ward—the most common grouping of Church members. Wards are groups of 300–500 Saints who are led by a bishop, his two counselors, and other ward leaders.

ward adviser—a member of the high council assigned to assist the leadership of a particular ward. The ward adviser can facilitate communications between the ward and the stake, answer questions raised by the leadership of the ward, and communicate instructions to the ward from the stake presidency.

ward budget—a yearly amount of funds given by the stake to each ward to finance their operations. The budget must be used to cover all ward expenses and finance activities planned by all ward organizations.

ward business—the name applied to the various announcements, sustainings, releases, and blessing of babies that occur in a typical ward sacrament meeting.

ward conference—a yearly conference where stake leaders attend and present a special program as part of sacrament meeting. Part of this meeting includes the yearly sustaining of ward, stake, and general church officers. Stake leaders may also make special presentations during other meetings, such as Sunday School or Relief Society.

ward council—a monthly meeting of ward leaders who come together to address the needs of the ward and make plans for future ward activities and programs.

ward mission leader—the man called to coordinate all missionary activity in the ward. He reports to the stake mission president and coordinates activities between ward members, stake missionaries, full-time missionaries, and other stake leaders.

ward organist—a member of the ward music committee who is assigned to play the organ in general ward meetings, primarily sacrament meeting.

Webelos—a rank in the Cub Scout program usually given to boys when they reach their 10th birthday. The acronym means "WE'll BE LOyal Scouts."

welfare—the general category of Church programs that are designed to look after the physical needs of members. The bishop is given the responsibility of looking after the physical needs of all ward members. At his disposal are a number of ward, stake, and general church services designed to promote the physical needs of Church members.

welfare committee—committees that exist at both the stake and ward levels and are designed to address the welfare needs of Church members. These committees often address such issues as unemployment, food production and storage, and financial planning.

welfare farm—a number of farms owned by the Church that produce food to be used in the welfare programs of the Church. Food produced on welfare farms may be sent to the local bishops' storehouse or may be processed at a local Church cannery.

welfare services—a stake program designed to educate ward leaders about the types of member assistance programs that are available at various levels within the Church.

welfare services mission—a type of full-time mission where the missionaries spend their time doing things that improve the welfare of the people they serve. Examples would include medical specialists who work in clinics and those who teach parents the proper care of infants.

welfare specialist—a ward calling that your bishop may or may not issue. It is associated with motivating members to become more self-sufficient. Welfare specialists attend the ward welfare committee meetings to determine the types of welfare problems that exist in the ward. The welfare specialists then assist in organizing programs to help members avoid or overcome such problems.

Wolf—one of the ranks within the Cub Scout program.

Word of Wisdom—a doctrine of health practiced by members of the Church. It gives guidelines for the use of certain foods and substances and prohibits the use of tobacco, alcohol, coffee, and tea. The Word of Wisdom is found in section 89 of the Doctrine and Covenants.

workfare—a principle associated with all Church welfare programs in that members are expected to perform work for the assistance they receive.

worthiness interview—one of several interviews designed to determine the worthiness of Church members. Examples of worthiness interviews include temple recommend interviews and the interview men and young men receive before being given the priesthood.

– Y –

year's supply—a Church welfare program designed to motivate members to maintain a year's supply of food and other necessities. These supplies help during individual emergencies, such as unemployment, and also help during local emergencies such as earthquakes.

Young Men—a program of the Church designed to instruct and motivate young men ages 12–18.

Young Men presidency—the adult leaders called to supervise the ward Young Men program. The presidency consists of a president and his two counselors.

young single adult—a member of the Church who is not married and is between the ages of 18 and 30.

young single adult council—a stake group that meets to consider the needs of the young single adults living in the stake.

young single adult representative—a young single adult called to represent all the young single adults in the ward. They are often asked to attend ward and stake meetings related to young single adults.

young single adult ward—*see* singles ward.

Young Women—an auxiliary Church program designed to instruct young women ages 12–18.

Young Women in Excellence—a program designed to let Young Women choose one of the Young Women values (see below) and set goals to help them develop that value in their lives.

Young Women presidency—the women called to provide leadership for the Young Women program. The presidency consists of the president and her two counselors.

Young Women values—a program designed to teach the Young Women to develop seven different values in their lives:

including faith, divine nature, individual worth, knowledge, choice and accountability, good works, and integrity.

youth conference—a planned program of speakers, seminars, and social activities designed to strengthen the testimonies of the youth. Youth conferences are usually organized at the stake or multistake level, and often involve traveling away from home for two to four days of activities.

youth interview—regular individual interviews conducted between the youth of the ward and a member of the bishopric.

– Z –

Zion—the origin of the word actually means "pure in heart," but it is usually used as a term to describe any location where the Saints of the Church are gathered.

zone—a unit of division within a mission. Each mission is usually made up of several zones, each of which is presided over by a missionary known as a zone leader.

INDEX